Women, Political Philosophy and Politics

Women, Political Philosophy and Politics

Liz Sperling

Edinburgh University Press

© Liz Sperling, 2001

Edinburgh University Press Ltd
22 George Square, Edinburgh

Typeset in Melior
by Hewer Text Ltd, Edinburgh, and
printed and bound in Great Britain by
MPG Books Ltd, Bodmin

A CIP Record for this book is
available from the British Library

ISBN 0 7486 1108 8 (paperback)

The right of Liz Sperling to be
identified as author of this work has
been asserted in accordance with the
Copyright, Designs and Patents Act 1988.

Contents

Preface and Acknowledgements

The original idea for this book arose from a third level course I taught at Liverpool John Moores University, on Women and Political Philosophy: from Plato to the New Right. As a specialist in British government and public administration at the time, the course was a bit of a luxury that allowed me to indulge my interest in political philosophy and how philosophers had been cardinal in the under-representation of women in contemporary British politics. The longevity of ideas about women and their relation to politics, the fact that arguments used by Aristotle are still sincerely held and articulated by people who stalk the corridors of power in ivory towers, is a fascinating and horrific phenomenon. I wanted to impress on the students the very origins of women's exclusion from politics; the history as told through mainstream political philosophy, and why it is so hard to make progress against such deeply entrenched ideas. After all, we all know about excuses made suggesting women's inability to think rationally, their unreliability and general dippiness that makes them unsuitable for responsible office. We also know that much of this is perceived as a function of biology; one cannot conceive, gestate, give birth and breastfeed, and not be an ideal house-keeper above all else. That such explanations are 'rationalised' by revered thinkers whose works have remained influential for hundreds, if not thousands, of years, makes traditional attitudes towards women seem almost intelligent. My objective has been to demonstrate that the arguments of the political philosophers, and the politicians who vene-rate them, are about as rational as they accuse women of being.

The book itself was the idea of Nicola Carr, Senior Commissioning Editor at Edinburgh University Press. As academics know, our meetings with commissioning editors often result, on our part, in the receipt of some useful books to assist with scholarly and research activities. From the publishers' side, they sometimes get books out of us! On this occasion the latter happened. Although I did my best to wrangle a book on women in political philosophy from Nicola she could not oblige, and after about a year asked if I knew anyone who might be able to write a book on the topic. Here is the result.

The book would not have been written without the extraordinary support of all my colleagues in the Politics Section of Liverpool John

Moores University: Martyn Nightingale, John Vogler, Charlotte Bretherton, Mike Mannin, Dennis Donnelly, Esther Jubb, Rex Li and more latterly, John Burchill, Simon Lightfoot and Mark Williams. Not only did they kindly agree to funding two semester-long sabbaticals, as well as other periods of teaching relief, with all this meant for them in added work as they absorbed some of my teaching and dealt with student issues that I was unavailable to handle, but they also had to cope with my incessant talk about my work, and the inevitable mood swings that seem to accompany writing, when we did meet up. Especial thanks go to Charlotte Bretherton who has read drafts of all chapters and given inestimable advice and encouragement. She gave me faith in myself to complete the book when I was wavering and has been a much valued friend throughout. Thanks also to Nader Fekri and Martyn Nightingale who read some of the chapters and proffered comments.

No acknowledgements would be complete without mention of family. Firstly to Paddy Sheehan who not only did the paintings for the book cover, for which I cannot thank or praise him enough, but who also provides ease of mind in knowing that my daughter, Hannah, is so happy in her life with him. To brother Colin and aunt Terry, a published author, who have both given constant support while I have been writing this book, and to brother Barry, despite his initial reaction when I told him about the book, which was, 'oh God, it leaves me cold'! Most importantly, my daughters, Hannah and Kate. They probably don't realise just how considerably they have assisted in this work. As any working parent knows, just by knowing when to interrupt and when not to, when to provide cups of tea, feed the cat, and intervene with a well-timed joke, children ease the stress of research and writing. However, like most working parents, I'm not sure that this was what really happened at the time – it's a lovely thought though. Certainly 'my girls' have been the mainstay of this project. They have consistently supported me during the two and a half years I have been working on the book and provided a source of joy and a harbour from the stresses of the work. Hannah and Kate are the most important people in my life and without whom the world and all its contents would be worthless.

Liz Sperling

Chapter 1: Women, Political Philosophy and Politics: Theory and Practice in Conflict?

The key to women's under-representation in modern liberal democratic polities rests between the lines of the works of major, mainstream political philosophers from Plato to Nozick. The great treatises of political philosophy that have shaped ideas of justice and laid the foundations for the good state are proclaimed as ubiquitous in their appeal and application. As pertinent aspects of different or successive philosophies are utilised, or rejected, to explain and respond to political events and circumstances, their profundity is assured. It is 'unfortunate' that political philosophers had so little to say about women, and that what they did suggest assured women's exclusion, progressing towards marginality in later years, in every manifestation and incremental advance of philosophy and politics *ad infinitum*.

This book is concerned with the salience of ideas that have shaped political structures and processes throughout the ages; ideas that are still relevant to contemporary politics and which systematically denigrate women, so affecting their relationship to politics, even in contemporary, 'enlightened' states. What is under scrutiny here is the perspicacity of the gendered nature of political philosophy in contrast with its more general political pretensions. In other words, can political philosophers and politicians ever achieve their objectives of instituting the 'good' state, in which justice is paramount, while such concepts are qualified by gender inequalities? In arguing that they cannot, the pronouncements on women, and justifications for women's political incapacity, will be subject to analysis within the terms that philosophers utilise in their treatises for instituting just political procedures.

While the supposition of the book is of particular relevance to feminism, it also, possibly more critically, addresses concerns for all liberals, democrats and Marxists, in their various forms. Liberty, democracy and communism are not complete if, wherever they pertain, their principles are applied selectively. In a sense, then, this is not strictly a 'feminist' book, although it written by a feminist and applies a gender analysis to common political concepts and familiar ideas. The aim is not to provide an exposition of liberal, radical, socialist or any variation of feminism. Nor is it to 'add women in' to mainstream liberal, democratic and Marxist theory. It is simply to look at customary political ideas and concepts that, as part of everyday political relations, are taken for granted, and consider the rationality of the origins and maintenance of the contentions that render them alien to women. Indeed, using the philosophers' own test of rationality, it is obvious that they do not live up to their own standards when referring to women.

What is the problem?

The origin of the interest in the causal effects of political philosophy on women's under-representation lies in the politics of feminism. It seems that whatever feminists argue in their struggle for justice, and whatever action is taken to ameliorate their demands, they hit a brick wall just below the surface of apparent comprehension of their contention that discrimination is intrinsic to socio-political relations in all organisations and ways of life. Not only are women not genuinely understood in any role other than their 'traditional' one, but their reasons for wanting change appear incomprehensible. When women challenge the status quo, they contest 'normality' – theirs, society's and history's. As such, concession can be made to their desires for more involvement in the state, recognition given of their work in servicing the state, family and men in their domestic capacity, and policies can be implemented that will satisfy an uncomprehending and superficial witness to women's inequality. However, the issue of women's intrinsic but unappreciated, in fact undiscerned, value to the state remains a mystery. When women claim that their work and achievements are not valued equally to men's, they are not referring only to unequal pay and treatment at work, the absence of value given to domestic work in either remuneration or the form of positive endorsement, or the feminisation of poverty. More intrinsically, women's value is not perceived in their equal contribution to the common wealth,[1] nor are they afforded the same liberty and privileges as men. Enduring differences between familiar concessions to women's demands for equality, and understanding of the fundamental causes of inequality, place women's and men's communication on parallel wavelengths.

Political Philosophy and Politics: fatale for femmes

There is obviously a fundamental contradiction within western liberal society concerning the situation of women in contemporary states. To claim that women are in the same position as they were one hundred and fifty, fifty or even twenty years ago appears nonsensical. Women have the right to vote, to stand for office, to paid employment, health care, education and all the accoutrements of citizenship. Moreover, they increasingly utilise these rights and demand fair treatment under them. After all, being relatively new holders of such rights, it is inevitable that there would be some teething problems in implementing them more comprehensively: it takes a long time to remedy the gender imbalances intrinsic for centuries in all fields. On the other hand, it can be argued that despite these rights, women's relation to all fields in which rights are evident remains that of newcomers and has not much improved, proportionally, since their accession. For example, women are grossly underrepresented in elected assemblies – even Scandinavian parliaments, in which representation has always outstripped others (Randall 1987: 103; UN 2000: 77), have not achieved full proportionality to population numbers.[2] The restriction of women's access to the highest positions in political and economic organisations is evident in the poverty of their numbers in government, on boards of directors, in professorships and as heads of state and companies (Parker and Fagenson 1994; Fawcett Society 2000: 5; UN 2000: 11) and the onus on them to maintain households and take major responsibility for childcare is unchanged.

In theory, therefore, women are not 'second-class', or even non-, citizens. They have the same rights and responsibilities to the state as anyone: in return for maintaining and obeying the law, and contributing to the common wealth as responsible members of the state, as paid and unpaid workers, women have the right to participate in, and engage with, the state and share in its benefits. Moreover, in their interactions with the state, women and men are desirous of pursuing interests that are of importance to them. These may be individualistic, or pertain to immediate family interests, or conceived on a more collectivist, even altruistic, basis. But they all depend on the eventual peace, security and stability within and between states that enable us to live the way we want without undue, arbitrary and discriminatory hindrance. This requires that all reasonable choices be granted equal value and chance of accomplishment. In practice, it is well-known and documented that, despite the formal right to equal treatment, women's rights within and from the state are not equal with others' (Lister 1997; Phillips 1999; UN 1991, 1995, 2000), nor are their contributions to, and choices within, the state the same. Women have the extra burden of domesticity placed on them by dint, it seems, of their capacity for gestation, parturition and nursing human offspring.

It may appear that the role of political philosophy is rather remote from the situation in which women find themselves in contemporary western polities. Philosophy requires equality among citizens; not absolute equality in terms of wealth and ownership, but in relation to liberty and the ability to understand, pursue and maintain the common good.[3] Although it has been granted rather late in the history of human society and politics, women have formally attained equal status as citizens. Moreover, politics is not necessarily determined by philosophy but by need. Fundamentally, need refers to the ability of individuals for self-preservation. This may just mean staying alive. But it also has other connotations in terms of posterity, or leaving an impression after we depart the world. We gather possessions, wealth, property and less tangible achievements so that, as well any physical comforts accruing from attainment, we gain self-respect, perhaps respect from others as well during our lifetimes, and leave something enduring of ourselves when we die. To do this, and to leave the best impression, order is required. Without order, attainments are under threat from individuals who are pursuing their own advantages. Without order, attainments may be gained in nefarious ways, and such acquisition will themselves be at risk. In other words, order prevents a free-for-all that is implied when the term 'anarchy' is invoked. Politics is a response to the need for order. But how order is supposed to be implemented, the extent of intervention in individuals' lives to obtain and maintain order, and the structures and processes on which order, and therefore politics, rests is an issue of ideas. It is contended here, that the form that politics takes to institute order within states is inextricably linked to underlying political philosophies.

The ideas on which contemporary politics is organised, and challenged, range from the liberal perception of provision of a basic framework which enables individuals to advance their interests secure from infringements by others doing the same (*Two Treatises*; *Anarchy, State and Utopia*),* to more interventionist models based on welfare or moral well-being within states (*Emile*; *Republic*). Varying levels of democratic involvement by 'ordinary' citizens may be prescribed, from full participatory democracy to exercising the right to vote periodically. Throughout, the concept of justice is apparent to ensure that the systems and processes prescribed for the 'good' state gain the hallmark of legitimacy from as wide a public as is feasible. When the development of states is considered, it becomes evident that they are built on the best, or the most appropriate, or perhaps the least worst, aspects of all the ideas that precede them. Over the centuries, as each stage of development substantiates or disavows the application of ideas, they are moderated, altered, adapted and incorporated to suit the circumstances and the exigencies of various states. Hence, it might be conjectured that

* The titles of texts will be used as references throughout the book. They are catalogued under the authors' names in the bibliography.

liberal democracy is the combination of ideas of democracy culled from ancient Greek philosophers, but which applied, then, only to a minority of full citizens, with notions of freedom developed from authoritarian through to more inclusive liberal conceptions of the people's relation to the good state. Citizens in western liberal democracies no longer belong to a small, elite, minority of landed or property-owning, exclusively educated men. Integral to this condition is that rulers are also no longer recruited from the same socio-economic background as their electors and legitimators. The historical incremental expansion of suffrage, and the concomitant increased breadth of state interests, are the expedient responses of politicians to crises of the state, supported by philosophers as silent mentors providing templates for the just state.

Common throughout the range and development of political philosophy is the apparently superficial treatment of women. To contemporary liberal democrats it is possible to interpret this as inclusion: what applies to citizens, other members of the state, and relations between rulers and the ruled is relevant to women. However, a not too strenuous reading of the philosophies' less 'political' passages abruptly disabuses any belief in the intention of philosophers to inclusiveness. For people concerned with the nuts and bolts of politics, who would rather leave the background justifications for political change and development to theorists, it is easy simply to browse through the passages in texts such as the *Two Treatises*, Book VI of *The Republic*, the incidental paragraphs in *The Politics*, and *Leviathan* that refer to women's relation to the state. Readers of Rousseau can find the task even more effortless, as his treatise on the unsuitability of women for politics and citizenship is annexed in a chapter of *Emile* and in part one of the *Discourse on Inequality* rather than appearing in the major political dissertation, the *Social Contract*. In contrast, those interested in the integrity of political philosophy and its comprehensive, authentic interpretation in the practical politics of secure, stable and just order will find in the brief but profound references to women, that they are 'different' from men in the state and that their distinctiveness is detrimental to the state if allowed to pollute its affairs. This is the one idea that is consistent, without adaptation, moderation or alteration, throughout all the stages of development of both politics and political philosophy.

It is interesting that women are singled-out for this treatment by the philosophers. Until the nineteenth century when representative democracy, in which all literate and numerate individuals of both sexes were ascribed a limited role in affairs of the state, no philosophy advocated full participation by the people who were affected by the decisions that rulers made. In other words, citizenship was a concept applicable to a limited, and select, group. And yet 'ordinary' men outside the elite citizenry were not overtly or indeterminately proscribed, although concerns about a possible tyranny of the majority substantially limited men's access while granting them the potential for citizenship. What the man in the field, factory, government and philosopher's den have in common is that they inhabit the public space. The political and economic interactions that they enjoy as sanctioned workers define them as significant players in the state. However, the ability to perform such public duties cannot be combined with meeting the more mundane necessities of life and remain unsullied. The most 'obvious' group of people to take on responsibility for the latter aspects of life in the state is women, who have to be confined occasionally for childbirth and can extend such confinement indefinitely based on the long period of dependency of human children. However, biological determinism would not necessarily be adequate to separate women from public decision-making, since the ability to think and suckle babies at the same time is not mutually exclusive. More intricate reasoning arising from women's natural abilities had, therefore, to be incorporated into political thought and practice. These tend to range from the fact of women's maternal role qualifying them as moral guardians, their unique talents in this area being required in the home, where they can remain uncorrupted, as a guide for children and a chaste anchor for men (*Emile*; *Discourse on Inequality*), to the need for constant replenishment of male babies which requires women to devote all their physical and mental energy to this task (*Politics*). So that there may be no misinterpretation of women's auxiliary relation to the state, accounts of their disqualification for political work are peppered with reference to their unreliability, weakness, selfishness and inability to perform for the wider good.

Had the division of labour that arose from the necessity for single-minded devotion to the state been within the code of political philosophy that liberty and justice be served, it would be assumed that it was the result of free choice: to achieve and maintain stability and security that enables free individuals to maximise their self-interests, or to meet their requirements for preservation, women and men agreed that the now familiar model of politico-economic/family unit was most appropriate, with women undertaking the domestic responsibilities. However, it is hard to conceive that whole populations of women and men, throughout the globe and not only in what became liberal democracies, would make the same choices. Men may not have the choice about whether to be public sphere participants, but they are able to make choices, however limited, concerning what they do and how they interact once there. In contrast, when it comes to the household and its role in the state, there are no choices available: men provide and protect, women have babies and maintain the domestic environment. Assuming that women have the same ability for self-preservation, with all this implies in terms of liberty and the freedom to make choices, it must be assumed that their universal domesticity and separation from the arena of decision-making is, somehow, devised. It now becomes clear why women require special consideration, however brief or implicit, by the philosophers: unlike other, male, individuals who are effectively free to pursue their interests, so contributing to the common wealth, women have to subsume personal interest in favour not only of the state but of male citizens and labourers. This may well be couched in terms of the good of the state and the common wealth; but considering that philosophers have traditionally belonged to the male elite, towards whom their writing is aimed, aspects of personal power that are intrinsic to the practice of politics, and that would have to be shared if women were granted equal citizenship rights, cannot be ignored.

Herein lies the explicit connection between political philosophy and politics that undermines women's attempts to relinquish their 'protected' and dependent condition and to participate as fully in the state as they may choose.[4] While it is not claimed that the gendered division of labour is the unique construction of political philosophers, they would have it in their power to influence a more tolerant and inclusive attitude towards women when they were advocating their ideal states. It is not beyond the bounds of possibility that women from the same background as that understood as a prerequisite for citizenship could be perceived as being equally adept in their contributions to the state as men. Instead, not only do the philosophers endorse the gendered relations within the state, but they justify them within limited parameters that demonstrate little thought or imagination, merely reflecting the traditional patterns of gender relations.

The main business of political philosophy is to prescribe the ideal state, much of which relies on women's subjugation in the domestic sphere, but which only needs a brief recapitulation to remind any uppity women of their place and to assure men of their rightful access to, and use of, political power. In other words, political philosophy reinforces the right of man *qua* man to sole political authority. This obviously has far-reaching effects as the history of political man cannot be challenged, women not having the authority to do so, and is embedded in the everyday consciousness of individuals within the state. Beyond the universe that political philosophy, in unification with politics, has decreed for centuries there lies only uncharted and outlandish incongruity. Thus, women who want more than superficial or formal acknowledgement of their rights, who know that their domestic role is not an auxiliary but an essential to the common wealth and who demand recognition of this, and those who demand treatment as bona fide participants in their public sphere activities, cannot settle for institutional and procedural adjustment, but are struggling against entrenched, habitual, even 'normal' ideas about their abilities as non-political beings. Without a fundamental understanding of the reasons for, and justice of, politics, and who and what is included in its objectives as well as its procedures to attain them, only minor modifications in institutional procedures to enable women's participation will be possible. This will amount to tolerance of women in affairs that are not really 'their' concern. For women to be accepted, rather than tolerated, there must be change at the very base of the chain of ideas and organisations that constitute politics.

Is the demand for basic analysis and change an entreaty or provocation for the development of new philosophies? In this case, it is not. As much as feminist theories of the state, citizenship, representation and society are essential to understanding the male dominance in these areas, and are a key to women's equal access to, and utilisation of them, the concern here is to understand the elementary basis of exclusion. In the way that feminism has always turned 'normality' on its head, illustrating the absurdity of many of the ideas, practices, arguments for women's exclusion and different treatment,[5] this book analyses the reasons for women's exclusion through reference to the aims that philosophers attempt to achieve. For example, if the secure and stable state is supported by legitimacy bestowed by a limited citizenry, the criteria for entry must be examined. If the limitations of citizenship are based on false premises, then the ensuing legitimacy cannot be genuine. Similarly, the exclusion of the female half of the population from 'universal' citizenship requires precise justification if the tenets of liberty and justice, or morality, are to be authenticated within states. If exclusion is to be justified, it must be shown that women are incapable of performing the tasks of citizenship that men are required to do. Not only is this book concerned with the authenticity of political philosophies and consequent political structures and processes, then, but it is also, tentatively, proposing that, despite their patriarchal roots, their objectives are potentially universal. After all, it is hardly radical to assume that women require liberty, justice, security and stability so that we may pursue our interests in the way that we choose without hindrance from others doing the same. Remove the patriarchy from liberal, socialist/Marxist or democratic theory and the universality of this aspiration becomes evident.

Women are Essentially Different

During the 1960s and 1970s, an assumption pervading feminism was that all women shared their oppression, or sense of it, that they understood their exclusion from politics and their secondary relationship to citizenship and its benefits. If they did not, they should have. Such unfortunate individuals were probably suffering from some form of false consciousness or the effects of ingrained patriarchy. It took the courage of black and working-class women to challenge the potential tyranny of white, middle-class feminism and to stimulate feminist conceptions of diversity.[6] It is now almost universally accepted that women not only experience inequalities, but have diverse ideals to which they aspire in equality. Consequently, they perceive different solutions appropriate to their objectives. This naturally causes problems for feminists, and others, who attempt to consider universal histories. Much as we might rail against philosophers who are obviously writing about middle-class women when they refer to 'women's' sedentary domestication, knowing that working-class women have always managed the double burden of domestic and public labour, we might also contest that generalised feminist analysis and feasible solutions to patriarchy address only particular segments of womankind. For example, reference to women's right to equal treatment at work may not include women's equal right to fair treatment if they decide to work in the domestic sphere, devoting themselves solely to family. Similarly, not all women are mothers and are discriminated against in the same way, or in the same arenas, as those with children. The danger with this kind of disaggregation is that a stage is reached in which there are no commonalities and issues of collective concern around which to organise. The feminism of the twentieth century was remarkable in its power to congregate women from diverse backgrounds and across interests around common issues. The fact that, like traditional philosophies, it has always been consti-tuted of more than one variant, even expanding in the late twentieth century to include, for example, black, lesbian and psychoanalytic feminisms, does not diminish the shared objective of achieving wo-men's full and equal rights. What must not be lost in the recognition of diversity are the elements of sameness that connect women, whatever their concerns.

Throughout this book, women are often referred to *qua* women, but with the understanding that they will appreciate different means and ends in pursuit of their interests. Thus, it does not take an essentialist standpoint, but starts from the view that all women are disadvantaged in relation to the state and citizenship. This cannot be avoided when studying the political philosophies, in which unconditional justification for women's universal exclusion is propounded. However, it must also be recognised that the political philosophers are products of their own time and experiences. Maybe, in the eras in which the philosophers worked, women's lives were more varied than is acknowledged in works such as *The Politics*, *Leviathan*, or *Emile*. However, the philosophers evidently were either unaware of this or their life circumstances would have protected them from this knowledge. Or perhaps it was merely expedient to ignore women's actual experience as it was inconsequential to the explication of the ideal and just state.

In the twenty-first century, women's secondary or marginal relationship to the state and citizenship is less pronounced. They are not excluded from political or economic participation, and it might be argued that politics has disregarded the inadequacies of political philosophy to accommodate women's rights as citizens. But, if gender equality had been achieved, not only would there be no need for books, papers and conferences on the subject of inequality, other than historical biographies and chronicles, but demonstrations and protests, legislation and initiatives to institute equal rights would be unnecessary. Moreover, the recently instituted trends in maintaining gender statistics provides empirical evidence of women's continuing under-representation in political and economic organisations, with analysis confirming fairly universal variables in its causation.[7] In other words, not only is it evident in works of political philosophy but also in contemporary political life that women are universally disadvantaged, even if in differing measures and by diverse means.

In this sense, then, women can certainly be subsumed under the label 'different' in relation to the state. Despite the fact that in liberal democracies many women may not perceive themselves as in any way disadvantaged by their sex and have succeeded in achieving, or working towards, their aspirations, it does not diminish the more prevalent experience of having at least some patriarchal obstacles and hindrances to contend with. In practical terms, it is essential to understand the common root of women's political inequality in terms of philosophy. Without this understanding women challenge the 'norms' of justice, morality and citizenship as embodied females, rather than as participants in their own right. This is evident when the 'neutrality' of citizenship is situated in a gendered context – male philosophers perceive citizens in their own image. Citizens not in that image are automatically visible, so disrupting the smooth efficiency of business that is the result of convention. Once difference is interposed, attention can be paid to physical differences and their implications rather than the fundamental sameness of citizens. Female citizens are perceived as women first, and their interests labelled 'women's issues'. Whereas, in reality, women's interests are as much the interest of the good state as so-called neutral interests which are, in fact, those of men. Inequality arises and persists, therefore, because women are as they are, not solely because their exclusion has been constructed on political grounds. Until this is acknowledged, women cannot argue their case in deliberative fora (Squires 1999) or in terms of multi-layered citizenship (Yuval-Davis 1999) on grounds that will be fully comprehended as petitions not just for policies to address evident inequalities and discrimination, but for full human rights.

As should be evident, there is no argument here for absolute uniformity among women. After all, different liberalisms or socialisms do not necessarily perceive their rationalisation in terms of unvaried humanity, occupation, situation and circumstance. Rather it is to ensure the same rights for women as men in whichever philosophy is concerned. Depending on the philosophy considered, this may not serve to equalise differences between socio-economic classes or races. But there is no philosophical reason for gender difference within such categories. Thus women should be able to act individually and collectively in the areas in which their interests converge (much as Young's (1997a) gender as seriality implies) as equals in their own right, not in the image of male citizenship and within the framework of patriarchal justice.

A Thematic Approach to
Political Philosophers' Influence on Contemporary Politics

The choice of political philosophers to illustrate the longevity, and the illogicality, of arguments for women's continuing political under-representation, was not intended to stretch the imagination or be in any way innovative. As the purpose of the book is to consider the everyday concepts of politics, and the customary excuses concerning why they do not apply to women, it seemed most appropriate to select well-known and mainstream influential thinkers. Of course, within these parameters choices were also made about whom to exclude, a rather ironic situation for a woman to be in, considering the nature of this book. As philosophers within the same traditions usually concur on the issue of women within their ideals, the choice was made easy; to exclude those with the least to say on women and those who were considered less engaging, or entertaining, in their treatment of women.

Aristotle may have little time to devote to women, but what consideration he does give them offers much for analysis. In particular, it is interesting that his work contains ideas that are familiar in contemporary arguments about women's maternity and inability to participate rationally in politics. Plato, Rousseau, Mill and Engels, together with Marx, are included as philosophers who had much to say about women. With these thinkers it is possible to see how 'progressive' arguments for equality are undermined by the inability to perceive women fully as equals, being unable to detach them from their maternal and domestic proclivities as well as, in Plato's case, blatant misogyny. Rousseau's argument for the separate but equal status of women, including their exclusion from politics, is a most entertaining example of double standards and illogical contention. Hobbes and Locke are rather interesting in their justification for excluding women from a new order of politics that would incorporate greater levels of democracy than had been proposed since the ancient Greeks. The contemporary philosophers, Rawls and Nozick, are included not only as examples of how political philosophy continues in the image that writers, since the time of Plato and Aristotle, have managed to sustain, but also for their remarkable attempt to circumvent the gender issue by not mentioning women at all. Unlike previous philosophers who knew the exigency of justifying women's exclusion from politics and, thus, sustaining the gendered status quo, the contemporary thinkers do so by assuming equality in societies in which women have the formal status of citizen without its full benefits.

Although within the work of each philosopher there is a complete story to tell about the exclusion of women from their ideal states, the format chosen for this book is more thematic. This satisfies two motives. The first is that it avoids excessive duplication. None of the political philosophers here manages, or even attempts, to justify women's exclusion on grounds other than their maternity and related domesticity. Certainly, their understanding of how this condition precludes political acuity and general development of intellect differs. It ranges from not having the time and leisure to develop and execute political acumen (*Politics*), and being unable to concentrate exclusively on affairs of the commonwealth (*Republic*), to being such precious moral beings that they should remain uncorrupted by the acerbity and depravity of the state and politics (*Emile*), to the 'fact' that having babies makes women dolts (implicit throughout). Therefore, although the theme of domesticity recurs throughout the book, the idea was not to reiterate philosophers' obsession with it. Instead, the traditional role of women, as advocated by the philosophers, is analysed in relation to some of the major objectives that the philosophers defended. The second explanation for using a more thematic approach is that it builds on the history of political philosophy, each theme emphasising a particular concept that has contributed to the modern cognition of politics. As such, it is intended to draw a picture illustrating the various aspects of women's exclusion, so adding to the understanding of the entrenched attitudes that perpetuate their under-representation today.

To set a context, the first three chapters of the book are concerned with the development of the state as the arena in which political relations are traditionally based. Chapter 2 is specifically concerned with humankind in pre-society, or the state of nature. Although this is a concept used by liberal contract theorists to show how the state and relations within it are the result of agreement between self-interested individuals (Ackerman 1980: 320; Vincent 1997: 15), presumably all political philosophies begin from a pre-civil condition from which gender relations are, apparently, determined. It is the philosopher's conception of humanity that ascertains their ideal state, based on relations that humanity can sustain. It would be a foolish man, indeed, who conceived of selfish and atomised individuals living in harmonious co-operation. If the basic nature of man is selfish and individualistic, then the ideal state must harness any propensity for egotism and vainglory to the common good while maintaining as much liberty for the satisfaction of self-interest as possible. On the other hand, if the unalloyed and extraordinarily selfish behaviour of an aberrant minority undermines the collective and sociable nature of the many to the detriment of society, being in contrast to human nature, then it is more likely that philosophers will advise a more communal form of state and government.

It is particularly interesting to see philosophers' opinions on the nature of humankind, before socio-political relations are established. For, as we know, gender relations are often more politically motivated and socialised than 'natural' (Millett 1977: 31–2; Wollstonecraft 1985). Thus, the perceptions of famous misogynists like Rousseau, or run-of-the-mill patriarchs like Locke, who discern women's and men's equality in the state of nature, are revealing of the very origins of political inequality as societies developed and politics was needed. Whilst submitting to the notion that women are capable of the same proficiency as men in their quest for self-preservation in pre-society, philosophers cannot fully conceive of any situation in which the traditional family, of wife, husband and offspring, did not exist. This was the 'earliest society' (*Discourse on Inequality*: 79–80; *Leviathan*: 87), and it seems that men were able to build commonwealths and govern in their own interests, of course including women and family under this umbrella, safe in the knowledge that they did not have to contend with the double burden of managing everyday life as well.

By the time the state was at its earliest stages of development, then, a division between the public and private had already been established. In the state of nature, male heads of families risked the hazards of the public world to provide for their dependants who remained safe in the private sphere of the household. Chapters 3 and 4 consider the pivotal role of women in the maintenance of order within states in their various conceptions. For example, in the Greek *polis*, and also evident in Rousseau's general will, women's virtue was in their traditional role, much as barrel-makers' virtue was in theirs. In states whose primary purpose is the regulation of economic or property relations, there is no reason for women to augment their domestic role with concerns of the state. Their lack of property, established in law, removes them from the need to interact as political participants in the public sphere. It is also evident that, whilst placing the family outside of the bounds of political interest, most philosophers place it at the pinnacle of political development. It is here that the relationships between ruler and ruled are most perfect, and on which relationships in the state should be modelled. The cynics amongst us might, at this point, begin to suspect that philoso- phers' praising of the family, and extrapolation of household hierarchies to the state, are instrumental in confirming and sustaining male power without much more justification than personal preference. However, this is to fall into the same lack of cognisance of which the philosophers are being accused.

Liberal democratic states are supposed to amalgamate the demands of liberalism and democracy: a comprehensive range of interests is ad- dressed by politicians who are elected and, therefore, legitimised by all individuals over the age of majority. The majority of 'ordinary' citizens also have the right to stand for election, to make representations to elected members of assemblies and appointed officials entrusted with policy implementation, and to protest or make their interests known by any legal means, so potentially influencing political agendas. However, based on the hypothesis that every new conception of the good state is developed on the strengths and weaknesses of those attempted pre- viously, when domestic affairs are considered to be the responsibility of members of the state as private individuals, they do not extend to the political agenda. Consequently, the failure of liberal democrats to apply a gender analysis to their ideas and policies, and their inability to listen to and understand feminist perspectives on the genuine application of liberal democratic objectives to women as full citizens, maintains the family and 'private' interests as separate from the state. In this case, it is possible for women to be perceived as 'equal' only in the context of the public sphere. In many ways, then, despite the advances of liberal democracy from the democratic ideals of the Greeks and Rousseau, and the liberal archetype which promotes the concept of pursuit of self- interest as essential to the interests of the state, it remains secure in the tradition of androcratic ideas which can only, by definition, be partial.

The concept of androcracy is one that is used throughout the book, complementing the understanding of patriarchy. Androcracy refers specifically to male-dominance in the traditional political arena with which this explication is concerned. In ethnographic terms, it is the foundation stone without which patriarchy cannot exist: in the absence of androcratic policy, patriarchs in the wider community have no exclusive claims to pre-eminence. Thus, a conscious decision was made not to use the term patriarchy in the context of contemporary politics. In addition, it is hard to argue against patriarchs who can point to the improved, and increasing, representation of women in elected assem- blies, administrations and economic organisations and say that women are not represented in their policy-making processes. Inevitably, the unthinking patriarch will assume that policy output is also representa- tive of the women who participate in it. However, it is not just old-fashioned patriarchs who perceive such phenomena. Young women do not necessarily appreciate their 'oppression' and believe that they are as free as men to pursue their interests; young and older feminists all know of men who are not archetypal patriarchs and who have supported the rights of women *qua* women and not as surrogate citizens; women who have 'made it' to the top of their professions may never have acknowledged any discrimination they have encountered, or may choose to perceive themselves as better for having overcome it.[8] The fact is that politics is no longer a male-only domain. Women are involved and 'women's issues' are on the political agenda and incorporated into 'relevant' policy. What remains constant is that the terms of engagement in the state, and its resulting policies and actions, are male-orientated. This is what the term androcracy, and its related androcentricity, is intended to convey.

Chapter 5 considers the origins of androcracy. The work of Plato and Aristotle proves fundamental to the notion that the good and just state is 'public' and that, although moral behaviour learnt and practised in the household is essential to the state, it is not *of* the state. In their different ways, both philosophers argue the 'truth' of women's place in the household. Plato, whose thesis in *The Republic* actually commends women as men's potential equals in identical occupations, argues in *The Laws* (1970: 445) that, in practice, women are men's inferiors and that it would take some stretch of credibility for them to be afforded equality. In contrast, Aristotle's teleological approach could not conceive of women as men's equals, the truth of their being, or the ends for which they exist, ascribing them the role of providers of healthy, male babies. In both cases, the foundations are laid for the social control of women to assure their supportive role. In the *polis* and succeeding states, in which order and security depend on individuals adhering to their 'natural' proclivities, control of those people forced into anomalous roles becomes inevitable. While domesticity may be the natural inclination for some women, it is unlikely that this pertains to all of them. Consequently, Plato and Aristotle's 'truths', and the justice which depends on these, prove somewhat partial.

The significance of political philosophy pertaining to ancient societies might not be of more than historical interest had not some of the key concepts they contained become so integrated into successive political ideas. By the time that Hobbes and Locke (Chapter 6) were expounding the virtues of earthly legitimacy for governments, it was accepted that women were not part of the political landscape. And yet, both philosophers felt compelled to justify women's exclusion from their illustrious ideas. Conceivably, by the seventeenth century, when they were producing their major political treatises, women were clearly dissatisfied with their circumstances, perhaps even supporting the 'wrong' ideas that Hobbes and Locke so eloquently challenged. For example, although much of women's history has been assigned to oblivion, we know that in the mid-seventeenth century, Aphra Behn, evidently suffering from a less than housewifely disposition, was prominent as a political actor, being a spy for Charles II and, as a playwright and political activist, overtly supporting the Catholic monarchy (Spender 1982; Behn 1992). The period of Behn's activism, and of her most prolific writing, would have coincided with Hobbes' and Locke's work, *Leviathan* being published in 1651 and the *Two Treatises* in 1690. Moreover, the legitimacy of Catholic kings rested on divine right, the very notion that Hobbes and Locke contested. It might be conjectured, accordingly, that the 'evidence' for women's unsuitability for politics required reiteration.

This was not too difficult for the early liberal writers who attempted to justify the dissolution of the divine right of kings without necessarily invalidating man's right to rule. The scriptures may not have given Adam, based on his relationship to God, dominion over all humankind, thus relegating women to the permanent status of ruled (*Two Treatises*), nor may man have been created in God's image (*Leviathan*) presenting the same implications for women. But, where political power is concerned, men created commonwealths (*Leviathan*) and are stronger and more able than women (*Two Treatises*) and, thus, merit the status of political rulers. Indeed, more than deserving to rule, it is imperative that they do so, since women's inability threatens civil disorder and a return to the state of nature. Consequently, when both Hobbes and Locke launch into the major contention of their dissertations, respectively, the achievement and maintenance of civil order and the regulation of private property as a means to just order, underpinned and legitimised by different measures of individual sovereignty consolidated in an original contract, the relevance of the state to women, and their potential for participation, have been dispensed with. This results in a distinct inconsistency in the basic doctrine concerning the type of liberal polities that both philosophers appeal to: that of women, who are equal in the state of nature, contracting with men to deny themselves the right to accumulate property, therefore abdicating their inalienable responsibility for self-preservation. In a polity that venerates individual liberty as the key to security and stability of the state, it can only be assumed that, as in the *polis*, women are somehow constrained in the, successful, attempt to domesticate them.

In many ways, Hobbes and Locke provide the template from which liberal democracies have developed. Hobbes was rather less 'democratic' than Locke who introduced to politics a more extensive concept of popular sovereignty than the Greeks had managed, and which was developed further by Rousseau in *The Social Contract*. Both perceived the good state to rest on the liberty of individuals to pursue their economic interests. Whether everything since then has been 'tinkering' to perfect the model (apart from the more revolutionary ideas that perceive liberal democracy as promoting the antithesis of freedom) is not a subject for debate in this context. For the purpose of this book, the progeniture of the model is accepted. This enables the analysis to progress to consideration of one of the essential elements of participatory citizenship: education. Indeed, it is not only participatory citizenship that relies on the education of citizens but, as Bernard Shaw (1944: 149) argued, without education there can be no progress. Chapter 7 explores some of the more remarkable expositions of Rousseau, who was convinced of women's simultaneous moral rectitude and malfeasance, in contrast with the more considered views of J. S. Mill who concluded that only socialisation differentiated women from men.

Although Plato first elucidated the importance of education to citizenship, and therefore the state, Rousseau's description of the education of his protégé, Emile, and his carefully selected partner, Sophy, is the definitive depiction of the necessary elements that contribute to the well-rounded, selfless citizen. It is a beautiful example of selective reasoning. Rousseau attempts to demonstrate how self-interest is utilised for the common good. Thus, *Emile* becomes a companion text to *The Social Contract*, which expounds the concept of the general will, by which each citizen subsumes their particular will for the benefit of the community. Unfortunately, it seems that women, by their nature, can never master this ability and are, therefore, disqualified from citizenship. The familiar theme of women's incarceration in the private sphere is, yet again, evident in Rousseau's work. Unlike boys, who are to be encouraged as the autonomous individuals that nature intends, education for girls is a masterpiece of constraint. Although girls seem naturally to evince more of the key criteria for citizenship than boys, for example, interest and enthusiasm for current affairs and learning, they are taught to curb their enquiring minds in the service of others. Most probably as a consequence of Rousseau's personal prejudices, the possibility that girls can be educated to be participants in the general will is not explored: they are, instead, to be both moral guardians and *in situ* paramours.

In contrast to Rousseau's doctrine of exclusive education for citizenship, J. S. Mill acknowledges the role of education in the exclusion from political activity of both women and men. Moreover, Mill was not only concerned with access of the traditional political 'class', but with extending participation to all individuals who had grasped the basic principles of literacy and numeracy provided *en masse* by affordable education. If it was possible for individuals to read of experiences broader than their own, to articulate interests and debate policy, there was no reason for their banishment from politics. Indeed, it was the carefully administered inclusion of people traditionally exempt from politics that would propel politics forward towards a greater legitimacy and a new vitality that limited citizenship could not hope to achieve. For Mill, education is not just concerned with the formal learning located in the classroom. His emphasis on female and male socialisation concentrated attention in the home as the breeding ground for traditional, gendered attitudes and behaviours. However, as such, it is also the potential forum for education for freedom and proper citizenship. Unlike Rousseau's household, in which traditional roles, manners and proclivities were to be strictly reinforced, for Mill it is in the family that boys and girls can learn equitability, which can then inform their equitable public behaviour. The more insightful strength of Mill's work is the linkage of women's liberation to the development of their political acumen. Together, his essays *On Liberty, On Representative Government* and *The Subjection of Women* present a potentially comprehensive picture of women's genuine inclusion in the political arena, although this is marred somewhat by Mill's inability fully to conceive that women's liberation might manifest itself in anything other than their choosing their traditional occupation in the private sphere.

Like Mill, Engels and Marx lived in a period when the economic contribution of women to the state, as well as their political activism, was undeniable, even if their domestic work remained unrecognised in economic and political terms. In Chapter 8, the apparent shift in political philosophy towards a more inclusive equalitarian perspective is considered. Engels presents an anthropological-economic explanation of inequality as a key to greater economic equality. Thus, *The Origin of the Family, Private Property and the State* is a map of human development from savagery to contemporary *homo economicus*. It is here that an explanation is attempted for the regression of women from primary economic participants, having control over the domestic production which sustained communities, to the proletarian equivalent of man as the bourgeoisie. In other words, once the deleterious effects of capitalism on the family are overcome, the potential exists for equal treatment and opportunity of women and men under communism. However, as with Mill's portrait of a polity or society defined by equal participation of all able adults, too much liberty for women poses an inherent threat: if women do not choose to maintain the services that they have traditionally and historically provided, who will? Marx and Engels offer an economically based solution to the housework problem, instituting a social industry that would undertake domestic tasks. Presumably this would include communal refectories, universal childcare and public laundries. Ideally, as in Plato's *Republic*, such services would be provided by those whose 'nature' was most suited to the work involved, whether they were women or men. But, as Plato discovered, such 'radical' ideas could not be sustained even in more revolutionary philosophies.

What cannot be denied, despite the evident discrepancies in the thoughts of philosophers who advocate more equal recognition in the state and, therefore, greater participation in politics, is that they at least attempted to explain women's historical exclusion as a means to remedy it. The tired old association of maternity with irrationality, selfishness and general lack of aptitude was, at last, subject to question. Of course, society and politics have progressed further since the nineteenth century, when Marx, Engels and Mill were first suggesting that women could be included as 'equal' participants in political, or socio-economic, decision-making. It appears from the contemporary philosophers that there is no need to mention women at all in their texts[9] and that the equalising task of their predecessors has been accomplished. Rawls and Nozick, the subjects of Chapter 9, were instrumental in revitalising political philosophy, and particularly liberalism, in the twentieth century. For Rawls, just political conditions are the culmination of deliberation in 'the original position', in which individuals, devoid of all particular knowledge of their status, wealth and personal preferences, determine the conditions under which they can gain most from society. The intention of this procedure is that, in ignorance of personal information but with knowledge of the general principles of society and economics, everyone will ensure that no one is unduly and hopelessly disadvantaged. Nozick immediately challenges Rawls' assumption of justice as fairness, arguing that no person can justly make claims of any others; the only means to justice is to remove the interventionist state and leave individuals to pursue their self-interests, subject only to the rule that they enable other people to do the same.

The problem that these thinkers encounter is that, unlike Hobbes and Locke, they are writing at a time when liberalism is well-established. They do not have the luxury of developing their ideas of the ideal state from its foundation in the state of nature. Of course, this does not prevent them from basing their ideas on their conception of human nature, Rawls apparently favouring a more co-operative notion than Nozick. But it does situate their theories in thriving liberal democratic polities in which traditions, attitudes, procedures and relations are relatively secure. The implications of this are profound but obviously veiled by convention. For example, as far as Rawls' 'veil of ignorance' is concerned, sex and gender are intrinsic to humanity and cannot be 'forgotten' when determining the conditions of justice. Women in the original position may not know whether they are unemployed single-parents, university professors or business owners, but many of them will know, within the general principles of society and politics, that they are disadvantaged compared to men in the same position.[10] Similarly, with reference to Nozick's deification of the economic market place, women have never been afforded equal access to, or opportunity in, markets. Not only are they are less propertied and less well paid than men, but also the market does not extend to the household. It is well known that the domestic sphere contribution to states' economies is unaccounted and unremunerated (UN 1995). Consequently, although Nozick refers to not equality but to the equal ability of all individuals to maximise their potential or interests within their circumstances, women remain universally disadvantaged within the minimal, regulatory, state that he advocates.

The significance of Rawls and Nozick is that they have both been influential in contemporary politics: the concept of deliberative democracy is one whose star is shining brightly (Squires 1999; Weale 2000) following nearly two decades of Nozickean Reaganonics and Thatcherism, when states have been 'rolled back' and markets reified. Here the significance of the hypothesis of this book becomes evident: if women, despite their formal citizenship status, are not perceived as sovereign individuals in their own right, their participation is in danger of androcratic assimilation. In other words, they will be perceived as 'women' bringing 'their' issues to the debate, not as citizens with inalienable rights to universal liberties, security and status in the state. The concluding chapter considers these issues. The main emphasis, here, is not to provide a prescription of how women can become sovereign citizens, but to consider the effects of their not being so. The omnipotence of the public-private divide that philosophers through the ages have reinforced is, of course, instrumental in women's lack of sovereignty: the 'domestication' of women, whatever else they may be permitted to do in addition, does not admit their genuine liberty in the way that philosophers have always perceived essential to individuals' sovereignty. As such, women can be granted the rights of citizenship, to add to the responsibilities that they have always maintained without the benefit of the status. What is at stake, however, is whether these can be utilised by women, and whether they are thoroughly enforced by the state.

Notes

1. The term common wealth attempts to breach the public-private divide by including all contributions towards the common good. It is intended to complete philosophers' use of 'commonwealth' which tends to refer only to the public sphere.

2. Admittedly, numerical proportionality is not evidence of political representation per se (Sperling 1997). It is used here simply to make a point
concerning the relatively slow progress towards full equality.

3. Phillips (1999) presents a clear and accessible argument that political
equality is unlikely to be achieved without economic equality.

4. Full participation is qualified here, as not everyone, female or male, is eager
for more than minimal political activity. On the other hand, the potential to
influence decision-makers, by even infrequent participation on issues of
personal interest, is possible in liberal democracies and must be available
equally to all.

5. The references for this are numerous. In particular, radical feminist texts
such as Millett (1977), Daly (1978), Firestone (1979), French (1992) and
Greer (2000) demonstrate this phenomenon most starkly.

6. The power of the feminist movement rested in its unity, as women from
diverse backgrounds and circumstances acknowledged their common disadvantages under patriarchy. Consequently, it can be conjectured that it
took a great deal of courage not only to argue that 'sisters' were not behaving
in a way to progress the needs and demands of others, but to risk any
solidarity that may have developed in a 'common' struggle. As women know
only too well, to assert the politics of difference is to risk established
relationships and friendship networks (Phillips 1991) as well as 'alienation'
from the familiar.

7. The United Nations produced the first global 'statistical portrait and analysis of the situation of women' in 1991, and has been instrumental in
maintaining statistical records since. However, it is obvious that many
countries are somewhat tardy in their attitude to gender statistics. In states
where gender, or sex, inequality is not perceived as a major issue by those in
power, a commitment to monitoring and evaluating the situation of women
is unlikely to be given priority.

8. This may be a tired example to British readers, but Mrs Thatcher, the longest
serving Prime Minister who won a record four consecutive general elections, was renowned for having little respect for the disadvantages that
women are required to confront when attempting to advance themselves in
careers. During her seemingly interminable reign at the head of British
government, more was accomplished in dismantling the infrastructure that
enabled women to participate in the public sphere than at any other time
since the beginning of the twentieth century (David 1986; Lovenduski and
Randall 1993).

9. John Rawls has been more or less shamed into the occasional reference
to women in his later works as a result of criticism from renowned
feminist writers such as Susan Moller Okin (1994; Frazer and Lacey
1995: 234fn).

10. It might be argued that unemployed, single-parent men are as disadvantaged
as their female counterparts. Certainly this will be true for some, even
though they form a far smaller proportion of single parents. However, I
attended a self-help seminar for single parents some years ago where the 99
per cent of women delegates were addressed by a man with a six-month
baby in tow. He informed us, in embarrassment, of the tremendous assis-

tance he was receiving from neighbours volunteering to meet his childcare needs, and housing and social service departments offering services to him. This constituted a radically different experience from that encountered by the women present.

Chapter 2: The State of Nature and the Origins of the Exclusionary State

The state of nature is essentially a tool used by some political philosophers as a foundation stone on which to build civil society. Whether this is a teleological device in which current political institutions, processes and relationships are justified by reference to the philosopher's view of pre-history, or whether it is a theoretical model explaining the evolution of political development is debateable (Schochet 1975: 11–12). The attempt to relate women's under-representation in the public sphere to political thought will probably call on both definitions. Male philosophers may attempt to use the dearth of women in the public sphere as a reason why women are, or should be, excluded from politics, justifying their absence on biological or other grounds; or it may be that the evolution of political institutions and processes did not include women for quite legitimate reasons.

For some, the difference between models will be of no consequence – contemporary under-representation of women results from both. However, the difference may be important in terms of how women tackle their under-representation in politics and in the development of political philosophy. The 'end view' would render women's apolitical stance or under-representation 'natural'. In this case it may be possible to tinker with numbers of women representatives to display a sense of equity, but this will have little substantive effect. On the other hand, if gender inequality is not 'natural', and politics has evolved from a state of universal equality, its patriarchalism will have been constructed, in part, by male philosophers who had access to dissemination channels, and who justified, through their subjectivity, limited participation in the public sphere. In this case, there is much scope for change to ensure better representation for women in the public sphere.

The state of nature presents a philosopher's perception of the conditions existing in pre-society. As social relations form and society develops, so the consummate freedom that is inherent in the state of nature is compromised, and philosophers who utilise the concept are concerned with preserving as much liberty as possible in the emerging civil society. Projecting from the hypothesised state of nature, it is possible to demonstrate how best society is to be governed to ensure citizens' liberty as they pursue their interests. The answers to what type of state is necessary as society matures will rely on the philosopher's understanding of human nature, as demonstrated in the state of nature in which raw human nature is exhibited. In other words, how humans are and how they behave in the state of nature will determine what political structures are required as society develops and matures.

Taking two quite different views of the state of nature, based on differing perceptions of humanity in the raw, and of the resultant state, should demonstrate this. The states of nature of Hobbes and Rousseau are perhaps best known. They demonstrate diverse, if not opposing, perceptions and attitudes towards how people behave and how they are to be governed: one preferring a more participative government based on the 'fact' that humans are naturally co-operative and will look after others' needs if necessary; the other insisting that greater control over people's natural avariciousness and downright nastiness is required if order is to be assured. However, a third theory, propounded by contemporary political philosopher Robert Nozick, argues against the premises of theories such as Hobbes' and Rousseau's. Instead, it is maintained that, whatever the origins of, and level of authority in, the state, individuals' liberty is unacceptably infringed. What is required is to restore as much of the freedom of the state of nature as possible to existing mass societies, leaving individuals' interactions, through their rational choices, to co-ordinate actions and maintain order.

Hobbes' War of All against All: The Basis for Voluntary Submission

A crass summation of Hobbes' view of human nature is that it is naturally selfish and that people are quite ruthless in defence of acquisitions. However, this is too trite. Rather, for Hobbes, individuals are governed by passions that may result in behaviour of different types. For example 'appetites' will inspire individuals to acquire that which they desire, while 'aversions' cause individuals to protect what is good and avoid what they dislike (*Leviathan* Ch.VI; Goldsmith 1966: 85). Thus, the fear of having something good taken away, or of physical harm from acquisitive others, may produce pre-emptive or defensive action. Indeed, Goldsmith (1966: 73) characterises Hobbes' state of nature as being governed by fear (*Leviathan*: 64), and the tableau in which,

it is manifest, that during the time men live without a common Power to keep them all in awe, they are in that condition which is called Warre; and such a warre, as is of every man against every man is easily perceived. This makes it quite easy to see why all individuals will prefer to submit to one relatively authoritarian sovereign as expounded in Hobbes' idea of civil society. It is better to be governed by the Leviathan, legitimised by citizens' consent, than to be subject to constant fear of losing one's possessions or of physical harm. In this way all individuals give up some of the powers of defence and retribution inherent in their person in the state of nature, to maintain as much freedom as possible in undertaking their affairs without constant fear.

Why the sovereign should be a male, as it almost invariably is, is not clear at this point. The philosophy of Hobbes' *Leviathan* refutes the divine right of kings that commanded male succession as a consequence of rulers being 'naturally' fashioned in God's image (Filmer in Locke *Two Treatises* Ch.III; Elshtain 1981: 102). Rather, Hobbes was concerned that the sovereign should be, in contemporary terms, 'the right person for the job', and, more importantly, that they be legitimised through a process of consent. In the state of nature everyone is considered equal, a convenient premise built on by contemporary philosophers such as Nozick in advocating its restoration. This does not mean that every individual was identical in terms of strength or ability, but that they had an equal chance of acquisition and defence of acquired goods: one person may be physically stronger than another, but a quick minded person has equal ability to provide for themselves and defend themselves against attack or threat (*Leviathan*: 63). It may be assumed, therefore, that what women lacked in strength, compared to males, they gained in cunning and guile. Indeed, Hobbes argues that men are not always stronger than women and that men and women can be in a state of 'war' with each other (*Leviathan*: 105). However, this did not appear to be taken into account beyond the state of nature and into civil society, leading Hobbes into considerable difficulty in justifying a contractual society generally. If people contract with others in their own self-interest, it would surely not be in women's interests universally to contract into, and consent to, subservience. This poses a problem that has not yet been resolved despite modern attempts to revive liberal society based on such perceived equalitarian dispositions.

Schochet (1975) and Pateman (1991) have both considered such anomalies in Hobbes' work by addressing the inherent patriarchalism in his writings. In these analyses the issue of whether Hobbes' social unit is the individual or the family is considered, offering a clear, although still incomplete, explanation of female exclusion from the public sphere. Hobbes notes that the family existed in pre-society, being the first form of organised co-operation, and that 'as small Familyes did then; so now do Cities and Kingdoms' (*Leviathan*: 87). He perceived the family as the model for political order, this being a microcosm of civil society. Moreover, members of family units consented to 'the absolute authority of the family head in exchange for the protection provided by membership' (Green 1995: 45). Therefore, as the state of nature began to evolve and transmute into civil society, rather than individuals being in a state of war against all others, it was the head of the household, who provided for and ensured the interests of his family, who could be so defined (Schochet 1975: 238).[1] Such an exposition suggests that women were already non-public actors in pre-society, further strengthening the case for their non-political role as civil society matured.

While Hobbes' description of the pre-civil family may explain why a sovereign should be male, it does not offer a reason for the basis of this; that heads of families are fathers rather than mothers. Indeed, in arguing against the lateral progression of paternal power to patriarchal power as a means to counter the postulate of divine right, Hobbes asserts that all children owe loyalty to their mothers. In the state of nature reproduction is not accompanied by 'matrimonial laws', and only the mother of a child can really be identified, or may be able genuinely to identify the father. In this case, women have the power to dispose of or to nurture their children as they wish. The children whose mothers choose to nurture them are said by Hobbes to have tacitly contracted with their mothers for protection (*Leviathan*: 105), and under the Fourth Law of Nature which obliges a recipient of 'good' to the giver (*Leviathan*: 78; Goldsmith 1966: 102), they cannot harm these mothers as they might do in a state of nature.[2] Why women should then feel safer under the protection of a male as head of household is not explained. The logical outcome of Hobbes' ideas on parental dominion lying foremost with the mother is that mothers are not in danger and do not need to contract with a man for protection. They are protected through their status as mother. A far from logical explanation is given by Hobbes, who simply states that 'if the Mother be the Fathers subject, the Child, is in the Fathers power' (*Leviathan*: 105). To complete the circle, Hobbes states that because 'no man can obey two masters', and 'because for the most part Commonwealths have been erected by the Fathers, not by the Mothers of families' (*Leviathan*: 105), familial and, therefore, political sovereignty belongs to men.

Hobbes apparently refutes biological causes of women's exclusion from political society arising from the state of nature and progressing to civil society. But he cannot overcome the tendency to employ 'natural', even divine, excuses for denying women equality in a mature society. Unlike the Greek philosophers, some of whom expounded a zero-sum equation in which use of women's mental faculties would reduce their physical strength in producing healthy, male babies (*Politics*: 443; Okin 1980: 83), or Rousseau who overtly argued women's inability to work continuously due to regular physical incapacities (Okin 1980: 146; McMillan 1982: 87), Hobbes at least perceives women in the state of nature as equal, even if different in ability, to men. However, he does not explain how women universally chose to subject themselves to contracts with men within family units in the state of nature and henceforward, in their self-interest. If self-interest is acquisition and defence in the cause of self-preservation, it does not make sense for beings of equal, if different, ability to subjugate themselves unless everyone is equally subjugated (*Leviathan* Ch.XVI and XXI). Hence, political sovereignty, while embodied in one person or assembly, is the sum of the consent of every individual in the commonwealth. Every person is equally subject to the power of the sovereign and/or has power *en masse* to withdraw that consent.

Contrarily, in a family, women's consent is not implied by nature of historical evolution, it is given openly and individually. Thus, the continuous, historical consent to a sovereign cannot be likened to the consent given by individual women to family units headed by men. This is more obvious when the continuity of the patriarchal family is placed in the context of sporadic but not infrequent rebellions against rulers. Moreover, if women's situation in the state of nature requires their submission to a male head of family, they cannot withdraw their consent, having nowhere else to go. Obviously a return to the state of nature would not be contemplated. If this were an option they would have continued to take their chances there. Sometime, and somehow, women must have decided that they were not equal in the state of nature and that they were, indeed, in need of male protection, this being translated into political domination in the broader society. It is reasonable to suspect that, implicitly, Hobbes does in fact subscribe to biological determinism. On the other hand, it may conceivably have been beyond his experience for women to participate in politics. Perhaps, then, it is unreasonable to expect him to consider equal participation, or the equal chance of female succession, in his ideal state, despite Plato setting a precedent for this, *circa* 375 BC (Introduction to *Republic* 1955: 19), when women in the Greek *polis* were situated very much apart from the political arena.

Discourse on Inequality or
Recourse to Subjugation: Rousseau's Idyll

While equality, for Hobbes, dissipates silently as society matures from the state of nature, for Rousseau the change from equality to women's subjection is quite explicit and justifiable on grounds other than divine right. This is not to deny that inequality, or difference, between the sexes is God-given. However, it has a political purpose in addition to the procreation and nurturance of children. As half of the 'citizenship partnership' necessary to develop and maintain civil society, women have a very definite and essential role to play.

Rousseau's state of nature, perhaps a modification of Hobbes' (Green 1995: 71), is expounded in its entirety in the *Discourse on the Origin of Inequality*. Rousseau's view of human nature creates a much more idyllic state of nature than that described by Hobbes, wherein individuals may display compassion for others whilst pursuing what is needed for their own survival. The continuous state of war which Hobbes envisages would be denied by Rousseau in consideration of the absence of language and reason in a pure state of nature that is required to understand the consequences of any action (*Discourse on Inequality*: 65–6). Thus, appetite for accumulation and aversion to fear are irrelevant when referring to pre-social individuals. There is no concept of good or bad, virtue or viciousness (*Discourse on Inequality*: 64),

each man, regarding his fellows almost as he regarded animals of different species, might seize the prey of a weaker or yield up his own to a stronger, and yet consider these acts of violence as mere natural occurrences, without the slightest emotion of insolence or despite, or any other feeling than the joy or grief of success or failure. (*Discourse on Inequality*: 66fn)

As with Hobbes, individuals have equal liberty and ability to survive whilst displaying different strengths and weaknesses. Women are no less able than men to survive, and Rousseau specifically considers women as mothers being capable of providing for themselves and their babies in the state of nature (*Discourse on Inequality*: 52). They do not even implicitly rely on male, or other female, patronage for survival: they are not in danger of their lives from acquisitive others, nor are they confined to intermittent disability as a result of pregnancy.[3] However, as society matures, the familiar tableau of women's subservience is created in Rousseau's work. The question again arises as to how women are transformed from naturally equal beings in atomistic pre-society to submissive homemakers and non-participants in political activity in civil society.

In common with Hobbes and other philosophers who retreat to the state of nature to explain, justify or forecast political relations in civil society, Rousseau perceives the family as the first form of society (*Discourse on Inequality*: 79–80). While such a unit is discussed as a consequence of a revolution which saw the development of the foundations of society, tools, permanent shelters and communication through language, it is not justified in terms of the state of nature. Rather,

the first expansions of the human heart were the effects of a novel situation, which united husbands and wives, fathers and children under one roof. The habit of living together soon gave rise to the finest feelings known to humanity, conjugal love and paternal affection. (*Discourse on Inequality*: 79)

No explanation is provided for the development from a state in which humans effectively 'mate' and have no further contact with each other, probably not even recognising each other should they somehow meet again, to one in which 'husbands and wives' come to live together with their children. Admittedly, female/male coupling may be seen as a result of nature, the physical attributes and functions of each sex being natural and indisputable. However, how one individual of each sex forms attachments under which they will share shelter and other more material resources is unresolved. This becomes more anomalous if consideration is made in respect to modern knowledge about the physiological and psychological aspects of sex and sexuality that may result in homosexuality, and, furthermore, the accepted ability for individuals to 'choose' their sexuality. Overall, Rousseau's recourse to nature does not explain the nuclear family.[4]

At this stage, such a justification may be superfluous. For Rousseau, the couple are still equal 'the more united because liberty and reciprocal attachment were the only bonds of its union' (Discourse on Inequality: 80). However, in time, and for no apparent reason, 'the women became more sedentary, and accustomed themselves to mind the hut and their children, while the men went abroad in search of their common subsistence' (Discourse on Inequality: 80). Green (1995: 76) asserts that Rousseau sees this development as a ploy by women to entrap men to their will. After all, why subject oneself to conditions in the state of nature when someone else will provide for you? Indeed, this is part of a trend in which the division of resources to private ownership leads to avarice, jealousy, pride and all the vices that Hobbes perceived to be inherent in human nature, thus requiring government. For Rousseau, such attributes were the result of society itself (Discourse on Inequality: Part II). Once property is introduced, the development of human nature from selfless to selfish individualism begins. Women as selfish individuals will do their best to ensure that their own, and their children's, interests are provided for with as little danger to themselves as possible. For men, the need to make certain that their property is preserved and remains to their posterity requires that they control women in the family to ensure correct inheritance.

It could be surmised, without further analysis, that Rousseau's thought epitomises male chauvinism, basing its ideas on female and male roles in civil society on his predilection for male superiority and women as sex objects. His resort to women's lack of reason could also be cited as evidence of Rousseau's prejudices in his justification of 'unnatural' conditions for women and men. However, Green considers Rousseau's basis for disparity between the sexes in a less confrontational way, suggesting that his emphasis on nature does not imply inequality per se, but difference. Women and men both give up liberty in the family unit: women so that they ensure a greater chance of survival for themselves and their children; and men to provide for their family. The requirement on a man to acquire a surplus, so that not just he as an individual but his dependants can survive, basically denies him the freedom of the pure state of nature. Consequently, 'since it is women who rob men of their original liberty it is only fair that women too renounce their liberty' (Green 1995: 76). Far from denying women's capacity for reason, this account stresses it. Moreover, nature does not make women weak, feeble and, hence, unable to participate in civil society. Both women and men lose their strength when 'living a softer life' in the family unit (*Discourse on Inequality*: 80). But reason led to the division of labour between the sexes in the family, women using this capacity to ensure their survival.

What such an account omits, of course, is that in choosing dependence, women are hostages to fortune, as the withdrawal of male provision is always an implicit threat (Green 1995: 77). In effect, then, women sacrifice more freedom than men as they move out of the state of nature. They cannot return there as the state of nature would no longer exist for individuals (*Discourse on Inequality*: 90), and if it did, women believed they were better off leaving. As women become dependent on males, they have to work to keep their favour and patronage (Archer 1928: 230; Lange 1991: 99; Coole 1993: 84). This is not, then, a relationship of separate but equal contribution. Indeed, the pattern of male provider and female homemaker is explained by Rousseau in terms of women's and men's different natures. In the state of nature where women's maternal care lasts only as long as a child is suckling, and is not a hindrance to her continuing pursuit for provisions and survival, there is no cause for suspecting that in the family unit whoever is the best provider should take that role. When each individual has their own strengths and weaknesses in different abilities, there is no reason why the males should become universal providers and women universally homemakers. While in later work it becomes obvious that women should be carers, their physiology and contrary nature requiring their training and education to the role of homemaker (*Emile*; Archer 1928: 219–20; McMillan 1982: 86), in the *Discourse on Inequality*, Rousseau merely notes that in mature societies in which family units have developed beyond the mutual assistance and co-operation that established them in the state of nature, women 'with much care and cleverness establish their empire' (*Discourse on Inequality*: 70). In other words, Rousseau cannot sustain the imaginative equality in the state of nature into civil society, and resorts to traditional views of the sexes based on lived experience. His own patronage by rich and powerful women enables him to see that women are able to control people, but that this in some way emasculates men or denies them their rightful role.[5] As in biblical stories, women's power is corrupt and also corrupts. Therefore, not only is it fair play that men be allowed public power and rights as citizens when civil society ensues, but it is necessary to ensure men of their rightful place and to provide honest government.

If, as the state of nature theories of Hobbes and Rousseau attest, the greater subjection of women cannot be justified then it is possible that even a mainstream philosophy based on recuperating the benefits of that condition could recreate the levels of freedom and liberty for all people. After all, in civil society everyone sacrifices a certain amount of freedom to ensure that the highest level of liberty possible is attained. It is just that women seem to make greater sacrifices for so much less liberty.

The State of Nature Revisited: Nozick and the Hidden Female

Writing from the vantage point of having experienced and analysed the consequences of the structures and processes advocated by traditional liberal theorists to maintain the liberty of the state of nature in civil society, Nozick asserts that the opposite effect has transpired. For him, to defend individuals' rights in a modern polity, the convictions about freedom in the state of nature need to be reinvigorated. The main problem with the development of the state as traditional contract theorists profess, is that the emphasis on 'rights' in modern civil society, wherein these rights become the focus of state activity, results in greater violation of the rights of others.[6] Where everyone has numerous rights, they will increasingly impinge on those of others, necessitating ever greater state intervention. In other words, to ensure all individuals' rights, the state has to enforce an unacceptable level of sacrifice by everyone. For example, taxation to pay for welfare 'rights' or other social goods is a sacrifice by every working person to pay for those who do not provide for themselves, and where 'taxation of earnings from labor [sic] is on a par with forced labor [sic]' (Anarchy, State and Utopia: 169). Rather than maintaining rights, defined as the inalienable rights that accrue to people by birth and so evident in the state of nature, the modern state has attempted to define and prioritise 'rights' and in so doing impinges continuously and increasingly upon them.

Where traditional contract theorists had erred, in Nozick's view, was by subscribing to the notion that a contract ensured that 'when everybody owns everybody, nobody owns anybody' (Anarchy, State and Utopia: 286). Thus, the contract represented a subtle but significant switch from the evolutionary, legitimate state to a contrived, interventionist one in which everybody is subservient. By basing the development of the state on Locke's state of nature, Nozick describes how states can evolve via the invisible hand of social and economic forces, resulting in a minimal state that remains a voluntary association. The familiar themes of equality are evident in Locke's description of the state of nature, but his particular interest in this condition lies with the executive powers that accrue to individuals as they pursue their interests. Every person has the right to exact punishment for infringements on their property, obviously favouring their own interests over those of actual or potential trespassers. Civil government, then, is considered as 'the proper remedy for the inconveniences of the state of Nature' (*Two Treatises*: 123), equality of executive power providing not justice but anarchy. From such a condition, Nozick speculates that individuals and groups in the state of nature would have co-operated to protect each other's property from threat or attack, developing mutual protective agencies to which other people could voluntarily contract. As such agencies grew and merged, a dominant agency evolved which provided protection for its clientele, including the right to exact punishment for rights' infringements, and to develop and publicise acceptable terms and conditions of engagement between individuals and communities within its territory (*Anarchy, State and Utopia*: Ch.2). By all definitions, Nozick notes that this is, in fact, a minimal state (*Anarchy, State and Utopia*: 118). However, it is not autarchic, being subject to the laws of competition wherein other protective agencies could challenge its position. In other words, the 'market' choices of individuals within the minimal state concerning their protection and self-preservation, unhindered by universal contracts and obligation to others, maintains the voluntary basis of relationships with the state, even to the extent that the minimal state is legitimate only as long as it maintains its market position.

For Nozick, therefore, the state cannot be legitimised beyond what is necessary to preserve the liberty experienced in a state of nature. The protection of individuals as they each exert their rights to the acquisition and maintenance of property is all that can be sanctioned. This is not to return to a war of all against all with its implications for human nature. Rather, it acknowledges that, either in error or deliberately, accumulation can result in violations of fundamental rights and that a minimal level of regulation and redress is required in public interactions. As such,

the minimal state treats us as inviolate individuals, who may not be used in certain ways by others as means or tools or instruments or resources; it treats us as persons having individual rights with the dignity this constitutes. Treating us with respect by respecting our rights, it allows us, individually or with whom we choose, to choose our life and to realize [sic] our ends and our conception of ourselves, insofar as we can, aided by the voluntary co-operation of other individuals possessing the same dignity. (*Anarchy, State and Utopia*: 333–4)

The solution to the insupportable intervention of the state in enforcing unjust 'rights' in contemporary society is to withdraw the state to its minimum, leaving a rump able to deal legitimately only with issues of law, order and defence, and enabling individuals voluntarily to contract together, and with agencies, to provide for their individual and common needs. Common needs are not to be confused with universal needs here. There are few, if any, needs that everyone experiences in equal measures if at all. Indeed, in Nozick's ideal civil society, no one is responsible for anyone else's needs.

Utopia will consist of utopias, of many different and divergent communities in which people lead different kinds of lives under different institutions. Some kinds of communities will be more attractive to most than others; communities will wax and wane . . . Utopia is a framework for utopias, a place where people are at liberty to join together voluntarily to pursue and attempt to realize [sic] their own vision of the good life in the ideal community but where no one can *impose* his own utopianism. (*Anarchy, State and Utopia*: 312)(original emphasis)

As women's nature or position is not mentioned at all in *Anarchy, State and Utopia* it could be assumed that Nozick includes women in his definition of 'individual', with all this implies for their interactions in the minimal state. However, as with any state of nature theory, the assumption that individuals have equal ability to pursue their interests cannot be sustained without considering their different situations in relation to others. For example, within the state of nature, Hobbes and Rousseau both introduce the family unit in which a division of labour occurs by whatever means. Such a separation, while not necessarily resulting in inequality, but difference, defines the relations of individuals to particular activities. Male heads of households acting in the state of nature become participating citizens as the civil state develops, and women within the household are 'evolved out' of public interaction beyond domestic need. Nozick does not take such a developmental line of argument in his theory. Rather, basing his theory of contemporary society on Locke's state of nature, he does not consider how social relations occurred. We can only assume that he accepts Locke's premise of the family, not questioning his theories on paternal and parental power (*Two Treatises*: Book II, Ch.VI), and supported by generations of tradition and socialisation.[7] However, this raises a problem in that social relations have changed, and continue to do so, since the traditional philosophers were propounding their ideas. For example, it is not certain whether Nozick accepts the decline of the two (heterosexual)-parent family so intrinsic to traditional theories, and the rise of woman-headed and single-parent households; whether he implicitly acknowledges the advantages of men in the public sphere, despite the participation of more women at all levels; or, indeed, if these are even important beyond the fact that attempts to produce change limit individuals' freedom and cannot legitimately be sustained.

For traditional theorists, and most clearly expounded by Rousseau, the state and relations within it rely on the division of labour between men and women. Male heads of household are able to operate outside the family more effectively because the division of labour enables them to be single-minded in their pursuits. In households with dependants and only one provider, the double burden of providing and caring must affect the ability to participate effectively and achieve full potential or pursuit of self-interest. This was clearly recognised by Hobbes, Locke and Rousseau in advocating the male/breadwinner-female/homemaker dichotomy. Nozick does not refer to this phenomenon, however, and we may assume either that it is taken for granted that traditional relations apply, or that they are unimportant to his theory of liberty in the minimal state, where women are as able as men to maximise their interests within their given circumstances.

The individualism in Nozick's theory assumes that every person is able to pursue their self-interests to their fullest potential. This departs significantly from equality or even equality of opportunity, concepts that require the curtailing of individuals' rights to support the less fortunate (*Anarchy, State and Utopia*: Ch.8). Therefore, it cannot matter that women, who universally undertake more caring and domestic responsibilities (UN 1995: 90), have less potential than others to pursue their own interests. This may even be expressed in terms of rights: if women's relation to the private sphere is endemic, based on how society is, it must be assumed that women have fewer inherent rights than men. This is not a consequence of their individuality but of their status in relation to their role in society – a rather odd condition in a theory that is vehemently individualistic. Although some women will be in possession of more rights than some men, resulting from their birth-right and acquisitions over time, this is not to dispute the near universality of women's poorer status, materially and in socio-political relations.

Of course, Nozick's theory of individuals' rights to pursue their interests without being forced into providing for others cannot be sustained when the modern family is taken into account. In a family unit, every member's rights are curtailed by the responsibility to provide for the needs of others. As with the older philosophers, it may be that such limitations on individual rights are consented to, every member giving up certain rights. However, the stipulation that no one can be made to do something that they would not have done voluntarily without their rights being violated creates the risk that everything is a violation of someone's rights. A marriage contract is not the same as a catering, cleaning, or laundering contract. However voluntarily, and to whatever extent women and men are willing to sacrifice their own

interests for those of their dependants, couples do not enter a relationship as provider and purchaser working to a delineated, working-day
timetable with a clear framework of job specifications. Without these,
prodigious potential for rights violations exists. For example, as male
breadwinner status diminishes in contemporary society, women no
longer, if they ever did, receive protection and provision in exchange
for their domestic labour.

Perhaps more significant for Nozick's framework theory is the emphasis placed on choice, and on individuals' freedom to determine goals
and objectives, as well as the means to achieve them. However, it is
unlikely that when individuals can freely, and without social stricture,
choose their routes to happiness that domestic and caring choices would
accrue mostly to women. Men would also surely choose communities in
which they could care for dependants physically and psychologically
rather than, mainly, materially. Or, perhaps, more women would not
choose to care for dependants, as Pateman (1991: 65) suggests in relation
to Hobbes' theory, preferring to pursue other interests, in which case
either the race would die out or individuals would contract with
commercial care facilities for the care of their dependants. Assuming
that such contracting would still be women's responsibility, they would
still have less resources with which to achieve their potential. Generally,
then, it can be argued that women's rights, assuming these are equivalent if not the same as men's, are constantly violated.

A possible conclusion to be drawn from Nozick's determination not to
consider social relations within the minimal state is that, as with Hobbes
and Rousseau, the family is the basic unit in utopia. As such, the people
entering into market exchanges with protective agencies and other
organisations will be heads of household. As civil society developed
it would have been the heads of household that determined the terms
and conditions of protective agencies, and who, in contemporary society, will decide for the household which agency or community to
contract with. Moreover, it is likely that the heads of household will, for
the most part, be male, ignoring changes in the family structure since
theorists like Hobbes and Locke wrote their treatises. The better economic conditions of men will enable them to contract with the 'better'
agencies which, in turn, will absorb the lesser ones consisting of the less
well off. Women will be able to pursue their interests within their
individual circumstances, which include domestic commitments and
their lesser economic status. For women with greater resources, their
potential for maximising their interests is better. However, no woman
will have the 'right' to pursue her self-interest if it requires compulsory
contributions from others: subsidised childcare or care for other dependants, and equal opportunity policies in the workplace to compensate
for her sacrifice to the family unit, is coercive and cannot be legitimised.

As with Hobbes' and Rousseau's states of nature, Nozick does not break away from the traditional family construct in attempting to demonstrate individual liberty, its pursuit and maintenance. If the family is perceived as a little utopia within the community of communities, then it is possible to imagine some negotiation between members as to which community is required in pursuit of the interests of the family. While this contrasts with families described by traditional philosophers in which the male had the final, or only, word, it is still not individualism. Each member of the family utopia is sacrificing individual interests to the others and is, by definition, enslaved. It may even be that one member dominates others, unduly restricting the rights of other members. In the larger communities, it is possible, although not always feasible, for dissenters to leave and find another community more in tune with their needs. In the family as a community, such mobility is not always possible. While the moral and legal obligations within families are not fully considered by Nozick, leaving this as one among many difficult areas 'of the thinking that needs to be done on the details of a framework' (*Anarchy, State and Utopia*: 330–1),[8] it is most likely that women remain with children. Thus, a woman with dependants and no means of contracting-in care to support her family may not have the opportunity to leave, unless she leaves the whole family to join another community, or the community accepts voluntary responsibility for her children, much as women friends and relatives do in contemporary society.

Paradise Lost: From the State of Nature to the State of Politics

At first sight, it would appear that the state of nature presents the ideal condition for women to fulfil their potential and to become fully participating citizens in any polity. The equality of potentialities that Hobbes and Rousseau describe in the state of nature, in which female and male qualities, even natures, are commensurate, should be the template for equitable relations in civil society, as well as the foundation for valuing socio-political contributions equally. The fact that neither philosopher is able to translate full individual liberty to civil society, curtailing this concept for women especially, may well be the result of a lack of imagination or the inability to understand how existing relationships at the time negatively affected the ideals that they were attempting to broadcast. Of course, it is also possible that to capture the attention of their audience, the radicalism of their treatises had to be limited to the acceptable parameters of politics, automatically relegating women to the margins. Whatever the reason for failing to extend the implicitly subversive ideas about gender in the state of nature to civil society in the seventeenth and eighteenth centuries, the fact that twentieth-century philosophers such as Nozick continue to ignore the gendered nature of political relations is not only testament to the power of socialisation, but to the continuing influence of traditional political philosophy. By building on Locke's work, without even considering the arguments that he propounded for women's exclusion from the state despite their equal parental status, let alone considering the situation of women in his own society, Nozick pays tribute to the partial arguments that traditional philosophers espoused. A return to the liberty enjoyed in the state of nature, even within the framework of the minimal state, would not extend to women.

That Nozick feels it unnecessary to analyse the nature of gendered power relations when advocating levels of liberty aligned to that of the state of nature, exudes an assumption of comfort with the 'natural' leadership of men. The fact that no mainstream philosopher appears able to conceive of a society with family structures and domestic, caring arrangements that are not woman-dependent does not lend optimism to the idea of a state of nature as a seedbed of equal political relations and opportunities. But this may be an irrelevant argument if consideration is given to the purposes of the original usage of the idea of a state of nature. Certainly, Hobbes and Locke were not concerned with gender relations and issues of equal participation per se. Their primary interest was the abolition of absolute monarchy and legitimisation of rule by consent. In some ways, then, the justifications for distinct, gendered political relations, or ignoring that these exist, so condoning the gendered status quo, can be interpreted as a means to serve political ambition. If men have power, why would male writers want to explain away their 'right' to govern? Hobbes' attempt to refute the divine right of kings, therefore, should not also be held to compromise the rights of men. Similarly, Locke's rebuttal of Filmer's thesis on the patriarchal right of succession arising from Adam's God-given sovereignty, allows maternal right in the family only to the extent that women share in progeniture and that children are required under the Commandments to honour their fathers and mothers (*Two Treatises*: 141–2). Filial duty is not aligned to political relations in which males are paramount.

The separation of the public and private is evident, with the philosophers effectively defining domestic life out of politics.[9] In Hobbes' state of nature it is the male head of the family unit who is in a state of war with other males; as civil society develops, the laws, processes and structures required to ensure peace are negotiated and maintained by men. It is their actions that define politics and political relations. Having made sure that, within a hierarchical structure, they are equal under the law in terms of rights of self-preservation and interest maximisation, every man's liberties are, in principle, equally curtailed as 'sacrifice' to civility. Out of the public sphere, men are rulers in their households, women having freely consented to dissolve their liberty in exchange for protection. Similarly with Rousseau, women's guile ensures that they do not have to contend in the state of nature. Accordingly, it is men's right, in return for their subjection to provide for dependants, to govern the wider society. For both authors it may be said that men are entitled to make the rules because of the severity of conditions in the state of nature in which they are competing for resources and for their, and their families', survival. In many ways, then, women are complicit in their own subjection, preferring domestic life to the stresses, strains and dangers of participation in the public sphere. It is not lack of reason but, rather, exertion of reason that led to the situation wherein women have been defined as carers and homemakers.

The underlying logic of this argument is that, because men are stupid enough to be beguiled by women, they can legitimately claim the right to rule, almost as consolation for the loss of liberty suffered by their foolishness. It is doubtful that such asinine discernment can sincerely explain centuries of patriarchal rule. More likely is the conquering of women in the state of nature and their captivity in some form of 'family' from the origin of organised society. As so easily achieved by political philosophers, the need for women's political exclusion can then be explained in terms of their inherent and incurable self-centredness, as opposed to men's natural predisposition to acknowledge the need for interdependence as essential to self-preservation.

The Power of Tradition: Languor and Radicalism

The mainstream philosophers' power to influence political develop-ment and subsequent political theories is evident from their continued popularity. Contemporary philosophy is based on foundations laid in centuries past. Hence, writings such as those of Hobbes and Rousseau, containing what may appear to be radical concepts and novel political relations, have become accepted as definitive statements on political development, each one modifying others without expounding funda-mental change. More recent writers, such as Nozick, also effectively modify rather than challenge accepted frameworks of modern politics. Very few mainstream theorists question relationships within the civil state to examine how individuals are able to utilise the conditions of citizenship. Indeed, perhaps the most invidious effect of political philosophy in relation to women and politics is the failure to step outside experience and consider 'real' alternatives. Even the language of traditional philosophy is rarely questioned or emended within the mainstream of political thought. The feminist debate about whether writers' references to 'he', 'man' and 'mankind' include women is pertinent here. As Phillips (1993: 46) argues, 'the individuals of liberal theory are presented as if they refer indiscriminately to women or men, but have written into them a masculine experience and a masculine norm'. Presumably, philosophers who specifically analyse the role of women in the state of nature and the earliest family units before civil society, and who then refer only to men in the public sphere, are doing so quite deliberately. They may not be able to justify this beyond recourse to God and nature, even if the premise of their great works is to refute such concepts in relation to men and politics, but they do so nevertheless. It is through, in particular, feminist analysis of political philosophy, processes and structures that the inherent partiality of arguments for 'natural' causes of inequality have been exposed. However, the use of generic language in a system that still demonstrates inequality based on gender difference runs the risk of repeating the injustice done to women by mainstream political philosophers through the ages.

As far as women as citizens are concerned, in contemporary political theory the absence of concern about their relation to politics may be explained by the notion of 'post-feminism'. It might be assumed that, after more than a century of struggle to be acknowledged and treated as equal citizens, and with a legislative framework in place intended to ensure equal treatment in the public sphere, opportunities are available for women should they wish to take them. Maybe, therefore, Nozick does not need to state a case specifically for women when he describes his ideal political framework. Women are as able as any other person, within their individual circumstances, to pursue their interests. However, it is equally possible that, without questioning the transformation of individuals as equals in the state of nature into families in civil society, modern philosophers are accepting an unjustifiable situation. Analysis suggests that the traditional theories cannot sustain a justification for the development of the two-parent, heterosexual nuclear family, with its gendered division of labour between male/breadwinner and political activist and woman/homemaker. A state of nature of different equals would more likely lead to a community in which individuals, within an organised group of whatever complexion, would undertake the work they are most able to do. This aligns more with Plato's Postulates of Specialised Nature in which the nature of the individual is the basis for their occupation (*Republic*: Part VI). It can only be assumed that philosophers such as Rousseau, Locke, Hobbes and Nozick, among many, accord with the less taxing and unimaginative notion of biological determinism, taking a purely teleological view of political relations.[10] Such a revelation, based on a logical progression from a state of equality, would be far-reaching. On the other hand, if the state of nature is taken as a basis, however theoretical, for the development and maintenance of political relations in developed states, then women's dependence, including their relation to politics, can only be the result of political impetus.

Notes

1. Schochet (1975: 238) discusses the issue of individual members of the family who leave the household for necessary excursions. As they leave the house, they too are in a state of nature and would need to fend for themselves, however temporarily.

2. The same relation exists whoever brings up a child should the natural mother not do so (*Leviathan*: 105).

3. They are, of course, temporarily confined during childbirth itself. It is possible that *pitié* or compassion will bring assistance at such a time from other individuals who will respond to cries of distress in the state of nature. However, this will be sustained only as long as necessary and does not place obligation on either party.

4. Explanations based on property are prescient. If women do become subservient partially as a means of ensuring heredity (Okin 1980: 147), it cannot be evident at this point in the development of civil society. Thus, female and male anatomy may result in heterosexual relations, but it does not justify monogamous ones.

5. 'It is easy to see that the moral part of love is a factitious feeling, born of social usage, and enhanced by the women with much care and cleverness, to establish their empire, and put in power the sex which ought to obey' (*Discourse on Inequality*: 70).

6. The decline of inalienable rights defined by the laws of nature (*Leviathan* Ch.XIV, XV; *De Cive* Ch.II, III, IV) or rule of law (Hayek 1976, Ch.VI and 1999, Ch.11, 16) has been precipitated by the desire to plan societies and dispense with discrepancies in social welfare rather than leave social co-ordination to the invisible hand of social and economic forces. Consequently, modern 'rights' have been contrived to ensure the achievement of desired socio-political and economic objectives.

7. Families are mentioned in a passing reference to how writers see the existence of the family as preventing equality of opportunity (*Anarchy, State and Utopia*: 235), a concept that Nozick believes cannot be justified in fairness.

8. However, Nozick does indicate that in any contractual arrangement, mobility may entail problems of obligation that are difficult to measure (*Anarchy, State and Utopia*: 330–1). The commitment to family is only mentioned in that a man wishing to leave a community may be abandoning family obligations.

9. This statement may be modified in the case of Rousseau, who perceives the public and private in tandem: the latter supports the role of the male in the former.

10. Rousseau overtly rejected Plato's proposed abolition of the family as a means of instilling a more genuine equalitarian and participative society (Green 1995: 79).

Chapter 3: The State that Ends at the Front Door

Debates about the nature of the state, its functions and parameters, are the spine from which political philosophy is sustained: the state is where politics takes place. What epitomises the good state is a synthesis of rulers and ruled, institutions, processes and people that enable citizens, other members and guests of the state to pursue their interests and occupations under conditions of security, stability and justice. When free individuals in the state are happy (Aristotle; Plato), and able to pursue their interests in security (Hobbes; Locke), under legitimate government that manages the internal and external security of the state, the components of the state are in concord. It is usually prevailing or potential discord within the state, in which the legitimacy of rule is questioned and civil equanimity is threatened, that stimulates political philosophers to elucidate solutions to maintain or restore order. If their ideas are implemented, the 'good' state will prevail to the benefit of all those people who belong to it, as well as to those who merely utilise its facilities on a temporary basis.

The genesis of the state in a form recognisable in function and structure is disputed by commentators, although it is generally agreed that the origins of the modern state date back to the sixteenth century (Vincent 1987: 14; Skinner 1997). From early beginnings, as disputed territories between self-preserving individuals became communities ruled by self-appointed, conquering rulers, to more sophisticated and highly populated states governed by democratically selected leaders, the state has been characterised as an hierarchical structure in which the 'masses' are governed by a small, relatively elite leadership. For traditional, mainstream political thinkers, this was the nature of politics and the state; the best organisation preferably being monarchies, aristocracies or oligarchies where strong leadership at the top would ensure sufficient unity to fulfil the purpose of security, stability and justice. Through time, the legitimacy of such systems of political leadership has been challenged; contentions usually concentrating on the nature of sovereignty and whether this should rest with rulers or ruled. In effect, the concern is with whom the interests of the state and its members are best placed, and how far leaders can be entrusted with the responsibility of maintaining the unity and security of the state without violating the rights of its members. As states and forms of government have adapted through history to accommodate such challenges, the locus of sovereign power has shifted. By the twentieth century, in which stable liberal democracies accommodated universal suffrage and notions of representation, enabling each person to participate at some level in affairs of the state, the issue of legitimate leadership was less contentious.

What has not generally been challenged in conceptions of the 'good' state are the public parameters of concern on which diverse theories of the state concentrate. The basis of philosophy in addressing problems presented by, for example, arbitrary rule occasioned by the divine right of sovereign rulers, or subterfuges of liberalism and democracy, ensures that it is only those parts of the state that philosophers find relevant to the preservation of peace and security that will be included in their theories; that is, interactions in the public sphere. Consequently, while the importance of private relationships and behaviours are universally accepted in political philosophy as being essential to the state, both as the foundation for the proper behaviour of public actors and as the support on which those actors rely, they are not considered the subject for analysis within the state. While philosophers may assert pertinent pretexts for the marginalisation of the private sphere in their theories, the problem remains that, while they effectively consider only the smaller part of the state, the conditions to which they address themselves in their attempts to develop the good state are evident in the private sphere. Whether a 'good' state can be proclaimed when only its public relations evince the essential criteria for security, stability and justice must be subject to some scepticism.

The Greek *Polis*:
A Good Life in the Good Community of Virtuous Folk

The origins of the debate about the public and private aspects of the state stretch back to the Greek philosophers and probably earlier.[1] For Aristotle and Plato the state was a moral entity, all individuals developing and contributing their virtues to it. Indeed, a symbiotic relation between state and members was perceived, in which the virtue of each side of the equation depended on the virtue of the other, and 'there were individuals distinct from the State, and yet in their communion forming the State' (Barker 1960: 2). Unlike contemporary ideas of the state which have effectively defined their purposes, for example, the provision of a legal framework to ensure relatively comfortable interactions between individuals and groups, the Greek city-state was an end in itself. Virtue was its objective and *raison d'être*, both as a state and as a collectivity of individuals, with security and benefits springing from this. Such a comprehensive application would tend towards an inclusiveness that, if developed by later philosophers, would pre-empt the need for analysis of mass exclusions, especially considering the favourable position that Greek philosophers traditionally hold as creators and defenders of democracy. Indeed, on reading texts such as *The Politics* and *The Laws*, it is hard to determine a separation of public and private, each being integral to the state. The problem is that, either the historical development of the state and state theory diversified considerably from the writing of Plato and Aristotle, tending to a more exclusionary concept (Saxonhouse 1991: 48), or the Greek city-state as described or 'improved' by Greek thinkers was not as inclusive as is commonly perceived.

Plato and Aristotle perceived a measure of unity within their states despite the presence of internal divisions or hierarchies. The concomitant outcome of this is that in the *polis* 'there was no such realm of privacy, personal rights or freedoms. Individuals only had claims as full citizens and there could be no conception of any distinction between public or private law' (Vincent 1987: 13). Indeed, Plato is quite explicit in *The Laws* (Book VI §11) regarding the expectations and behaviour of people on even intimate issues: choosing a marriage partner; failure to marry and setting fines for such anti-social behaviour; correct procreation, including punishment for not producing children of accepted quality or quantity; consideration of the best ages for reproduction and fines for not reproducing within the specified ages or reproducing outside them. Throughout the rest of *The Laws* less intimate but still personal behaviour is regulated and, of course, Plato's pupil, while rebelling somewhat against his teacher, includes similar areas for consideration by the state in the *The Politics* (Book VII, VIII). The point here is that, in the Greek city-states, laws covered the whole of the territory, both sides of the front door, as it is behaviour in all aspects of relations within the state that contribute to the good of the whole. And yet, the nature of political decision-making was such that in practice a separation of the public and private existed so that 'claims as full citizens' did not extend to those in the latter sphere: slaves, children (although at least some male children would eventually legitimately become full citizens) and women. To be generous in interpreting Greek ideas, women did have rights as free persons, together with non-citizen males.[2] However, they were still excluded from participating in the decision-making that determined their roles, behaviour and relationships in the virtuous state. Thus, Barker (1960: 235) willingly concedes that 'marriage was regarded as a means, and a wife as an instrument, for the procreation of lawful issue for the service of the State', implictly diminishing the role of women as free persons within the state and overtly reducing them to subjects, if not slaves.[3]

In general, it is clear that women were necessary for the unity and virtue, as well as to the happiness, of those in the *polis*. Essentially, the state could not continue without women to produce, or assist in the production of, future generations of good citizens or other essential members of the population. For Plato (*Republic*: Book VI), women were also needed in the Guardian classes, partly for eugenic purposes but also to fulfil their individual inherent talents to the benefit of the state. However, apart from Plato's utopian ideas, which were later diluted to less Olympian standards, the role of women in relation to the state was not one of statespersonship, or in any way concerned with what we would now see as affairs of state. Even in a state so integrated that the lines are not yet clearly drawn between public and private, women's role was as an auxiliary; their stake in achieving and benefiting from outcomes was not accompanied by a stake in decision-making. From a contemporary point of view, this argument may, of course, be considered erroneous. As Raphael (1976: 39) and Vincent (1987: 12) point out, the *polis*, rather than being a state, was more properly a community. City-states were relatively small both in territory and population, as would be required for such an integrated approach to organisation. Moreover, the *polis* was an ethical community in which defined moral behaviours would presumably confine different status-holders to their role. One only has to glance at contemporary writer Amitai Etzioni's *Spirit of Community* (1993) to understand the importance of sustaining 'proper' roles in the maintenance of community. Women's status, and the issue of the public and the private, are, therefore, issues of state only in order to ensure correct behaviour and relations so that the state may endure.

The idea of community maintains its importance in relation to women as state theory and practice develop. Throughout political thought and consequent practice to the present day, women are entrenched in the 'community'. They may not be completely forgotten or excluded by political philosophers or practitioners in relation to the state: they merely interact in the community rather than actively participating in the state. Undoubtedly, any sensible person analysing community and state in the context of the public and private would notice that the community is still in the public domain. 'The community' interacts in public, uses public services and spaces, and is essentially the basis of the state. It originates only as humanity rises from the state of nature, and the need for the state is perceived. It is fallacious, therefore, to have recourse to the public and private for preventing women's participation in the former.

Explanation of why community members are excluded from decision-making has therefore to move to individual characteristics (discussed in Chapter 4) and to the characteristics of the state, community and private domains. For Plato, setting the scene for writers who follow, the differences between rulers and ruled tend to revolve around what may generally be called appetites and rationality. On these grounds, the majority will be exempt from decision-making on state issues because,

the greatest number and variety of desires and pleasures and pains is generally to be found in children and women and slaves, and in the less respectable majority of so-called free men . . . While the simple and moderate desires, guided by reason and right judgement and reflection, are to be found in a minority who have the best natural gifts and best education. (*Republic*: 202)

The latter virtues are required to maintain the virtuous state, and as virtuous members of the state the majority of people, including all women, will recognise that their role in the community is enough, leaving it to those possessing the higher virtues to perform state functions.

For the, generally more democratic, political thinkers who attempt to conflate community and state, the difficulty is to close off routes to universal participation at state level 'legitimately' while presenting a perceptibly inclusive model. For many later thinkers, such as Hobbes and Nozick, the task is made easier as the community becomes merely an adjunct to the state and it is possible to define it out of the political public arena. Thus, as community becomes a less coherent form and individualism becomes *de rigeur* in political thinking through time, the clear divisions of public and private become visible.

The People's Authority: For the Good of the Propertied

The state has come to be seen less as a moral and coherent singularity, and more as a framework for resolving, if not preventing, conflict in a crowded world of people who are accumulating and protecting possessions. The idea that individual good contributes to the common wealth remains intact, but a definite distinction between individual and state is apparent by the time liberal thinkers are espousing their views. Having noted this, though, within the hemisphere that is the state, unity is necessary.

For Hobbes the state is the corrective to the war of all against all present in the state of nature. Accordingly, the type of state required is one in which order and obedience is paramount. After all, there is little use in a state that permits, indeed encourages, conflict when its purpose is to prevent such. It is, therefore, a small and logical step to the leviathan in which everyone consents, or contracts, to submit their individual authority to a sovereign person or assembly. An enigmatic entity, the sovereign becomes judge of what is good, bad, legal or unlawful in subject relations, it holds the rights of war and peace with other states, bestows honours and decides punishments and, 'as the Power, so also the Honour of the Soveraign, ought to be greater, than that, of any, or all the Subjects' (*Leviathan*: 95). The only way that a sovereign can do wrong is to compromise the self-preservation of any individual, a blanket cover in that damage to the state impacts on the individuals within the state. Moreover, as every person consents to the sovereign, and thereafter whatever the sovereign does, then 'whatsoever he doth, it can be no injury to any of his Subjects; nor ought he to be by any of them accused of Injustice' (*Leviathan*: 92). The final irony is that only the sovereign has the right to choose its successor.[4] Once authority has been given to the sovereign by the citizen/subjects their work as statespersons is done.

While Locke disputes with Hobbes on the grounds that leaving the perfect freedom of the state of nature to submit to such a strong sovereign would be somewhat anomalous (*Two Treatises*: 163), he too perceives the need for a sovereign body, although one firmly rooted in more continuous popular consent. However, as with Hobbes, the safety valves preventing decline into autocracy are unclear. Certainly, to curb the excesses of self-interest that destroy the state of nature, a defined set of laws administered by known judges and accompanied by suitable punishments and sanctions is understandable (*Two Treatises*: 180). In Locke's commonwealth, laws and punishments are agreed by common consent and power is limited by reason. If the state neglects its duties or otherwise violates the people's trust, power reverts to the people. However, concern remains that if there is disunity within the state, this would allow arbitrary power to be sustained.

For both these liberal thinkers[5] the basis of their idea of the state lies in ownership. This may be in terms of property (as land and/or other assets) as well as liberty itself. The political relations that are governed by the state are those based on property and the right to accumulate, distribute or conserve it. While this may appear unproblematic, and political philosophers tend to treat it as such, ownership in relation to the state is quite complex. For example, what is it that people own and what happens to those who own nothing or very little? It is of great significance to women that, historically, not only have they owned less property than men, including liberty (Brennan and Pateman 1979; Stacey and Price 1981; Grimke 1991), but they have been designated as property. This phenomenon has been well rehearsed: the subsumation of women as guarantee of heredity (Millet 1977: 33–4; Okin 1980: 147); that as property is passed to male heirs so, too, sisters, mothers and other female relations are handed on or 'given away' in propitious unions (Miles 1989; French 1992; Mies 1998); and women taken as historical spoils of war (Pettman 1996). Consequently, men of all classes are, in a sense, property owners. Not only would this promote male property interests over those of women in the development and maintenance of the liberal state as proposed by Hobbes and Locke, it also overtly limits 'universal' concepts such as sovereignty and mutual consent. Perhaps the blatantly inequitable socio-economic conditions of the seventeenth century enabled Hobbes and Locke to address a specific audience to which their wisdom would appeal. However, in the twenty-first century, where political equality is presumed essential to liberal democracy, traditions persist whereby the people with the greatest interests in conserving and building their accumulation are the most vociferous and eminent in the law-making process (Dunn 1991: 335). Exclusion based on property is evidently an integral part of our philosophical and political tradition, potentially preserving archaic political hierarchies that require justification in terms of sovereignty.

The idea that 'property' is a state issue ignores the location of property in the private sphere, much as the relationship between 'community' and the public is taken for granted. Although the liberal state is concerned only with the public rights of property, preventing or resolving dispute and enabling self-maximisation in terms of accumulation and distribution, it is unclear how this can be separated from the social aspects of property and, hence, the private domain. At a fundamental level the state is intimately involved in the private sphere when pronouncing on the rights of private citizens to private property and its usage, including allowing property owners to do as they will with their possessions. If they want to smash their priceless Ming vases that is their prerogative. Similarly, presumably, if they want to beat their wives and abuse their children, it is their business, as long as they have the right to accumulate such possessions in the first place. However, women clearly are not goods in the sense of farm animals or china ornaments, although Rousseau's work conjures up pictures of the latter. Moreover, they have reason and a stake in much of what the state is concerned with, even if not as primary actors.[6] More particularly, and with concern that the logic of the liberal argument may be inconsistent, private actions impact further on the private accumulation patterns of others. The more Ming vases that are smashed the fewer property rights for collectors, requiring the state to intervene. Similarly, if women and children are essential to property accumulation then their ill-treatment cannot be sanctioned by the state, even if that sanction is inferred by the absence of law. Moreover, if a wider definition of property is taken, as philosophers would need to do to create inclusivity, the diminished ownership of liberty by individuals cannot be sustained in a private context when this further infringes public accumulation of material goods.

Overall, the emphasis on the public duties of the state does not absolve philosophers from considering the state in the private sphere. When philosophers such as Hobbes and Locke dismiss the private from state intervention, they do so by giving men the natural rights to ownership and liberty as well as control of property. They base this on premises such as men's superior physical strength (*Leviathan*: 105) and, 'being of the more excellent Sex' (*Two Treatises*: 157), their greater capacity for understanding and sound decision-making regarding property relations. Consequently, it can be argued that concepts such as Locke's mutual consent and Hobbes' unified sovereign are only mutual and unified in a very restricted sense. Any other interpretation of consensus would not permit such a limited conception of the state, its officers or its laws. In addition, without a reasonable analysis of the interconnection of public and private, an inescapable situation is established, or unchallenged, by political philosophers. That is, only those people whose interests lie in the deceptive immobility of the public and the private are involved in the processes by which legitimacy is conferred on the state. By defining the private out of the sphere of the state the historically acknowledged limited state is legitimised.

However, as we have seen, the state is intimately involved in the private sphere already. Thus, in a liberal state claiming any level of participation at any stage in the legitimating process, it is fantastical to exclude those actors involved in the private sphere. And yet, if these were not excluded the potential to difference and conflict is greatly increased. For Hobbes (*Leviathan*: Ch.XIX), any disagreement with the sovereign power is key to the dissolution of the state and a return to the state of nature. The nature of property interests, and government of ensuing political relations, is enough potentially to cause such friction. How much more so if the interests of those acting within the private sphere and without protection in their lives were to be included? Why and how women (who philosophers admit are, by nature, equally capable of self-sustenance and preservation) would overwhelmingly support male authority and legitimise a state that condoned their own subjection and absence of protection in law within the home, is equivocal.[7] Continued voluntary submission of women can be explained only by appeal to what we now know as myths of male protection through their greater physical strength and superior mental capacities. But evidence of male violence as opposed to protection, together with the arguments of philosophers such as Hobbes (*Leviathan*: 105) and Plato (*Laws*: 192) who noted that good physique was not essential to the good statesman, and the equality of psychological traits depicted for men and women in the state of nature, in addition to

common sense, render the correlation of such variables with statespersonship invalid. It would seem, therefore, that artificial means to prevent women's participation in the legitimation processes of the state
were required to prevent issues and interests being introduced that,
while integral to the functioning of the good state, would threaten its
harmony and continuity. Only by such means can agreement on defence
of, and security within, the realm be assured, further assuming women's
fundamental opposition to male opinions and knowledge.

The Inclusive State: From General Will to General Market

Perhaps the greatest exponents of participatory states in traditional
political thought, after the Greek classical theorists, are Rousseau and
J. S. Mill. A general reading of the latter is enough to reveal that
overlaying the more inclusive aspects of his ideas is an entrenched
elitism. Mill is concerned not with participatory democracy but with
representative government, whereas Rousseau treads a middle but
confusing line between the two.

The major concept that Rousseau depicts in *The Social Contract* is
that of the general will, a social compact that involves all individuals as
citizens in determination of the common good, each submitting 'only
such part of his powers, goods, and liberty as it is important for the
community to control' (*Social Contract*: 186) to ensure continuity of the
good state. Achievement of the general will is an exercise in convoluted
thinking finally simplified by the exercise of a vote. The legislative or
sovereign assembly, consisting of all citizens bringing their own influence to bear, is periodically convened to determine law (*Social Contract*:
237–8), necessitating administration by a representative government
intermediate between people and sovereign (*Social Contract*: 209). And
yet, Rousseau is acutely aware that in large states individual sovereignty
is diluted in direct proportion to the numbers in, and growth of, the
population (*Social Contract*: 210). Hence the need for an electoral
system to determine the general will, 'the vote of the majority always
binds all the rest' (*Social Contract*: 250). However, to avoid potentially
disastrous disputes, the people are not asked for their opinions on issues
of state, but whether proposed laws conform with the common good or
the general will, which is the will of all the people. If this is not
complicated enough, one has to ask where do these proposals for laws
come from? Obviously, the magistrates or governors, entrusted with
administration, are also those who present proposals for confirmation
by the general will.

The same issues arise concerning who legitimates the sovereign
power in Hobbes' and Locke's work. Rousseau's tenet is that everyone

is an inalienable part of the sovereign and, therefore, subject to their own laws and restrictions which all agree to suffer (*Social Contract*: 188). However, not everyone is bound by the same conditions nor do they enjoy the same rights. Perhaps Rousseau's claim that 'the essence of the body politic lies in the reconciliation of obedience and liberty' (*Social Contract*: 237) also reconciles women to their lot in terms of the general good. But it is difficult to see that womankind would understand their seclusion, the interment of their talents, and public declamation of their wickedness as beneficial to the community and a legitimate part of the sovereign general will. On the other hand, in an astute move Rousseau appears to encompass full participation, which potentially includes women, while ensuring that private interests are exempt from consideration, and, in the name of community, effectively ruling out much community interest. The claim that the 'difference between the will of all and the general will; the latter considers only the common interests, while the former takes private interest into account, and is no more than a sum of particular wills' (*Social Contract*: 185) does not permit the inclusion of any collective interests, whether these be of race, sex, geographical location or relation to the state. Only when all such interests are removed from the equation does the general will remain as residue.

One might wonder what constitutes a common denominator on which a society could agree. Certainly in many communities it would be difficult to obtain agreement on the state of the weather without private will intervening: gardeners, against common opinion, may like summer rain and skiers cheer when it snows, whereas most people might prefer sunshine and warmth. But what Rousseau achieves is a state based on the minutest of agreement. This becomes even more evident when his sovereign powers are considered beyond the universal. Not only must it 'be granted that the Sovereign is sole judge of what is important' (*Social Contract*: 186) and that 'what makes the will general is less the number of voters than the common interest uniting them' (*Social Contract*: 187), but that when a majority as low as one votes for a proposal, the rest are bound by it (*Social Contract*: 250). If the sovereign will is overruled then no one is free, even if they were amongst the people who voted against the general will, or majority. Quite simply, they are wrong.

In practice, of course, it is rare for a clear victory by majority to be gained, and it is here that the dilemma for women's representation in the general will occurs. More generally, 'pluralities', whereby more people vote for one proposition than for any other single proposal, the majority voting for the other alternatives or abstaining, are mistaken for majority votes (McLean 1991: 174). The majority, therefore, becomes a majority of those who vote, not of a living general will. People who do not vote, and those who vote differently from the plurality, have agreed to the general will simply by their presence in the community. The convenience and political expediency of championing a majority vote is clear. Even if half the electorate minus one voted positively on 'social' issues such as women's rights, they would not be perceived as acting in the general will.

It would be unlikely that a majority or a plurality of women, or supporters of domestic representation in the general will, would occur. Even though women constitute more than half, or a majority, of the population of many states, this does not guarantee homogeneity of ideas and interests (Sperling 1997: 121). Moreover, it does not assure a unity of perceptions of the common good among women which differs from those of men. Nevertheless, as a majority placed in a specific location in relation to the state, women's interests would certainly have an impressive level of 'particularity' about them. It may not be that as a majority they would want to change their position. But it is reasonable to suppose that many, if not all, women would want some accommodation within the general will pertaining to their circumstances. With regard to the assimilation of domestic interests, the contortions of Rousseau's general will ensures that, even if it gained the support of a large minority, it is unlikely to mobilise support of half the population of women, let alone of the whole population. A simple majority race is more suited to maintaining traditional political parameters. This suggests that Rousseau's general will is particular to him, and to supporters of this theory, and can be used to good effect to maintain traditional political power and terms of reference. While women's virtue in the good home is necessary, it is only through regulation by statesmen within the public sphere that this is ensured.

The twists and turns of Rousseau's general will are put into relief by the work of J. S. Mill (*Representative Government*), who advocates a representative system in which all classes and both sexes participate in state decisions, provided they are educated to the extent that they are able to evaluate issues and make informed contributions. Plato and Mill are possibly the only mainstream philosophers who consider the relation of women to the state in a positive manner. For Mill, it is interest in good government that determines participation, and every person has such an interest not 'in order that they may govern, but in order that they may not be misgoverned' (*Representative Government*: 342). This certainly has connotations for women in the home, upon which Mill elaborates in *The Subjection of Women*. However, Mill advocates participatory democracy only up to a point, beyond which the mass of people are not equipped for political decision-making. Participation for most people extends to choosing their representatives based on informed judgements on affairs of state. How refreshing to see elitism undisguised without the agonies and contradictions that philosophers put themselves through to assert any level of equalitarianism.[8] For Mill, there will always be 'superior minds' better able to determine issues of state, but superiority, whether intellectual or numerical, does not justify power. What must be assured is a defence against a tyranny of the majority, who are of lesser intellect and liable to make unsuitable decisions, by ensuring that, even as a minority, those of greater intellect are present to inject sense into collective decision-making and determination (*Representative Government*: 315). As with the Greek philosophers, for Mill the democratic state has a moral role with participation having a moral function. Not only,

among the foremost benefits of free government is that education of the intelligence and of the sentiments, which is carried down to the very lowest ranks of the people when they are called to take a part in acts which directly affect the great interests of their country (*Representative Government*: 327),

but for the state itself, it is immoral to exclude the governed from affairs of state. Thus, 'every one is degraded, whether aware of it or not, when other people, without consulting him, take upon themselves unlimited power to regulate his destiny' (*Representative Government*: 329). Presumably, it is equally degrading to those who assert such power, although they are even less likely to be aware of it, as they are without a moral foundation to their powers. In such a view, no matter how much thinkers such as Hobbes and Rousseau claim their sovereign powers are based on a collective legitimacy, where exclusions persist a moral vacuum is created that denies the cohesion of their states.

In Mill's state, women's role, like that of all people, is both educative and moral. Women's perspectives, not as women but as social actors, add to the quality of political deliberation in that men and women would be able to discuss issues based on different opinions, all of value, and men would have to reconsider and justify views historically taken for granted (*Representative Government*: 343). In this way women are not only educated in politics in the same way that the lower classes are, by participation and exerting influence itself, but they are perceived and perceive themselves as holding legitimate opinions, with all this entails for exerting rationality and behaving responsibly within the state. Improving women's condition in the state contributes to the progress of the state itself, doubling the mental faculties available in the service of the state, raising levels of debate and discourse and, frankly, achieving justice (*Subjection of Women*: 298–9).

Of course, Mill cannot unpick the line between the public and the private. 'Personal interest or worldly vanity of the family' (*Representative Government*: 343) is not the stuff of politics, and women's political education wrought by their activity informs them that that their influence in these areas, already exercised on political man via the home, is not a concern of the state. And yet, Mill is quite clearly concerned with issues that his predecessors would not contemplate as part of their theories. For example, in *The Subjection of Women*, he expounds his belief in the moral powers of the public sphere, when women are represented, to overcome the abhorrent arbitrary powers of men over women in the home. Similarly, it is in the home that political manners are learnt, that boys are taught that they are not natural rulers but must earn their place in society (*Subjection of Women*: 296), and that men are educated to a level of humility deserving of their status. This is an interesting stance: women are part of the state and yet their predominantly private interests are irrelevant to it. If it is accepted that what goes on in the state has an effect on the private sphere, then Mill's inclusion of women is significant in that women will be able, potentially, to influence economic and political decisions that impact on their daily lives. Obviously the state has a stake in women's well-being and treatment within the private sphere too. Moreover, in the nineteenth century, women were quite clearly working in the public sphere in large numbers and would be seen to have a part to play in the workplace as well as in governmental democracy as it affected their work and their lives.

Despite Coole's (1993) and Okin's (1980) analyses of the shortcomings of Mill's work, based on his failure to dismantle traditional domestic relations, *Representative Government* potentially spreads the net wider. If Mill can speak of the 'lowest classes' of workers contributing to government, dependent on literacy and basic numeracy (*Representative Government*: 330),[9] then women will be included, being present throughout the class structure in the public sphere. Moreover, unlike Rousseau's general will, Mill's analysis of plurality and proportionality in voting would not exclude issues of importance as they relate to women. On the other hand, in not releasing women from the burden of domestic duty, Mill not only limits their opportunities for participation but also maintains the traditional spread of interests that are applicable to the state, with all this implies for restrictions on women's liberty and their rights. Admittedly, he allows for women to have choice, better education presenting choices to them. Indeed, the advent of women MPs and other professionals would be predicated on a choice between career or marriage (*Subjection of Women*: 315). This is in stark contrast to male politicians and professionals who could have both (Okin 1980: 230). But not only would most women freely choose marriage in preference to a public career, Mill does not clearly define what happens to women who 'choose' both as would have been common in the working classes. It is evident that women in the home carry the responsibility for domestic affairs, and that this is both time consuming and prevails on women's faculties (*Subjection of Women*: 290–1). Moreover, Mill does not break

through the psychological barrier that would dispense with the traditional, gendered division of labour, the male-breadwinner/female-
homemaker being 'most suitable' (*Subjection of Women*: 264). Generally, it is just common sense that as homemaking is a vocation, one
either chooses it or some other occupation. The discrepancy between
male and female career 'choices', and that most homemakers are women, does not appear to register with Mill beyond recourse to nature.
Despite the enlightened approach of Mill in incorporating women to his
state, therefore, the majority remain in the traditional model.

The End is Nigh: Time for Women's Redemption?

If detailed theories of the state do not or cannot include women as equal
partners in defining legitimate parameters and/or determining suitable
representatives of sovereign power, the potential for theories of 'no state'
or minimal state either provide the solution or exacerbate the problem.
The basis for such theories is not that there should be the same start or
finish lines for all people, but that all individuals have the same
opportunities either to maximise their self-interests or to contribute
to the collective good, something that states deny them. For example,
Marx's dictum 'from each according to their ability, to each according to
their need' ('Critique of the Gotha Programme': 533) is not, as is
popularly perceived, and in some cases brutally enforced, a call to
uniformity. Instead it is recognition of difference accommodating the
diverse faculties and capabilities of individuals within a community.
Along the spectrum to the right, Nozick's minimal state lauds inequality
but will not artificially limit anyone's legitimate activities to attain their
personal level of achievement. Such theories may be a solution to
gender inequality and women's relation to the state, not only by dis-
solving such an entity, but by releasing women from the bonds on which
states exist. Without a state or with a minimal state, any issues relevant
to individuals' actions are to be dealt with as necessary by those
involved. As the state exacerbates gender issues, no or minimal state
theories could provide the antidote to the socio-political inequalities
that permeate, but are ignored in, state theories. However, a familiar
filter that concentrates the vision on the arena of public interactions,
historically the purview of traditional state theories, is firmly in place in
the challenge presented by writers such as Marx and Nozick.

The premise of optimism for women in the 'no state' society and in the
minimal state is that, as in Plato's writing, all individuals have their
talents and abilities which are not gender dependent. For Marxists this is
further underpinned by the belief that people are co-operative and not
self-seeking to the detriment of others, whereas right-wing libertarians

completely condone self-aggrandisement as long as everyone has the opportunity to compete. In both cases, politics is abolished as the basis for political action and relations is removed from the frame. For Marx, the conditions that create politics are removed from the state when private accumulation based on exploitation of others, and the means of production that allow private accumulation, are socialised and centralised, so ending class division. The 'state' then becomes 'an association in which the free development of each is the condition for the free development of all' ('Communist Manifesto': 228). Women, who had hitherto been 'mere instruments of production' ('Communist Manifesto': 224) in a bourgeois family structure based on property relations and ownership within the state, are also freed. Where no private property can occur there is no call for private accumulation, no need to exploit women in the home, and women are not tied to marriage due to poor economic prospects. Consequently, marriage can be based on sexual love rather than economic necessity for both partners, and women are as able as men to contribute to the community to their best capacity whatever that may be (*Origin:* 1979). It may seem an anomalous comparison, but similarly, in Nozick's minimal state in which private accumulation is the basis of public interaction, the universal concept of equality of opportunity does away with politics, leaving a minimal state to administer markets. In a state in which everyone is imbued with inherent and indissoluble rights, the only conflict that is possible is that of encroachment on economic liberty, and the minimal state exists purely to resolve such problems. In all other respects, women and men, whatever their economic circumstances, are as free as possible in a crowded community.

For most political theorists, one of the primary functions of the state is to resolve conflict arising from the struggle to accumulate and maintain scarce resources, or, where power is exerted[10], either in that struggle or in asserting other real or imagined rights which are under threat (Mabbott 1967: 98–9; Lukes 1974; Barry 1981: 50–1, 72). In the context of the 'no state' society, communal access to resources must delete the first aspect of politics, and impinges on the second as no one has rights to more than they can use. Moreover, any person's rights cannot infringe those of others', whether to exploit another person or their 'possessions'. The latter argument must also attach to people in the minimal state although, of course, their rights are concerned with property and pursuit of personal, often materialistic, goals. In this case, activity is regulated through market exchanges in which all action is reduced to the agreement between individuals determined to effect the best deal for themselves (Haworth 1994: 13). The state has only a regulatory role ensuring freedom of markets, and 'politics' is contained within this ambit. For the rest, the 'invisible hand' or 'impersonal forces' of the market are what determine the satisfaction of people's wants (Nozick 1974; Hayek 1976; Haworth 1994: 30). In both scenarios what is left when the state 'withers away', or is reduced to a skeletal legal entity, is society, although Nozick emphatically denies society as a legitimate concept because of the connotations of collectivity attached to it (*Anarchy, State and Utopia*: 33). The implication here, asserted by contemporary writers like Raphael (1976: 31), is that politics does not occur in society but only in political, or state, contexts.

What 'no state' and minimal state theories ignore is that conflict does occur in private situations and that often these impact, either directly or indirectly, on the public, or economic, activities of those concerned. This renders such acts political. Theories that concentrate on ending economic exploitation or sustaining individualism in economic markets disregard a long history of gender differentiation in which the benefits of one sex are based not on economics and ownership but on the luxury of avoiding menial, ceaseless and boring domestic tasks that have no extrinsic value attached to them, whether economic or not. Both Marx's prediction that the end of the class-based state will augur the end of politics, and right-wing, libertarian, market-based, individualist proclamations of equality of opportunity and depoliticisation, are, therefore, somewhat premature. Wherever the actions of free individuals are hindered by artificial (political) restraints, the invisible hand, whether of the market or of collective good, becomes a glaring beacon of injustice.

Where the domestic constraints of women are not accounted for in 'no state' and minimal state theories, the theory cannot apply to them. They will not be free individuals as are others who do not have those constraints. The socialisation of the domestic industry (*Origin* 1978: 87) cannot completely eliminate domestic labour even within marriages and personal relationships based on love rather than economic necessity: the most personal aspects of domestic labour will still be private. And the assertion of writers like Nozick that unequal outcomes are inevitable as long as opportunity is available, within the constraints to which a person is subject, is an excuse not to deal with the circumstances of the majority of the population that have such constraints placed on them by dint of their sex. It may be that in these new societies domestic labour will be shared between the sexes, and women can take their place performing to their best potential in whatever field their individual talents lie. But, as a market exchange or as a loving gesture, it is still women who would have to bargain themselves out of their traditional 'vocation'. Thus, they are still coming to these apolitical societies from a position of weakness. Moreover, no matter how inefficient states have proved in relation to women's rights historically, without a state, or with only a minimal state exercising a severely restricted remit, any channels offering hope of redress of such mass injustice, however remote, are removed.

Moral Fibre – State Constipation

In many ways, the state can be seen as a mechanism for organising political interactions and relations. For Greek philosophers, good state relations arose from suitable behaviour throughout all the groups and associations of which the state consisted, including those now perceived as 'private'. As history unfolded, new ideas of the state were expounded, shifting the focus from the collective to the individual, on whose behaviour the good of all rested. Alternatives to atomised individualism, demonstrated in the works of democractic theorists such as Rousseau, and later collectivists like Marx, recognised the potential for the non-neutrality of the state as an organising framework.

Despite the differences in the state, and 'no state', theories through the ages, variables common to them all are concerned with creating totems around which people can congregate, endorsing a sense of belonging and ensuring security both within and against outside intrusions. As such it is not a giant step to perceiving the state as 'a mental category which informs the attitudes of individuals towards authority' (Vincent 1987: 224). Such a perception incorporates the types of state espoused by various philosophies as well as potentially explaining the relative stability of political relations evident throughout philosophy and political development, somewhat graphically depicted in gender as well as class relations to the state. The idea that the state is, if not neutral, at least acting in the interests of its constituents, serves as an antidote to vexatious claims by those not susceptible to the anaesthetising properties of ubiquity. This may well explain the *ennui* with which many social movements are confronted until they become serious contenders for state attention. What it does not explain is how the state originally became male, class and race dominated, and torpid. It could be argued that those governing the state have been able to accumulate the ideas of generations of similarly disposed thinkers and rulers, and thus retain the aspects that serve their purposes in the guise of state unity and security.

The relations of women to the state are ambiguous. While Rousseau is quite explicit about this, other philosophers indicate that women are virtuous members of the state, although not citizens, when doing what is deemed good, and amoral when challenging accepted parameters of female activity and attitudes which are determined by an authority in which they have little, or no, part. In many ways, as long as what the state does is seen to be for the benefit of the state and its people, then it is accepted. Hence Pierson's (1996: 25) assertion that 'the argument is not that states in modernity are genuinely an expression of the will of their peoples, but rather that it is perceived to be important that they should present themselves as such'. In other words, if, for the good of the state, it is seen to be right that women are subject to stricter limitations, being remote from centres of power and open to the abuses that power often brings in its wake, then this is what must be. That such a situation can be wrapped in the cloth of 'protection' and snug domesticity further serves the purpose of maintaining unity within the state.

Of course, what mainstream political philosophers are actually arguing in their theories of the state is the case for maintaining as much of the existing state as possible, merely relocating sovereignty wherever is required to support their ideal. That states, in the experience of philosophers, are generally ruled by men is not what is at issue and, therefore, not the subject of concern. However, in arguing for the equal spread of sovereignty, it is necessary to explain the exclusion of people who are essential to the state without according them requisite rights of sovereign individuals in the state. Women can, therefore, be contained within the family and the private or domestic sphere; part of the state but separate from it. Custom, eulogies to the honour and necessity of women's roles and the inevitability not only of one's necessary station but the improbability of change in the non-existence of opportunity to participate in decisions that could influence change, embed the parameters of the state and the concept of the political in the common wealth.

It could be argued that the exclusion of private politics from the domain of state activity is made possible by placing it at the apex of political development. Therefore, the family and the political relations it portends never have to change; they are the epitome of good government. The separation of the state from the private, then, places the family beyond the reach of imperfect politics. Women are clearly protected in such a theory. They do not have to be concerned with the troubled world of the state, living within a mini-state that provides for their needs without having to represent their interests outside their immediate domain; confident in their role and expectations of them, and others they interact with. Of course, by defining the private, domestic realm outside the political sphere of the state, the absence of any measure of accountability, provided by the concept of common or equal sovereignty, occasions potential for hidden, or even open but uncensured, abuse taking place behind the front door. That rulers of the state may be corrupt, with the occasional need for sovereign citizens to take them to task, or even replace them, is not reflected in the closed family. Moreover, such a justification for separate spheres does not account for the interaction of family and state that constantly occurs, whether this is defined as political or not. For example, that the essential private, domestic sphere is conterminous with the state in terms of moral education and sustenance of full, and future full citizens, requires that the domestic, private sphere is intimately involved with the state and vice versa. Consequently, it can be argued that attempts by political philosophers through the ages to justify a state limited to public, political concerns is not only unwarranted but unsustainable, and that the public-private divide is clearly a political construction which perpetuates particular embedded interests in state affairs.

That the inclusion of more than a minority of members of a state as full citizens may threaten the smooth running, security and unity of the state, suggests that these concepts are achieved at the expense of the majority of members of the state who have no say in what constitutes a unified system of values. Indeed, it would seem that any objection to what the state is, how it is run and the values it incorporates, risks the security and happiness of those who challenge it. And yet, without debate, challenge and the introduction of new ideas, a state may well become stagnant, so threatening the very things it is proclaimed to protect. Therefore, it may be asserted that the full inclusion of the private political sphere in the realms of state affairs would prove the purgative necessary adequately to address the issues that philosophers raise in progressing ideas of the good state.

Notes

1. Plato's inclusion of women in *The Republic* and *The Laws* attracted a response from Aristotle who appealed to 'nature' in his pleading for normal socio-political relations within the state. Both theorists refer to pre-existing states in which the position of women was more advanced than in Athens. Moreover, writers such as Hesiod, who was fervently anti-feminist, pre-date Plato and Aristotle by some centuries.

2. While Plato implies women's freedom throughout both *The Republic* and *The Laws,* Aristotle specifically refers to women being ruled in the household by their husbands 'as free persons . . . as by a statesman' (*Politics*: 92).

3. Aristotle's (*Politics*: 65) definition of slaves as 'a sort of living piece of property; and like any other servant is a tool in charge of other tools' certainly suggests that women's status would align with that of slavery if subjected to cold analysis. Perhaps only the 'sentiment' attached to marriage preserves them from such a destiny.

4. *Leviathan* (Ch.XIX) considers forms of succession to the sovereign power, although ultimately if the sovereign does not choose a successor the commonwealth is dissolved and a state of nature resumes.

5. Their liberalism may differ and, indeed, some question Hobbes' liberalism (Mabbott 1967: 20). However, the basic premise of self-maximisation within the parameters of the state tends to support this definition of both Hobbes and Locke.

6. Locke states clearly that women should be allowed to own and control property in their own right, men only having the 'natural' right to the final say in issues involving communal property. Women were even allowed the potential to leave relationships and revert to independent living when their children became independent, although most would prefer to stay with their husbands, of course (*Two Treatises*: 157).

7. It can be argued that women are complicit in their subjection, not only by the historic, and contemporary, failures to mount successful mass movements against 'male oppression', by accepting their role as housewives and mothers in addition to their public economic contributions, but also by participating in liberal democratic processes that legitimate the state (Spooner 1991).

8. This is not to advocate blatant discrimination. But if discrimination exists it is better to see it and to tackle it in the open than for it to remain hidden, active and unchallengeable.

9. This may well be seen as an exclusionary tactic. But Mill intends public education, or education at a price that the lowest paid workers can afford, to bring most workers into the frame (*Representative Government*: 330).

10. The exertion or threat of power need not be overt. Much power is implicit in both public and private relations without the need, indeed circumventing the need, for overt usage (Pierson 1996: 10).

Chapter 4: Citizenship and Representation: A Case of Protective Custody?

A contemporary definition of citizenship has been built on the relationship between mass participation and capitalist liberal democracy. In the 1950s T. H. Marshall (1950) identified a series of social, political and civil rights applicable to individuals in return for their meeting certain obligations. Thus, individuals have the right to participate in certain areas of decision-making, often narrowed down to voting; they have the right to protection from undesirable behaviours from the state and from other individuals; and they have rights to particular freedoms, such as to speech, association and worship. However, such rights arise from a particular political arrangement in which evident socio-political inequalities have to be matched to a system which purports to maximise equality of opportunity. In other words, modern definitions of citizenship are an attempt to reconcile the inherent inequalities on which capitalism relies whilst pertaining to equality of political status (Hay 1996: 72).

Once again, the authority of traditional philosophy is manifest. Hay's analysis of Marshall's definition of citizenship goes some way to uncover the patriarchalism of the concept. However, this is based on inequalities of citizenship within a liberal democratic state boasting a mature welfare system, itself a legacy of gendered divisions of labour and attitudes concerning acceptable socio-economic roles for women and men (Hay 1996: 86). Consideration of citizenship in traditional mainstream political philosophy will determine how inclusive or otherwise the concept is. Moreover, the extent to which citizenship is inclusive necessarily determines how far political institutions and actions are representative. Modern notions of representation tend to be coupled with citizenship in that citizens are supposed to be represented as well as having access to, and the potential to become, representatives. In mature liberal democracies every adult citizen, with some notable exceptions,[1] is an essential part of the representative system or process, whether that representation is passive or active.[2]

However, the history of the development of such representation, like that of citizenship per se, does not necessarily fit with such broad definitions of the concept. By considering the philosophical foundations of citizenship and representation, it should be possible to explore the parameters of accepted inclusiveness and apply these to women's relation to political institutions and activities.

A Community of Citizens in a Representative Framework

Comprehensive citizenship has usually been identified with democracy and can be traced back to the Greek *polis*. Such states are commonly heralded as genuinely equalitarian, participatory and, in modern parlance, representative although, as Wolff (1996: 69) notes, the model only lasted briefly. This triptych is painted in clear colours: citizens' duty is to the state and constitution (*Politics*: 179; *Republic*: 178); despite differences in such things as profession and personality, citizens are equal in status or have the ability and opportunity to hold higher offices of state (*Politics*: 413; *Republic*: Book I); the *polis* is arranged so that citizens can perform their duties by meeting and discussing affairs of state (Barker 1960: 21). As every citizen is involved in decision-making, the representation of their views and opinions is assured. Every citizen's opinion is given at some time in the process of decision-making, whether directly in assemblies or in pre-meeting caucuses and discussions which enable compromise, or consensus, positions to be reached. Furthermore, we have established that the state has a duty to protect its people, having been developed by the people for their own preservation. In return, the people have an obligation to obey the rules and regulations of the state, including fighting for its defence: after all, these are fundamentally the rules and regulations of the people.

Here is possibly the first problem of definition concerned with citizenship: are 'the people' citizens? If the role of citizen is to obey laws and get on with the life of virtue that supports the state, then surely all law-abiding people can be labelled citizens. Their obedience and pursuit of honest occupations necessary within the state is what maintains the constitution. Political philosophy throughout history tends to ambiguity about such issues. Certainly interpretations of Greek, early liberal and later democratic philosophies can presume universal citizenship of those born with the necessary qualifications by residence, birthright or 'gift', and who maintain the constitution. However, within such encompassing definitions other criteria are posited. Citizens are law-makers and/or keepers of the law. Indeed, citizens are states*men* in the sense that they are the politicians dealing with the affairs of state. Again, anomalies occur in such definitions of citizenship. What is 'keeping the law' if not maintaining the constitution which, it has been established, is the duty or virtue of all free people and other inhabitants of a state? As in most, if not all, states the laws are not made on a day by day basis but were originated in the past, to last in perpetuity, and framed in such a way as to provide general rules to accommodate unforeseen circumstances and natural advances in society. Thus, the original legislators are long dead, leaving all later generations to maintain the good state. Consequently, there should be little difference in citizenship status between state officials and other occupations necessary to the state. Of course, such a logical analysis is not sustained within any political philosophy until, ostensibly, twentieth-century liberal democracy. The hierarchical nature of the states envisioned by traditional philosophers automatically restricts attempts to equality of citizenship. In addition, the conceptions of human nature apparent in the works of the political thinkers mitigates against full citizenship for the majority of people within the confines of the state. That the nature of hierarchy would place most women at equal non-citizenship with men would be a reasonable assumption. In most cases, by concentrating purely on the philosophical text, such reasoning is upheld. However, when philosophy becomes enshrined in political institutions and behaviours, it becomes evident that women are perceived as lesser citizens even than the majority of men.

For the Greek philosophers only those people demonstrating the necessary virtues, and with time or leisure to devote to the affairs of state single-mindedly, were deemed admissible to the realms of full citizenship. For Aristotle, citizens may display diverse virtues and even participate in different occupations, but they must be predominantly public minded (*Politics*: 179). Indeed, the virtue that all citizens hold in common is that they put the state equal to, if not above, self.[3] As a result, citizenship becomes a limited association of members. People undertaking functions which, although vital to the well-being of the state, are of primary concern to the individual, are not admitted to this association. Therefore, a citizen may not be of good personal virtue but can still be a good citizen (*Politics*: 179). Conversely, not all good people have the primary virtue necessary for citizenship.

Similarly, Plato confines the status of citizen to a particular class of people, building an elaborate myth of origin[4] to justify hierarchical differentiation. Plato's ideal citizens, described in *The Republic*, are the Guardians, in turn subdivided into Auxiliaries (silver people) who hold an executive function, and Philosophers (gold people), occupying the legislative role. The Guardians are effectively separated from the rest of society – manifested in ordinary (iron and bronze) people subject to the whims and wiles of commonplace circumstances and characteristics. Being so situated, the Guardians are in a better position to control and maintain the laws that support the virtuous state. The specialised nature of the Guardians is their skill in watching over the community. This obviously includes elements such as intelligence and rationality, to be able to understand and uphold the laws, and physical strength to defend the state from external and internal insurrection.

As with Aristotle's citizens, in *The Republic* there is no division in the Guardians' minds between state and self-interest (*Republic*: 178). To ensure that potential Guardians can live up to the requirements of the job, and maintain their integrity and principles in the face of persuasion, temptation and provocation, they are tested from their youth (*Republic*: 180). The metal elements of Guardianship, and their superior role in the state, tends towards a perception of privilege. However, certainly for the Auxiliaries, whose function is to counter the potential corruption of the state inherent in usual practices and interactions between individuals of different wealth and ownership status, they are held to rectitude by relative poverty and vigorous restrictions (*Republic*: 184–5). The potential elegance of communal living actually manifests itself as the bare essentials of life. The Guardians are provided only with such food as people will exchange in return for care and protection, their sexual activity is controlled to ensure the propagation of future generations of 'gold and silver' people, private property is prohibited due to its corrupting influence in diverting attention away from the good of the state and, being constituted of precious metals themselves, they are forbidden to wear or touch such metals. The wealth and privilege of the Guardians and, therefore, of full citizens is in the position itself and not in material gains that accompany the role and status. Indeed, the materialism of non-citizens is precisely why a class of Guardians is needed.

For the Greek political philosophers, then, citizenship is concerned with safeguarding the virtues of the state and with defence of the constitution and its residents. Not everyone living in the confines of the state is capable of being a citizen: citizens are effectively people of special virtue who are able to move beyond the motivations of personal gain and to see a comprehensive view of the state and of relations to it. Greek democracy may be concerned with inclusiveness, but the framework for this is hierarchical and admits only certain people to the upper echelons in which citizenship is said to reside. The influence of Greek political thought is clearly evident throughout later writings of such philosophers as Rousseau and lays the foundations for all later philosophies concerned with citizenship and politics in more 'developed' states. Consequently, it may be argued that later philosophies and the political processes and relations that these spawn are premised on misconceptions of a limited democracy and/or citizenry that are chosen to be interpreted as more inclusive than they actually were. For example, Rousseau is able to laud the work of Aristotle without fully having to compensate for the society for which he was writing. After all, the myth of a connection between social class and levels of intelligence, or levels of required virtue for citizenship, can surely withstand any amount of population growth, economic development and political change. How much more so when citizenship is able to ignore other factors such as gender? In other words, limited citizenship is convenient. Political thinkers are able to expound their views without the added complications of a multitude of opinions on what is, or is not, right for the virtuous state.

This theme is clearly continued by liberal philosophers such as Hobbes who, taking a negative perspective of Greek political arrangements, states that 'it is the *Unity* of the Representer, not the *Unity* of the Represented, that maketh the Person *One*' (*Leviathan:* 85)(original emphasis). The good liberal state, concerned with maximising liberty within civil society, again assumes universal citizenship in that all people are responsible for the maintenance of laws which ensure liberty. As with the Greeks, the original laws stand and need only tweaking to meet changing conditions in society. There is little actual law-making to be done and everyone is involved in executing those laws in abiding by them. However, for the early liberal thinkers, quite the reverse seems to be true. For Hobbes in the *Leviathan* and Locke in the *Two Treatises*, there does not appear to be anything called citizenship.[5] Rather, everyone except the sovereign is a subject. It could be construed that more than one person comprises the sovereign, as in Rousseau's general will, to be discussed below. However, Hobbes is quite specific that all persons give their innate authority and liberty to the sovereign. Given his predilection for a strong monarchy, Hobbes' sovereign is one person, albeit supported by executives of its choosing (Gavre 1974). However, every subject is represented in the sovereign, each one having consented to the authority of the sovereign which speaks for all (*Leviathan*: 84–5). Similarly, Locke submits to the authority of a monarch, although one that, through the shared responsibility of subjects, appears less able to resort to tyranny than in Hobbes' state. While Locke openly refers to the concept of 'tacit consent' in which every 'citizen' approves the sovereign and transfers consent to them (*Two Treatises*: 153), Hobbes implies such throughout. By being born into, or remaining in, a society a person has performed their role in supporting the constitution. Other than that, the sovereign power can make decisions on affairs of state, demand calls to arms and choose successors knowing that the subjects consent to any decisions made. As long as such decisions preserve the liberty of subjects, and in Locke's case their property, they are legitimate (*Two Treatises*: 184).

These views contrast strongly with later liberal theories in which elements of democracy are introduced and citizenship aligns rather more with that of the Greeks. For example, for Rousseau the foundation of the social contract is that sovereignty is inalienable and cannot be detached from the persons contributing to the general will (*Social Contract*: 182). Of course, he is rather vague about who actually does constitute the general will. Certainly in *Emile* (passim) familiar patterns of citizenship appear: devotion to the state and the common good; indivisibility of state and personal interests; and perfectibility of citizens. Consequently, despite the general will being hailed as the constant will of all members of the state (*Social Contract*: 250), only certain persons will have the capacity to be full contributory citizens. While Rousseau does not expand on this in terms of social class, he certainly defines women out of the zone of capability for citizenship. However, limited citizenship does not necessarily correlate to limited, or non, representation under the social contract. Mutuality of sovereignty and government translates as a bond of representation in that decisions may be deemed collective. Thus, a person can be represented by themselves and no one else (*Social Contract*: 182) and, even though each individual has yielded up as much liberty as is necessary to support the civil state, the state can demand only reasonable duties from them, to which reasonable citizens would, of course, agree (*Social Contract*: 186).

Political thinkers, from Plato to Rousseau and beyond, appear to have great difficulty in reconciling their ideal states to the fact that the people inhabiting such states are not all ideal people. Indeed, Plato is probably the only one, until J. S. Mill, to attempt a comprehensive analysis of a state and citizenship whereby imperfect people are given an essential role in the maintenance of the state, both as full citizens and as subjects (Okin 1991a: 19). Most of the philosophers present a partial construction leaving a vague notion of equality of citizenship and representation but, when analysed a little, within a small sub-section of society. Nineteenth-century philosophers attempted to redress such a notion by presenting a more participatory depiction of decision-making and politics. For writers such as Mill, there was little justice apparent in a system that subjected the majority to laws which they had little, or no, part in making. His process of representative decision-making, while still presenting an elitist pyramidal framework with 'natural leaders' at the top (*Representative Government*: Ch.VII), was far more inclusive than that suggested by any of the previous writers considered here. However, this does not go as far as Marxist representation which may be interpreted as giving every citizen complete control over the decisions that affect them. What Gourevitch (1998: 546) refers to as 'polymorphous realisation' allows individuals to suit their actions and the timing of them to meet self and communal needs. As the need for a 'state' becomes redundant, individuals contributing according to their abilities and taking accord-

ing to their needs ('Critique of the Gotha Programme': 541), the need for
institutional representation appears to be void. Of course, until such
conditions are met, some sort of institutions are necessary and thus, in a
pre-Marxist transitional state, the problems of representation persist.
The replacement of one set of citizens as decision-makers by another
cannot alleviate the contradictions inherent in the concept. Moreover,
Marxist-feminism acknowledges that within the post-capitalist condition, gender, recognised by Marx and Engels ('The German Ideology':
176) as the first division of labour and hence oppression, will persist
unless specifically tackled (Hartmann 1992a; Barrett 1992). Even in a
new epoch depicted in post-political relations, the relationship between
gender, liberty and citizenship remains a political issue.

Universality and Difference in Citizenship and Representation

The fact that citizenship does not extend to everyone resident within a
state has been established by all the pre-nineteenth century traditional
philosophers discussed. However, so far there is no reason to believe
that within the community of citizens inequality of status pertains, or
that the virtues necessary for full citizenship are specific to certain types
of people beyond the possession of the virtues themselves. Cursory
reading and malestream interpretation of the philosophical texts would
tend towards the view that citizenship is open to any person meeting the
necessary criteria, and that these are neutral with respect to whom they
are attached. Indeed, contemporary commentators, when waxing lyrical
on the gender issue, often maintain that the philosophies are inclusive,
and that when writers constantly refer to 'he' in their discourses, they
are merely using generic terms that ultimately include 'she' as well.[6]
Feminists, however, have provided significant analyses of language and
gender, such as is evident in political philosophy, arguing that systems
and processes built on male experience and verified only by males serve
not only to exclude women but to nullify the legitimacy of female
experience (Spender 1985; Daly 1986; Phillips 1993). This is an essential
analysis in relation to the conjoined concepts of citizenship and representation. For if citizenship is concerned with the support and maintenance of the virtuous state, and the state requires unity, 'difference'
will be perceived as a destructive force.

By locking diverse and, therefore, possibly disruptive interests in the
private, domestic sphere, political philosophers alleviate much of the
potential for difference that can damage, if not destroy, the civil state.
For example, Locke's deconstruction of paternalism is firmly entrenched in political relations. His critique of Filmer's justification of
the divine right of kings in the first book of the *Two Treatises* clearly

argues the absurdity of royal lineage traced to God's appointment of
Adam by negating the rights of dominion over humankind. God may
have granted Adam the right to use animals for self-preservation but
Locke does not see how this translates into dominion over humans.
Indeed, surely the means of sustenance were given to earth and all
people, not just Adam (*Two Treatises*: 18, 29). Moreover, the Fall was a
punishment of Adam as well as Eve. As such, it is nonsensical to
presume that at the same time as banishing Adam from Eden he, and
his posterity for eternity, should be granted dominion over all humankind (*Two Treatises*: 31–2). For Locke, women are no more subject to
Adam's divine, or man's, rule (*Two Treatises*: 33), and they cannot be
obliged to subjugation. Within the family, mothers are owed as much
loyalty and obedience as fathers. However, Locke recognises that 'the
husband and wife, though they have but one common concern, yet
having different understandings, will unavoidably sometimes have
different wills too' (*Two Treatises*: 156–7). The ugly head of difference
is reared only to be subdued, 'it therefore being necessary that the last
determination (i.e., the rule) should be placed somewhere, it naturally
falls to the man's share as the abler and the stronger' (*Two Treatises*:
156–7). While in the political sphere women may well have determination over their own interests, where common interests are concerned
men naturally have the power of representation.

As Locke's state is concerned primarily with the preservation of
property rights, and as the family is the basic political unit in the state
(Okin 1980: 282), it follows that the common property interests of the
family are represented in the political sphere by male heads of family.
Any differences of opinion between men and women are easily subsumed within the framework of political representation that Locke
admits. Of course, this does not necessarily guarantee unity. Men, as
individuals and as heads of household, may disagree over issues and
solutions. As before, such dilemmas are dealt with by recourse to
sovereignty. In a state based on property rights, individuals quit their
natural rights to judgement and exacting punishment for offences to
property, giving authority to the community to regulate such matters
(*Two Treatises*: 159). Again, individuals are united in the sovereign,
each having surrendered power to the commonwealth. The state as such
has a limited remit, and it is unlikely that there are major differences
between men within this. Moreover, the differences between men may
not be as great as those between women and men, as the quotation from
Locke suggests: if men relate to experience as men, as heads of household and property owners, they are more likely to hold similar opinions
on issues of public import. The different interests that women will have
in their position as non-property owners, silent partners in the public
arena and in the family on issues of common interest would more

probably create divisions that citizens and the state would have difficulty in containing.

The liberal thinkers of the seventeenth and eighteenth centuries did
not really move far from the perceptions of politics and citizenship
expressed in mainstream Greek thought. However, while they acknowledged the interaction, but not the interchangeability, of state and
society, for Greek political thinkers society and state interacted to the
extent that there should be no differentiation (Barker 1960: 12). For such
unity to prevail the potential for political opinion to be translated into
political action needs to be checked. Barker (1960: 14) argues that Plato's
The Republic and Aristotle's *The Politics* aim to create institutions and
processes to obtain harmony and protect differing interests without
preference. An ideal model for such states is that of the family, in
which the interests of all members supposedly coincide. As such, a
detached echelon, or attached but 'special' group, of citizens can be
characterised as parents with their children's and each others' well-
being in mind. However, the analogy to parenthood and the family is
still somewhat schismatic. Citizens may perceive people in the state as
their children. But, for example, Aristotle's definition of citizenship by
virtue of public spiritedness excludes women and labourers, in that
such people cannot put state affairs above other priorities (*Politics*: 183).
Not only are their capacities for official public service diverted to
personal, own family or occupational issues, but the practical demands
of citizenship do not admit them. They do not have the leisure to pursue
state affairs by meeting and discussing issues in market squares and
gymnasia (Barker 1960: 254), and, for women, access to such arenas was
restricted, if not denied. But more fundamentally, the virtues of women,
being inferior to male virtues, would not meet the criteria for citizenship. Spinning, weaving, household management and beauty (Okin
1980) did not qualify for admission to the ranks of the citizenry, despite
being vital to the virtuous state.

The method by which Plato excludes women from full citizenship
stands in sharp contrast to his theory of non-gendered specialised
natures propounded in *The Republic*. By the time he wrote his last
dialogue, *The Laws*, in which a 'real' as opposed to an ideal type of state
was described, women had been relegated to less important roles than
men. For example, unlike the Republic in which 'gold' philosopher
rulers may be women endowed with the 'requisite natural capacities'
(*Republic:* 354), in Magnesia the thirty seven 'philosopher kings' of the
Nocturnal Council are all to be men (*Laws*: 224). Membership of this
ruling council will consist of people having held high office in the state
and with the education and moral character suitable to their position
(*Laws*: 516). It is unlikely that, in a society differentiated by sex, any
women will qualify for a position on the Council. The division of labour

is justified by recourse to custom and the fact that people would probably not accept women as equals (*Laws*: 294) even though it effectively robs the state of much talent.

Of course, excluding the argument that not ensuring the status of women's parenting role actually infantilises them, if the family model is legitimate the fact that women are not in the role of equal parent is not important. What is good for the family is essential to the state, to the extent that the first laws Plato enumerates are those of marriage. No family member is excluded from this good and no one can place their interests above that of the state. Any decisions made, even by an all male citizenry, will incorporate the good of the family and its members within the state. Aristotle mirrors such sentiments in his argument that the best state is one in which individuals are happy (*Politics*: 395). Therefore, the role of legislators is to ensure the good life for individuals whether they are citizens or not (*Politics*: 398). However, as Plato acknowledges (*Laws*: 294), different occupations for women and men result in different interests and prevent unity of thought and action. The dilemma of the mismatch of gendered citizenship and neutral laws is never resolved in Greek or later thought, beyond iteration of arguments about the unity of the state. Saxonhouse (1991: 47) notes that, for Aristotle, each member of the family knows their differences and observes a distribution of tasks working to their common good, and then goes on to note that the family model alluded to was not that of the Greek model in practice. The implication of this assertion is that philosophers' family model of citizenship, and subsumation of interests under the head of household, is not sufficient explanation for the exclusion of women as citizens. The efforts that are involved in reinforcing males as heads of households further indicates the political nature of limited citizenship based on family relations. Indeed, it is common knowledge that families are often not havens of tranquillity and members can, and do, put their interests above those of the group. The unchallenged authority of male citizens may quite conceivably misconstrue common interests (Phillips 1991: 63), leaving the small association of citizens quite happy, but not necessarily presenting unity overall.

Without explanation of how or why the family, as an essential unit of society, and its non-citizen members should be unrepresented in the state, political thinkers often resort to the sophism of separate but equal. While men are full citizens embued with the characteristics enabling their role, women are playing a support role suited to their equally important but inferior virtues. Such a picture is perfectly painted by Rousseau in *Emile*. Here, Emile, a child from a wealthy family, is trained and educated by his tutor, a thinly disguised Rousseau, to citizenship. His character is moulded to suit the rigours and requirements of self-discipline and self-sacrifice, to the point of leaving his beloved with whom he is infatuated, necessary to pursue his role within the social contract. Sophy, on the other hand, being naturally more concerned with social niceties, is trained and educated to alleviate the domestic concerns of the male citizen, and to complement his role in observing social behaviour. Her proper behaviour preserves her husband's good reputation (*Emile*: 352), and she is in a position to analyse the behaviours of others to be used in the pursuit of her husband's role (*Emile*: 415). Women's role in men's citizenship is essential, to the point where Rousseau (*Emile*: 531) can assert that they are each half of the whole person: Sophy is the hands and eyes; Emile is the head. How this translates into separate but equal is perplexing. At a basic, physical level of analysis one can note that it is possible to live without eyes or hands, but not without a head! The head is somewhat more than the sum of body parts and cannot be deemed 'equal to' the extremities or to individual organs. As the hands and eyes cannot function without the head, but not the reverse, so the civil society cannot function without citizens. The highest political honour surely cannot be deemed equal to the supporting role.

In justifying difference and the related exclusion of women from the upper echelons of the state, Rousseau conjures up contradictions that would alert logical minds to the unsuitability of men for any position of responsibility, let alone that of citizenship. There is no doubt in his opinion, that private interests in the home are not the concern of politics other than in terms of protection of property which, for men, would include the protection of their rights as heads of household. Indeed, a contented and comfortable home is the basis on which citizens can go into the outside world and perform their duties to the state. However, Rousseau's comparison of girls and boys indicates that girls are more enthusiastic and eager to learn than boys, they are more curious, attentive and persuasive than boys (*Emile*: 399) and, as they grow up, women have greater power over men, since they know what they want and how to get men to provide it. A situation in which, against appearances, women are actually naturally stronger than men pertains (*Emile*: 387, passim).

The reason why the strengths that women possess are inappropriate for public service can be explained in physical terms: the regular suffering of women through childbirth and menstruation (*Discourse on Political Economy*: 118) would interfere with their public duties. But also, girls get enthusiastic and eager about the wrong things. They are concerned with detail and practicalities, not with general principles and abstract concepts necessary to cultural, scientific and social progress. Hence, 'woman has more wit, man more genius; woman observes, man reasons; together they provide the clearest light and the profoundest knowledge which is possible to the unaided human mind' (*Emile*: 419).

However, as Wollstonecraft (1985: Ch.6) so clearly argues, it is separate education that harnesses girls' enthusiasm and dexterity to what Rousseau suggests the state requires of them: submission and domesticity. 'A woman's education must therefore be planned in relation to man' (*Emile*: 393) so that they can attract and retain a husband. Moreover, far from being dolts, it appears that women understand the injustice of their position from an early age and as such they 'should learn early to submit to injustice and to suffer the wrongs inflicted on her by her husband' (*Emile*: 399). In other words, as Rousseau cannot exclude women on grounds of insufficient ability, he stoops to physical restraint and psychological coercion to maintain social and political divisions between women and men.

Rousseau's schizophrenic annunciations of women as the fount of moral correctitude for society, and as the base of moral depravity of men, demands their governance and their solitude, reducing the separate but equal thesis to absurdity. Indeed, according to Vogel (1995: 215–19) it is precisely the separation of women in the home and men in public that ensures liberty of men as citizens and the good of the state. Mixed society only enables women to lure men into behaviour directed at meeting women's needs and expectations as a diversion from the serious business of the state. Consequently, it is 'the good son, the good husband, the good father, who makes the good citizen' (*Emile*: 390), a sentiment, and practice, that appears in political philosophy throughout the ages but is articulated by Rousseau with the clarity that others appear loath, or perhaps afraid, to utilise.

Women and Citizenship: the Costs and Benefits of Exclusion

If the motivations of citizens are built around the desire and need to ensure unity and/or happiness of the state, it may be believed either that non-citizens are unified and happy, or at least content, even in ignorance, under the aegis of a limited citizenry; or that they are not but are unable to do much about it. One of the benefits of a relatively closed or select hierarchy, with a citizen-elite at the top, is that it is self-legitimating as well as the arbiter of what is and is not acceptable for consideration in the political arena. Another aspect of this equation is that the citizens themselves may not be too happy in their role, carrying responsibility for the state and its people and possibly having to divert attention from their occupation that may be more to their preference than politicking. Indeed, Wolin (1960: 55) points out that Plato recognises a dilemma of this kind in that, if the highest and noblest occupation is philosophy, why would philosophers want to devote themselves to Guardian duties? Plato is required, therefore, to invent a rotational duty rosta whereby politics becomes an honoured but temporary duty experienced intermittently by those qualified for the job (*Laws*: 231). In other words, citizenship may be a cleft stick: it offers status but not more, and probably less, freedom than non-citizens. In this way citizenship may be perceived as just another job, albeit the most prestigious one, with the limitations that any occupation accrues and with greater responsibility attached to it. As such, the status of non-citizens is less damning and women, as most people, hold valued positions within society. But, as Wolin (1960: 57) notes,

Plato did not deny that each member of the community, no matter how humble his contribution, had a right to share the benefits of the community; what he did deny was that this contribution could be erected into a claim to share in political decision-making.

It may be from a contemporary perspective that citizenship has become idealised as essential to membership of a state. The dichotomy of citizen/subject is one that would not have substance for Greek nor, perhaps, liberal political thinkers. For Plato and Aristotle, citizenship was not just a function of being born within the boundaries of a state. But those born non-citizens were still free people, with slaves occupying their particular place in the hierarchy. Similarly, later liberal thinkers in the seventeenth and eighteenth centuries held to be implicit a minimal level of what modern political thinkers would call 'citizenship'. By 'being there' people within the state proffered legitimacy to the work of decision-makers, although not everyone was a fully participating decision-maker. This did not render them unfree or slaves with no rights or responsibilities. Rousseau clearly articulates this argument in terms of gender, in his belief that women are far better off than men precisely because they do not hold the responsibilities of citizenship and statesmanship. Women accrue all the benefits of living in a civil society without bearing the costs on their lives. Furthermore, they do not necessarily forego the advantages of political representation in the deliberations of citizens as their skills of persuasion, indeed manipulation, afford them indirect access through their menfolk who are too weak to resist feminine wiles (*Discourse on Inequality*: 70; *Emile*, Book V; Okin 1980: 145).

The fact that, historically, political philosophers perceive most people as non-citizens, may be offered as an example of why women are not a special case in any analysis of citizenship and representation. As the few people who are qualified for citizenship are almost certainly, although from different occupations, from a particular echelon in the state, very few people or groups in the state are 'represented' in the citizenry and its decisions. However, the reason why gender is an important variable in citizenship is that the constitution of the citizenry affects what is perceived as necessary for the good state and acceptable political relations within it. In Greek states, what contributes virtue and, in liberal states, levels of liberty, and the political frameworks in which each are contained, are in the gift of the citizenry. For example, a simplistic job description for citizens in nascent, and even mature, liberal states would be the determination of legitimate levels of unfreedom for people within the confines of the state. Hay (1996: 68) also notes that a function of citizenship is in defining who is, and who is not, part of a community. Indeed, 'politics' is often about ensuring the legitimacy of a state which provides a framework in which individuals are able to maximise their self-interests.

Self-interest in the context of citizenship may be communal and synonymous with the state, as for Plato and Aristotle, or more individualistic and concerned with material, economic interests which, in turn, contribute to the good state. For liberals, then, the maximisation of self-interest and the maintenance of the good state, requires that individuals are *as free as possible* to pursue their personal, familial and/or community-wide objectives according to their interests. Obviously, *as free as possible* cannot translate to absolute freedom as one person's freedom is another's restriction, and it is the citizenry, itself not absolutely free, which determines the levels of unfreedom for the rest, as well as the form of the framework within the state that upholds rights within the parameters and definitions of 'freedom'. It would appear that for the traditional citizenry in political philosophies, women's lack of liberty, whatever the cause, and however spuriously justified, is an acceptable level of unfreedom. Indeed, even within the household it is accepted by mainstream political theorists that women's liberty should be restricted, women usually being ruled by men as sovereign within their mini-state/households (*Leviathan*: 195; *Two Treatises*: 154). Only one mainstream writer, Mill (*Subjection of Women*: 223), has likened such unfreedom to slavery and it is open to speculation whether, had women been citizens, levels of unfreedom for half or more of a state's free population would have been deemed legitimate.

In a citizenry that is unrepresentative of most free people but in which men as a whole are evident, not only will the commonalties of men across classes be relatively well represented, but this may be interpreted as an expression of more legitimate unfreedom for women across classes. This can be further entrenched in the knowledge that 'current' citizens are not the originators but guardians and upholders of laws laid down by the first law-givers. Their interpretations of, and increments to, law can be situated within a particularistic, gendered and opportunistic framework. Logically, if more people have greater freedom, the likelihood of infringements on all individuals' actions is increased. Even though a writer as overtly patriarchal or masculinist as Aristotle notes that men's and women's public interests differ (*Politics*: 94), to include women in the echelons of the less unfree would add further potential barriers to the levels of freedom of others.

Partial Citizenship and the Art of Politics

The compelling feature of citizenship posited by mainstream political thinkers throughout history is that it is self-serving, self-legitimating and enclosed. It is difficult to challenge as 'not a good thing' because the writers convincingly interrelate the good of the state and its members, the majority of whom are not citizens, and the role of citizenship. More than this, though, is the historical entrenchment of the concept of citizenship, despite changes in its definition and parameters, as 'good'. Failure to investigate where this 'good' originates and how it is maintained may, in fact, be perpetuating something that is not as good as it could, and should, be. If politics is the realm of the citizen, then non-citizens have little or no role to play and their concerns, whether about the legitimacy of the state per se or the actions and decisions of citizens, are not legitimate or within the sphere of politics. Breaking into political territory, if possible, is not easy as citizens are effectively the gate-keepers to what is and is not legitimate for the state to deal with. Even in cases, such as in Plato's city states, where new citizens are welcomed to the fold and, presumably, new blood brings new ideas, new citizens are still males with all this implies for gendered discussion and decision-making. Hence, domestic issues, and women who are defined as being concerned with such issues, are outside politics. Moreover, any maverick females, such as Wollstonecraft and later feminists, who dare to question the time-honoured arrangements of mainstream political thought and its ensuing organisation, can be easily dismissed as being undemocratic 'hyenas in petticoats'.

Of course, the meaning of citizenship and its parameters has changed since the Greek classical philosophers, and the later liberals, were plying their views. Now citizenship incorporates the rights of all people holding membership of a state. In modern liberal democracies it is accepted that citizens not only have formally equal rights before the law and to public services, but that they can also participate to a greater or lesser extent in affairs of state should they so wish. For most citizens this may manifest itself in intermittent voting when required, weather conditions and interest levels permitting. For others, more active involvement in political parties, issue groups or other fora may be undertaken, even to the point of standing for office in local or national government. However, the legacy of traditional political thought can be perceived, not only in the lateness of women's admission to the realm of citizenship and politics, but in their continuing low representation in political and business decision-making processes, persisting attitudes towards and about women in office and the public sphere, and the boundaries of politics itself.

Contemporary mainstream theorists do nothing to alleviate the inequities that abound in politics as a result of the enclosure of 'legitimate' ideas, evidenced in lack of insight or imagination beyond the most basic and evident partiality. It may be surmised that, for many writers, the evidence that women are 'out there' in the public sphere, even if somewhat lagging behind, is an affirmation that citizenship is working as an inclusive concept. Or, alternatively, that it does not matter that a mass section of state members are inherently disadvantaged by the omission of a proper analysis to place them squarely within the legitimate confines of citizenship and its benefits. For example, as Locke clearly, if unjustifiably, wrote women out of his sphere of citizenship, his twentieth century myrmidon, Nozick, simply fails to mention women at all in his attempt to reinstate a Lockean perception of the legitimate state. As such, women are left to sink or swim in a minimal state with legitimate functions designed only for the protection of individual liberty and property. And yet, as a consequence of women's historical exclusion from the realms of property ownership and their predominance in the domestic sphere, nowadays often alongside public economic activity, the premise that Nozick lays down cannot properly include women. Although most political thinkers accept that inequality is an inevitability, whether natural or politically manipulated, the situation of women renders them far less equal than others *en masse*.

At least one contemporary writer overtly uses women's traditional status and relation to political institutions as a means of improving life and values in western liberal democracies. Etzioni (1993) claims that it is women's assertion to the rights of citizenship and public activity that has damaged the 'good' state. Although the formal status of citizenship should not be confiscated from them, they should realise and accept that, as underadvantaged actors in the public sphere, they would be better in their traditional sphere of activity, and that society would benefit as a consequence. Admittedly, the breakdown of social values and the consequent effects on the nuclear family results in some women being unable to be fully private sphere citizens. However, as long as their public activity is kept to a bare minimum some improvement to a society in strife will ensue. How clear the imprint of the traditional political thinkers is here. And how evident the reference to male experience throughout history. Rousseau's prediction of social breakdown and moral degeneration should women be allowed into the public sphere (Vogel 1995) is writ large in Etzioni's thesis. In postulating not his ideal society, but a solution to the problems of modern liberal democ-

racies, Etzioni assumes traditional male rights to public access, decision-making and, effectively, citizenship. Women may still have rights
before the law and to public services, but their separate but equal place
is within the family. Beyond the acceptance that women's desertion of
the domestic sphere is to blame for all social breakdown, no analysis is
attempted of other potential causes: much male social violence is
ascribed to women; but scrutiny of such things as the irrationality of
traditional decision-makers leading to poor decisions and the possible
deleterious effects of restricted citizenship on decision-making despite
social change is never ventured. Indeed, despite numerous studies of
such phenomena which provide sufficient evidence to cast doubt upon
Etzioni's findings, he leans heavily for support on those that prove his
point, the fact that some of the authors of such studies are women
apparently adding weight to his thesis.

Citizenship as a Closed Universe

The growth of the state over time, with regard to both population and
terms of reference, has obviously required reconsideration of citizenship
and this is, indeed, a contested concept. However, in failing to analyse
fully the original concept in relation to different groups incorporated in
the state, the old errors, misnomers and exclusionary attitudes and
practices appear to have survived its development. As Barker (1960:
18) eloquently states, 'the problems of Greek citizenship touch us today
because they are ours; and they are ours because the experience of the
Greeks has passed into our substance and merged into our being'.
Consequently, by necessity, in modern times women and other historically unrepresented groups may be tolerated in the offices traditionally
reserved for 'citizens'. But, in struggling against millennia of entrenched
'truths' and accompanying attitudes about the role, it is a difficult task to
be fully incorporated and accepted as bona fide active citizens in their
own right. The task of broadening the political agenda to include
citizenship issues pertaining to women is laborious and slow, the
potential for upsetting the real work of institutions, and the traditional
incumbents of office, remaining ever present.

An obvious paradox is evident when considering the extent of citizenship proposed, even by the limited parameters defended by political
philosophers. As they all note that domestic service is vital to the
development and maintenance of the good state, then surely domestic
issues, historically so vehemently proclaimed by male decision-makers
as 'women's issues', are political. There is no logical explanation for the
exclusion of domestic issues from the sphere of politics, or of women
from full citizenship. Indeed, there is no reason for men not being

involved in the domestic sphere, so vital is it to the state. Again, the logic of male philosophers cannot stand up to scrutiny. And yet women are in the situation where they have to justify their right to citizenship and inclusion of their rights in the political realm. Effectively, the history of citizenship, its knights and disciples, has created a universe beyond which nothing can reasonably exist. It therefore becomes relatively easy to dismiss arguments concerning the fundamental injustice of the concept. Perhaps it is irrelevant whether a root-and-branch restructuring of citizenship is required, or desired, or a genuinely inclusive model along the lines that political philosophers envision is developed. It is unlikely that the former is feasible. Certainly, judging by levels of apathy or non-participation in advanced democracies, most people are satisfied with formal citizenship, not desiring more involvement in decision-making than is absolutely necessary but at least having the opportunity should they so wish. The issue for women is that they should be able to participate if and when they want and that their concerns, whether domestic or not, receive not just adequate but honest and scrupulous consideration as legitimate issues within a state of citizens.

Notes

1. People may choose not to place themselves on the electoral register, of course. However, in the UK, certain people such as peers, convicts serving their sentences, non-voluntary psychiatric patients and foreign residents or visitors are ineligible (Peele 1995: 274).
2. Representation as a system could be defined as requiring a passive citizenship in which participation is preferably confined to politicking at election times and to voting. In contrast, an active representative process would require greater levels of participation from citizens.
3. Citizens may follow any occupation, as long as their chief focus of attention is the state. However, the functions of citizenship will involve holding office (*Politics*: 169) and participating in public judgements or affairs of state at some time, if not being a full-time occupation.
4. Plato invents a story of how different people are embued with different precious metals indicating their character and, hence, their roles in the state. He notes that most myths probably originate as a political exercise and trusts that his will be held in posterity (*Republic*: 181).
5. This is despite the title of Hobbes' treatise on *Citizen*, the precursor to *Leviathan*, in which subjection to the sovereign is first justified.
6. I have found this to be the case in personal discussions with commentators who, when engaged to explain the inherent patriarchalism of citizenship treatises assert their prowess on all things philosophical, including the complexities of non-gendered linguistics.

Chapter 5: Plato and Aristotle: Androcracy Incarnate

Although scholars decry the notion that Greek political philosophers expounded the ideal of democracy, common understanding is that democracy was indeed perfected by the ancient Greeks and had its heyday more than two millennia ago. The difference between theory and practice is evident here in that philosophers such as Plato and Aristotle were teaching and writing at a time when Greek politics was far from perfect, or democratic; their purpose being to improve the situation rather than describe it (Sabine 1951: 27; Myers 1968; Thomas 1981). Not believing that democracy was required for such improvement, Greek political thinkers were open in their scepticism about its qualities. As Thomas (1981: 49) notes, while they worked towards the democratisation of Greek politics, they did not see democracy as the ideal.

Of course, modern democracy, its processes and ideas, differs somewhat from those expounded by Greek political philosophers, but it still tends to look to ancient Greece for its foundation and, to some extent, philosophical legitimacy. Democracy in contemporary polities is defined by levels of sovereignty of the people, lending them political, civil and social rights in return for certain obligations.[1] For the ancient Greeks, democracy per se was only the best model from a bad bunch, including oligarchy and tyranny (*Politics*: 239; *Republic*: Book VIII). The more people involved in decision-making or holding rights, the more likely the potential for disharmony and fragmentation as specific interests take precedence over the good of all (Barker 1960: 174; Field 1969: 58; Elshtain 1981: 25). Indeed, rights may be viewed as practically synonymous with self-interest, the opposite of what is required for the good state wherein control of personal appetite is necessary if the good of the whole is to be understood, attained and maintained.

The best model for Greek political thinkers, after monarchy by the perfect, and therefore non-existent, ruler, was aristocracy. This enabled the moral, intellectual and strategic leadership necessary for the good state to survive and flourish with less than perfect beings, but all with the necessary virtues for leadership, balancing out excess and inclinations to protect vested or specific interests. However, within such a model, the non-aristocrats would still have their place, essential to the state. But an interesting, if not unsurprising, characteristic of all the states that Plato and Aristotle perceived as in some way better than others, is that they were all ruled by males. In other words, whatever the constitution, they could all be described as androcratic. The important aspect of Greek rule was that the 'right' people be enabled to govern (Barker 1960: 176; Elshtain 1981: 30; Thomas 1981: 47). In a system in which all input to the state has its place, and those able to perform specialist tasks are encouraged to achieve their potential, people with the ability to rule should do so. Allowing non-specialists the role of ruler cannot suffice and can do only damage to the good state.

The stage is set wherein contemporary democracy can look to Greek ideas to legitimise current practices. In terms of institutions, both Plato and Aristotle recommend what we would now see as a system of legislature and executive (Sabine 1951: 20–3). Moreover, for the Greek political thinkers, as now, everyone is essential to the state in their everyday role and relationships (Morrow 1998: 23). Moreover, although the Greek citizenry was limited compared to that of modern democracies, one of the tasks of ancient and modern citizens is to choose rulers from those who are deemed so suited. The fact that in contemporary democracies practically anyone is able to stand for office only obscures the profile of rulers which tends to be fairly consistent, especially at the national level of government.[2] This further reflects the continuation of limiting full citizenship in the *polis* to those with 'natural' talents, as well as the problems of meritocracy that Plato demonstrated in *The Laws*. Indeed, the greater opportunity to participate in the decision-making process nowadays owes more to the liberal influence of the seventeenth century than to Greek ideas which assumed the rules of civil and political life to be static, rulers guarding and enforcing them. Of course, one cannot in modern times argue that the Greek androcracy in which citizen electors and rulers were male has been wholly reproduced throughout the ages. The fact that, universally, women have been considered suitable citizen material for less than 200 years does not alter the fact that women are now able to vote and to stand for election in western liberal democracies and most 'third world' polities (UN 1991). It may even explain the proportionate dearth of women in political office as they have a couple of millennia of 'catching up' to do. The question arises, though, as to why women were not properly included in any of the forms of polity that the Greeks described, let alone championed, as the solution to their political problems at the time.

The Language of Exclusion: Greek Misogyny in Words if not Deeds

The debate about whether or not Plato and Aristotle are misogynists is both interesting and diverting. Plato's ideas may cause confusion: his insistence on specialised natures regardless of sex, running alongside the notion that women per se are created from the reincarnated souls of evil men (*Timaeus*: 122), does little to ease the concerns of women that women are, basically, unfit for public life. More clues about Plato's attitude to women can be seen in the language used to describe them, either regarding their own abilities or as descriptions of men who do not fully meet the requirements of the androcracy. For example, in *Phaedo*, a dialogue set in Socrates' death cell, women are sent away from the scene as their hysterical behaviour is disturbing to the last lesson Socrates teaches before taking poison. Indeed, as he lies dying he berates his young followers for crying, it being 'mainly for that reason that I sent the women away, so that they shouldn't make this kind of trouble' (*Phaedo*: 78). Throughout the dialogues, less than ideal conditions are often referred to as feminine. For example, the Persian monarchy was poorly managed as a result of the 'womanish education' of princes (*Laws*: 145); ill treatment of corpses after a battle is described as being 'low and mean . . . a kind of feminine small-mindedness' (*Republic*: 257); and cowardice in battle is the mark of womanliness (*Laws*: 492–3). On the other hand, some of the values Plato holds most high are given feminine references: excellence and justice are referred to as 'she' (*Laws*: 390, 373). Whether this is a considered conjunction or akin to modern notions of inanimate objects, such as cars, ships and countries, being given feminine status, the difference is clear between merely labelling something good female and purposeful analysis of less than adequate behaviours as feminine.

In his response to, and development from, Plato, Aristotle unashamedly assigns women a supporting role. As all things have their nature pertaining to the ultimate that they are able to achieve in life, women's nature is not to rule but to be ruled (*Politics*: 68). For some commentators, this is not to assign women a lesser role but a different one (Dobbs 1996; Mulgan 1994). Levy (1990) even goes so far as to suggest that Aristotle is rather more publicly inclusive of women, taking for granted that they will share the benefits of the state, including office holding, equally with men. This contrasts with feminist, and many malestream, analyses of Aristotle's failure to discuss women, other than as domestic actors and incubators, as a sign of his championing an early division of labour that excludes women from politics.[3]

It is possible that Plato's and Aristotle's unfortunate use of language and feminine labels, as well as their common placement of women as secondary to men, is not a sign of misogyny but acceptance of the status quo in this particular area of political theory and practice. Putting a neat label, such as misogyny, on anyone who decries women's worth does not assist in understanding more pressing reasons for exclusion. It is more necessary to consider the fundamental reasons why women were perceived as unfit for leadership and/or citizenship or, in Plato's case, less likely than men to be able to fulfil the criteria for the ultimate designation of philosopher king. After all, it is not compulsory to like one's rulers, as long as they are able and willing to do their job well. Misogyny, while on a grand scale of dislike, should not itself disqualify women from political activity within the state any more than having the 'wrong' colour skin or being from an unfavourable socio-economic background. It is possible that women's role in support of the state was equally valued by the philosophers. But this is unlikely to be more than platitude when the hierarchical nature of their socio-political ideals is considered. Unless, that is, the political values of ancient Greek polities differed from what we have come to expect, even as we have built on the legacy of Greek androcracy.

Truth, Justice and the Western Liberal Democratic Way

One of the most noticeable developments in political ideas through the ages has been in how politics is actually perceived. Contemporary ideas of politics as being concerned with good government, ensuring justice based on often volatile, intellectualised values and economic management, may be an evolutionary progression from ancient Greek ideas. It is not necessarily a 'natural' one, however, nor one that is particularly fair to women. However much Greek philosophers' values are repugnant to modern women, and to what extent they are responsible for the continued exclusion, or marginalisation, of women to politics, it is more possible that their belief in specialism per se rendered women greater respect and import than can be claimed by later thinkers who simply take for granted the inferiority of those who are not politically active or, for whatever reason, able.

A more credible evolution of political ideas from the ancient Greeks would include women's needs and abilities, even if not to the extent of 'allowing' political participation, at least valuing women's role as essential to the state far more than modern and contemporary polities manage. Understandably, this would still not be enough. Wherever a hierarchy exists, the exclusive prerogative of a particular group to membership of its hallowed halls implicitly denigrates less exalted positions, however loud the chorus of approval claiming esteem of the lesser. Of course, not only women inhabit the lower socio-political levels in Greek thought. Most men are also unable to progress beyond everyday work to participate in the state's political activity. However, although for Aristotle most men are in this position, all women are. For Plato it is less likely that women will have innate abilities for politics, although enough to reproduce the generations of Guardians will just about be found (Coole 1993: 23). It is evident, then, that there must be something, either in women's essence and/or in politics itself, that makes them unsuitable for politics or that ensures that their place within the state is satisfactory both to them and to the state itself.

Truth and Teleology: Women Cannot Pass Muster

Although Aristotle rejects Plato's concept of the one and only truth, both philosophers expound a notion of truth within their work. Aristotle's teleological approach presents the true nature of any animate object, allowing a more tangible and diverse feast than Plato's beauty and true knowledge. But whatever the definition, a major problem with 'truth' is its irrefutability. Rather like the Marxist recourse to false consciousness, against which it is not possible to argue precisely because one is deluded into a perfidious material existence, it is not possible to argue against 'truth'. To argue that truth is wrong in some way is not to possess truth, although, as Plato demonstrates, Socratic method consists of argument to discover truth (Crombie 1964: 136–7).[4] Moreover, to rail against truth is to challenge nature and even justice. Therefore, if women's *telos*, or true nature, is inferior to men's, to attempt to extend it is unnatural, wrong and harmful to the state, as well as unhealthy for the individual.[5]

Whether the 'truth' pertaining to women is perceived as natural or resulting from the political endeavours of the androcracy to exclude them is important. As far as Plato is concerned, the truth is that, beyond the fact that 'the female bears and the male begets' (*Republic*: 232), women and men are different only in the same way that men may differ from each other. Thus, 'we should regard a man and a woman with medical ability as having the same nature . . . but a doctor and a carpenter we should reckon as having different natures' (*Republic*: 232–3). This implies that women are as able as men to learn the necessary skills and abilities required for any occupation, including Guardianship. However, outside Book VI of *The Republic,* while Plato sometimes appends a statement saying that his arguments or pronouncements also apply to women, women tend to be forgotten, unless they are being used as examples of poor behaviour by citizens and other members of the population. It is interesting that a philosopher so engaged with truth and justice, and one who so meticulously analyses each relevant proposition, is so uncritical, or opinionated, where attitudes towards women are concerned.

Perhaps the most indicative text to consider is *Timaeus* in which Plato considers the nature of creation. Needless to say, a male divinity is responsible for all creation and, therefore, it may seem only natural that when humans were created the better of the two sexes 'was that which in future would be called man' (*Timaeus*: 58). Moreover, as a believer in the eternal soul, Plato's understanding of reincarnation, documented in *The Republic*, and *Phaedo*, as well as *Timaeus*, is that one reaps in future lives what one sows in the current one. Consequently, 'anyone who lives well for his appointed time would return home to his native star and live an appropriately happy life; but anyone who failed to do so would be changed into a woman at his second birth' (*Timaeus*: 58). The *Timaeus* is one of Plato's shorter dialogues, each dialogue concentrating on a particular philosophical aspect and not all directly concerned with politics of the state, although feminists would not distinguish between direct governmental issues and 'non-political' issues that contribute to them. However, the ideas contained in the separate dialogues should not necessarily be seen in isolation. If Plato's pronouncements on the souls of women are now placed against his theory of knowledge, expounded in *The Republic*, he does not meet his own criteria of truth and knowledge so to disparage womankind.

For Plato, knowledge can be either visible and surface knowledge, equated with opinion, or a deeper and fuller knowledge that penetrates to what is not visible, the truth or essence of what is being studied. Most people will be able to pass opinion by superficial analysis of beauty in, for example, attractive paintings, scenery and even people. Crombie (1964: 158) gives the example that, whereas a philosopher will hear pure musicality, a non-philosopher may like different types of music according to mood, fashion or the company they are with. Very few, that is the philosophers, will have the ability to see the essential nature of beauty itself, or any characteristic, in whatever frame it is presented. Such ability cannot be acquired through training. Rather, training can be given to perfect innate ability in those individuals displaying aptitude to philosophical matters. The difference between philosophers and non-philosophers is that the former desire knowledge and to see truth, and are willing to study to reach such goals. Moreover, knowledge is eternally immutable. The rest languish in surface knowledge which enables them to change their minds about issues and objects. Accordingly, based on *Timaeus*, as far as women are concerned, whatever each individual's nature, the truth is that they are essentially evil. How does this conform with Plato's argument that women should be active throughout his state, from producer to philosopher, and indeed, with the good state itself? At a basic level it could be argued that Plato is certainly swayed by opinion rather than knowledge as he changes his mind about the nature and role of women. At any time they may be worthy of Guardianship or become a potential source of disruption in the state and in need of strong control (Coole 1993: 34). But, however unfortunate, women are a necessary part of human life and, in Plato's vision, must also be part of his politics if his theory is to be consistent (Okin 1991a: 19).

A corollary of the reincarnation theory is that experiencing life as a woman is training for the male soul to be redeemed in a later life when it can return in a male body. This really means that all souls are male and that women are only bodies to house them as a means of punishment and rehabilitation. As such, it is not surprising that physically female beings are present throughout the social strata. But it does not solve the dilemma for Plato of allowing evil people, even in the process of recuperation, such a central role in the *polis*. If the essence of women is that they possess male souls, such souls are still not in a condition to rule or defend the good state. On the other hand, does philosophy and its study require goodness? It is perfectly possible that evil people are able to sift through surface emotions and characteristics to perceive and understand essential natures. Women's place in the *polis* is justified. However, for Plato, knowledge of the good as a pure concept is an inalienable part of philosophy and Guardianship (*Republic*: 304). So, again, his 'knowledge' about women is questionable. They cannot in all truth be both evil, or rehabilitating, souls and capable of goodness in the sense that Guardians exemplify. Paradoxically, Plato may claim to be able to see and understand the essence of women but, if he believes that his knowledge of women is correct, he cannot then include them in his political structures. Based on the fundamental tenets of Plato's ideas, the two are mutually exclusive. His real choice, therefore, is to either exclude women altogether or include them as fully equal, except perhaps in physical strength, which would surely not include using them as examples of citizens' shortcomings.

In many ways, Aristotle's teleological approach renders the truth much more tangible and comprehensible. As every being or type of being has an ultimate end-form it is relatively easy to see whether, or when, it achieves its own true self. For example, when a seed has fully developed into a shrub it has reached its end state, or *telos*. All internal growth processes and externalities, such as environmental conditions, available nutrition and pollination, that are required for it to achieve this end-state are components of the finished product. Analogous to plant life, humans and human relations also have defined ends to which Aristotle refers in his political writings.[6] Certainly, as biological organisms, human *telos* is irrefutable: to become an adult with all its physical and psychological components. However, unlike a plant, which is self-sufficient, humans are usually dependant on others to satisfy their requirements, and Aristotle describes the natural progression from solitary individual to the formation of self-sufficient associations: men and women, to procreate, form a household, also containing slaves; households form villages to provide for more strategic needs; and villages form states to complete the circle in which self-sufficiency is achieved (*Politics*: 56–9). The state is clearly a finished product and 'belongs to the class of objects which exist by nature' (*Politics*: 59). Consequently, humans are, by nature, beings that exist within states. Moreover, as natural components of the state they also all have their own functions determined by intrinsic moral and deliberative virtues, such as temperance, reason, bravery and justice (*Politics*: 94–5; *Ethics*: passim). As virtue develops according to purpose, it is not the same in all people and, therefore, human *telos* is not uniform.

Through his considerable constitutional, as well as biological, studies Aristotle was able to determine that the ultimate aim of human beings was to achieve happiness, the state being the vehicle for its attainment in individuals and as a community. While sub-categories of material or altruistic concepts and objects, such as wealth, power or charity, may appear to end in happiness, they are in fact only components of the end-state. True happiness as *telos* is self-sufficient wherein people will 'always choose it for itself and never for any other reason' (*Ethics*: 73). For individuals, true happiness is attained when they are fully utilising their virtues to the moral good (*Politics*: 428), thus contributing to the common good. However, while all free people possess such moral virtues as temperance, reason, bravery and justice, they are differently distributed according to need and not always fully developed. For example, deliberative virtues are absent in slaves, ineffective in women and undeveloped in, presumably male, children while they are fully developed in men (*Politics*: 95). It must be assumed, then, that only men can attain full happiness, being aptly endowed with those virtues that enable them to contribute to the state and maintain the conditions in which happiness can ensue. Hence, androcracy is a *telos* by nature.

Of course, as with all end-states, the component parts are necessary, if often not essential. At a basic level, man's happiness cannot be sustained without replenishment of the base unit, man himself. In relation to this, women are essential and necessary to the continuation of the good state, their *telos,* and presumably happiness, being to reproduce male babies who will eventually take their place in future generations of statesmen. Should women exceed their natural functions and try to determine their own fate by, perhaps, ignoring eugenic rules on which way the wind is blowing when attempting to conceive, or exerting their mental faculties while pregnant, depleting the amount of strength devoted to the gestating foetus, they may well produce female babies

(*Politics*: 439–44). While some girls are necessary, of course, they are not templates for the perfect future. Although continuous or fairly regular pregnancies after the age of eighteen may be the fate of the good woman, they do not live in the Greek equivalent of a plastic bubble during this time and, therefore, are allowed some other functions. But these are only as a husband 'hands over to his wife such matters as are suitable for her' (*Ethics*: 276). The upshot of this is that, either women cannot be happy, because they do not have full use of their moral virtues and are at the behest of those who do, or that they are contented precisely because their virtue does not allow them to contemplate their situation as unjust or in any way less than their potentiality. Another interpretation could be, of course, that they have full use of their faculties, perceiving their best interests in not pursuing any other course and allowing the men the onerous tasks of the androcracy.[7] But if this is wrong and women did understand their *telos* to be something other than what Aristotle portrayed, they were effectively under an obligation not to pursue it. Not only is it a fundamental rule of Greek political philosophers generally that doing what one wants is not consistent with happiness or, therefore, moral or communal good, but because Aristotle's teleological knowledge fixes a definition of happiness in the good state as he describes it, it would not be in the common interest for women to pursue a different *telos*.

Where female *telos* is concerned, Aristotle appears to bend the rules of nature to suit a particularly androcratic model of politics. Perhaps the most blatant abuse is in the deconstruction of humanity to its parts. Humans are subdivided into men, women, slaves and children, each with their function within the family and the state. Why the ultimate happiness of men and women should differ is not explained by allusions to different development of the same virtues. Indeed, Dobbs (1996: 79) argues that interpretations of Aristotle's ideas as proclaiming women's inferiority are incorrect, implying that they are propounded only by ardent feminists. For Dobbs the only difference between men and women accruing from the differing distributions of virtues is that women cannot start a pregnancy, male semen being required to provide the heat necessary to spark the process. For the rest, difference leads to mutuality, male and female roles complementing each other. The problem with this interpretation is that it does not explain why the mutuality lies with citizen man and homebound woman and not with political, as well as domestic, complementarity.[8] Furthermore, it does not tackle the question of nature or nurture which Aristotle's methodology circumvents. While the physical functions of animate beings can be tested and substantiated, although many of these are still being discovered and debated even with the technological progress made in the last two thousand years, moral virtues are not subject to such certainty.

Considering Aristotle's fastidious vivisection of constitutions, he is remarkably credulous in his perceptions of human nature.

In many ways Aristotle falls into the same trap as Plato in that, to fulfil the conditions of the good state, certain imperatives have to be justified. For Plato, communism and justice determined women's place among the Guardians whether he believed they could live up to that status or not. In the same way, Aristotle's good state, in which the common interest is paramount, depends on women's inferiority. His refutation of states depending on common ownership of property and a community of wives, as well as those in which women hold political power, supports the notion that property and family is an integral part of the natural state, provided that private ownership meets communal requirements (*Politics*: 115). It must be presumed that in the many states he observed, the androcratic pattern of human and political relations prevailed. Indeed, wherever exceptions were noted they were usually due to extraordinary conditions such as the absence of control over women after wars in Sparta (*Politics*: 143) or where only a female beneficiary is available to inherit wealth and position (*Ethics*: 276). In all such cases the state is diminished. However, rather than analysing the reasons for the circumstance of female domesticity, and the results of its desecration, recourse is taken to different distributions of virtues. Rather as now, where women's under-representation in any field or organisation can be excused by reference to their special talents being excellent, but unsuitable for the specific task at hand, Aristotle also patronises women by allocation of their part in the good state. And as Aristotle was not concerned with change for change's sake, but with considering what was good in existing states and building on them (*Politics*: 114), it is 'natural' that major changes to social structures and relations would not enter the equation. Indeed, Saxonhouse (1991: 36) notes that, for Aristotle, equality only leads to problems within any state. It can be surmised that once everyone is granted equal *telos* then more material concerns come under scrutiny, such as why only men hold political honours. This is synonymous with Aristotle's explanation of the deterioration from the best constitutions through the power of avarice among groups bent on specific interests, even where these are mistakenly believed to be for the common good. In other words, it is in the common interest that virtue is depicted as different for women, men and slaves; even so far as attributing it to nature itself.

Justice and Androcratic Politics

So far, then, it can be seen that although both Plato and Aristotle perceive deficiencies in women that would justify the development and maintenance of androcracies, these are not sustained through the methodologies both philosophers utilise. It is also possible that politics, by its nature, is ripe for androcratic governance. Here reference to politics concerns not only organisational arrangements but the purpose of the political, which for both philosophers is the pursuit of the good life. Above all the elements that contribute to this concept, the notion of justice presides: what people do and how they do it are essential to the development of the just state and, of course, Greek prescription determines the nature of just relationships and behaviours.

In Plato's taxonomy, justice consists of wisdom, courage and self-discipline (*Republic*: 198–202). Within the state these attributes are evident to a greater or lesser degree in the different classes and, in individuals, their distribution determines the class to which one justly belongs. Plato confirms this when he says that 'justice is keeping what is properly one's own and doing one's own job' (*Republic*: 205). By accepting limitations arising from innate virtue and socio-economic position, the wise are able to act for the common good and not specific interests, the courageous keep the state safe, and the temperate or self-disciplined maintain order and harmony between the weakest and strongest elements of the state. The distribution of elements contributing to the good state is clearly defined in Guardian philosophers, auxiliaries and the common people. Knowing that Plato includes women as able participants in all classes necessarily means that a just state is one in which women perform their tasks according to their natural abilities. However, as Sabine (1951: 72) notes, Plato, realising that human nature would not admit to the potential that his ideas held, felt it expedient to adapt his ideas to accommodate the intellectual and political sensitivities of his time.

While *The Laws* may be seen to extricate Plato from the radicalism of *The Republic,* in fact it also does a great deal, within the confines of omniscient androcratic qualifications, to create a public role for women in a state that is more realisable than his ideal republic. Women may be junior members of the executive, children's play supervisors and marriage supervisors (*Laws*: 279, 267) but, apparently to his chagrin, not legislators (*Laws*: 295). This obviously does not lend itself to justice, and although Plato still refers to this constitution as a just one, he also understands it to be a second best option (*Laws*: 296; Sabine 1951: 91). Having noted this, probably closely aligned to his underlying wariness of female virtue, Plato adeptly justifies women's inferiority in *The Laws*. The reversion to a more recognisable state grounded in custom and convention (Sabine 1951: 96; Bowle 1961: 46) enables the full extent of man's imaginative deficit to flourish, eventually leading to the comment that 'the "superiors" of bad men are the good, and of the young their elders (usually) – which means that parents are the superiors of their offspring, men are (of course) the superiors of women and children, and rulers of their subjects' (*Laws*: 455). Does this eliminate Plato's concept of an inclusive justice? Among the usual derogatory feminine labels attached to substandard behaviours, Plato is keen to assure his audience that women do have a place 'so far as possible . . . on the same footing as the male' (*Laws*: 294) in the second-best city state. They are to be trained as defenders, participate in mixed and single-sex sporting competitions and festivals, and receive education. The grounds for this, even where their path to the highest official positions is blocked, is that a state where women are not afforded such benefits 'is only half a state, and develops only half its potentialities, whereas with the same cost and effort, it could double its achievement' (*Laws*: 294).

It is not justice per se that requires women's equal participation but the good state. However, a good state is also a just state. This leads to two conclusions: firstly, a state that does not admit women is unjust and, therefore, despite their supposed deficiencies women must be trained and educated to a standard which enables their participation. Secondly, it may be that the state prevents women from achieving their potential, and thus, from pursuing their just roles. Therefore, the state itself acts unjustly and cannot be a good and just state. Indeed, Plato, in modern parlance, acknowledges that women are socialised into much of their unvirtuous behaviour and that this renders them reluctant to participate in public affairs (*Laws*: 263). The solution to this problem is to regulate women closely and carefully, forcing them into behaviours suitable for citizens (Elshtain 1981: 40; Coole 1993). Of course, education is essential to this process as is participation in communal meals which, as Coole (1993: 27) notes, is a means to train people to good public behaviour in that, through contributing to the meal, women will also learn the value of community.[9] In a way then, Plato is suggesting that women, despite their inferiority, are not as fundamentally bad as they appear in existing states and can be trained, educated and regulated to become, and remain, good citizens. While this effectively countervails his arguments on justice, by having to include women in the *polis* he can also justify androcratic politics only on the grounds that the human psyche is, unjustly, unprepared to accept women, even in their trained condition.

Naturally, Aristotle does not have the same problems as Plato in attempting to defend the unequal status of women in his state. The problem for Aristotle is to explain why women who possess the same virtues as men, albeit in different distribution, cannot participate in public affairs and are permanently ruled by men. This becomes important in the context of justice within the state, which is defined as equality among equals (*Politics*: 193). Here, equality does not refer to a universal absolute but 'it is relative to people, and applies in the same ratio to the things and to the persons' (*Politics*: 195). Anyone attempting to skew processes and outcomes to reach a form of equality for all, or between groups, is acting in specific interests, usually their own, and not for the common good. Hence, women, who may be of the same class and virtue as men, who want to share political honours with them, would be considered selfishly motivated and unjust. It becomes necessary, therefore, to consider what, for Aristotle, has to be equal in order to achieve justice.

Certainly there is an unarguable progression of political relations as experience develops virtues in respect to citizenship. Obviously the young, whose virtues are not fully functional, are ruled by older people, effecting an apprenticeship in which good virtues are developed through emulation (*Politics*: 182). Similarly, productive and mechanical classes will be ruled by those whose virtues render them apt to rule. Among the ruling class itself, justice requires rotation of rule, no one having just right to permanent office. Justice further ensures that people recognise and acknowledge the just positions and prerogatives of others (*Politics*: 405): the young know and understand why they are ruled by their elders, the same applied to producers and citizens, and to rulers and ruled, even to levels of seniority among the ruling classes. But this lends itself to critical analysis in the case of women and men who actually share class attributes and, therefore, virtues, however differently distributed they may be. Women cannot justly possess equal virtue and not share in the rotation of rule where this may apply. Moreover, it does not conform to definitions of justice for women to have the virtues necessary to rule in aspects of the household and not in the state. Aristotle clearly designates the household not just as a component, but a microcosm of the state. Although this is circumvented to some extent by the proviso that women can have control only over the areas of the household that men designate for them, the evidence must be that women have the capability to undertake such jobs. The argument that household rule is not one of master over slaves but statesman over subject (*Politics*: 92) does little to alleviate this conundrum. Men cannot justly permanently rule over women because they are free. But as free persons, a level of equality is present that demands rotation of rule. Aristotle's further recourse to reason does not suffice to untangle the web as women, to perform their tasks, must utilise reason to ensure achievement. Thus, any level of responsibility within the household must exercise the deliberative faculties to the common good of those in the household. If deliberative faculties can be used in such a way in private then, by Aristotle's own reasoning, they must be suitable for use to the broader common good too.

The conclusion must be that it is only 'natural' that men rule permanently over women because of experience and not innate ability. Indeed,

Levy's (1990) attempts to counter feminist criticism of Aristotle by reference to women's moral superiority in the presence of men's intemperate pursuit of public honours, only serves to strengthen arguments that men should share rule with women in public. Dobbs (1996: 86) even goes so far as to say that citizenship is not a prize for men's greater virtue but therapy, public office serving to regulate their unfettered appetites. Basically, in the household women demonstrate all the virtues, suitable self-restraint, prudence and reason, among others, to perform their tasks, in addition subsuming any possible desire to exceed their role where they feel this is possible. All this is to the common good. One would imagine, therefore, that justice would demand their equal opportunity to share in public honours, and Aristotle does not prove irrefutably that this should not be the case. Indeed, the state is inherently unjust when it does not allow equals to partake of the honours suitable to their rank.

The impact of 'justice' on women is that it effectively limits not only their functions but any attempt to argue that they are being repressed and under-utilised, either in an individual capacity or within the context of the state. In other words, justice essentially becomes a form of social control. For the Greek political thinkers considered here, this is overtly the case: people must be educated not only to their role and to accepting that this is all they can attain, but that this is essential to the state and the well-being of all those residing in it. Political relations are cast within this framework with the ruled acknowledging the propriety, or justice, of their circumstances. Where such circumstances do not pertain, states become, or remain, dysfunctional.[10]

The methods for supporting 'just' relations, then, are to enforce the idea of their centrality to justice, and the state's ends, within the objective of achieving happiness. A happy person is one who performs the function for which they were born and who provides for the happiness of all others by performing their function. The whole edifice relies on the stability, unity of purpose and goodness that each person, happily performing their tasks, contributes. We have already considered issues allocating all women to domestic tasks and that this is probably not a natural or just situation. However, the concept of justice is such that if women are unhappy in their allotted role, it is not because they are in the wrong job but that they are wrong-headed and want what they cannot 'rightfully' have in all justice. In drawing a parallel between relations in households and states, Aristotle provides the perfect foil for such women, or rather for their husbands. Although the best constitution is determined by the circumstances in which the state exists (*Politics*: 242), good constitutions always have the most suitable person, or group of rulers, in power. Where this does not pertain, factions vie for power causing disruption and, eventually, constitutional change for the worse. For example, democracies occur where the poorer free majority hold power, oligarchies where the fewer rich do so (*Politics*: 245). In each case, those in power are motivated by the desire to gain honours for themselves and those like them, and where a less than perfect and just constitution exists, correct leadership is absent. When this is translated to the household, wherein women transcend their *telos* either to claim equality with men or to rule over them, a situation in which some heiresses may find themselves, not only will women's happiness be impaired, but the household will not run efficiently. Consequently, a part of the state is not performing to its full potential in the service of the whole. After all, justice and politics are not about doing what one wants, but what is good.

The First Brick in the Wall: Once Analysed – Thereafter Forgotten

The heritage of Greek political philosophy is profound. After two and a half thousand years we still utilise Greek ideas in politics, whether as a benchmark or a model, our political vocabulary is defined by the Greek, and political ethics and behaviours are measured by the standards set by ancient Greek political philosophy. Although not without change and adaptation, 'that these ideals should have been stated in the idiom and within the limitations of the *polis* does not make them less permanently valid or incapable of adaptation and enlargement to a wider setting' (Bowle 1961: 43). At the very least, Greek ideas situated politics in the *polis* as the realm of justice (Saxonhouse 1986: 403), effectively defining the concept and the arena in which it legitimately occurs, in perpetuity. As commentators point out (Crick 1964; Raphael 1976; Randall 1987; Lister 1997), politics has traditionally been perceived as a public activity executed by public actors. Moreover, the parameters of politics have remained virtually unchallenged: internal order and external defence, dependent on the welfare of citizens. Although the citizenry may have broadened with different approaches developed to accommodate these changes, the basic framework would be recognisable to past philosophers.

Integral to this continuity of philosophy is that private relationships and occupations are necessary, indeed essential, to the state. However, although these pursuits are *in* the state as part of its geography and infrastructure, they are not *of* the state as political constituents. The result of this arrangement, for the state as well as for women, is that not only has politics been historically and almost universally seen as a particularly male-centred activity, but also, inevitably, it has become narrowly focused on the interests of a relatively closed ruling group (Millett 1977; French 1992). Consequently, wherever an attempt is made to include women in politics, it is done on androcratic terms and conditions, adhering to the true nature of politics as defined by Plato and Aristotle. This becomes obvious when considering Plato's female Guardians. Coole and Elshtain highlight that Plato's method of instilling equality is not to have recourse to nature but to strong control through education to purpose and enforcement of law. This does not necessarily amount to defeminisation (Coole 1993: 34), but to deprivatisation (Elshtain 1991: 70) whereby women's contribution to the state is forced to conformity with current practices. In other words, women's equality as Guardians depends on their meeting male norms, accepting existing agendas and practices. A clear distinction arises here between women being accepted as citizens versus women's true citizenship in which they bring issues to the agenda. A more comprehensive politics is not just concerned with including numbers of women but also their inter-ests. The power of the knowledge and truth passed down through the generations from the Greeks is evident. By Plato's, Aristotle's and their disciples' understanding, androcracy is 'natural', reflecting men's sup-posed ability to see the big picture and make decisions based on common interests. Anything that claims that the common interest is, in fact, particular is itself particular and a danger to stability. In this analysis, the 'narrow focus' of androcrats can be described as a figment of the slighted female imagination.

What appears to be missing from mainstream political philosophy after the Greeks is scepticism about many of the pronouncements of the Greek foundationalists. Indeed, another profound legacy of Greek phi-losophy with regard to women and politics is that it appears to have given licence to later philosophers not to give women due consideration in their treatises. But, as Elshtain (1981: 26) notes, the good state is really only a creation in speech not an existing entity. Taken with Wolin's (1960: 6) announcement that politics comes before philosophy, the latter being based on existing order, then we cannot place Greek philosophy in the category of definitive knowledge or truth. Nevertheless, this is exactly what mainstream political philosophers have done. Hobbes' and Locke's perfunctory dismissal of women as worthy of equal parental loyalties but incapable of political undertakings have no need of further explanation. Aristotle has provided this for them. Rousseau's lengthy treatise on Sophy also owes much to Aristotle although the depth of 'analysis' presented is worthy of Plato in its detail if not in its findings. In fact, Plato is the only mainstream political philosopher, until perhaps the nineteenth century, who attempts an analysis of the relation of women to politics. But as Bluestone (1988) found in her study of historical scholarship on Plato, his writings on women have been systematically ignored or denigrated. In fact, her comments about Plato scholars, in reference to Plato's writing on women, is generally applicable: 'it is striking that scholars whose interpretations make Platonic text vital and comprehensible in many respects, are so much less careful when dealing with matters of female equality' (Bluestone 1988: 54). In other words, where women are involved, the methods that are otherwise used by political philosophers to explain, analyse and expound complex political relations are suspended.

It can certainly be argued that the legacy of the Greeks is generally positive. Democracy is globally cherished and fought for, and as socio-economic conditions have changed, the democratic framework has incorporated more and more citizens into its sanctum, including women. However, inheritors of the Greek traditions have failed to solve, or even consider, fundamental issues concerning the basic tenets of politics and the nature of political relations. Consequently, the inadequacies of democracy remain unresolved. The unsatisfactory condition whereby interests, and people, deemed essential to the state are not represented in decision-making cannot be perceived as just. Moreover, such exclusions can only be to the detriment of the good state. Members of the state who are disqualified from making representations as citizens, and who are effectively, if passively, compelled to perform roles that may not meet their full potential, are unlikely to be the happy and content inhabitants that maintain the state as Plato and Aristotle foretell. Perhaps the demands that democracy and democratic theorists make on states are too exacting. The breadth of relevant interests cannot ensure comprehensive inclusion as well as stability. This would explain the need for restricting access to citizenship, including offices of state and channels of representation, so justifying later political developments in which citizens became the legitimators of otherwise autocratic rulers.

Notes

1. Debate concerning the parameters and measures of democracy in contemporary politics is continuous. The difficulties of meeting the standards set by the definition of democracy as government for the people, by the people are further intensified by the rapidity of change in domestic polities and in the global economy (Wollheim 1969; Roche 1992; Wright 1994). However, certain criteria appear in all contemporary claims to democracy, although in different amounts: basic welfare provision, legal and participatory rights of citizens are twinned with citizen obligations to contribute to the common wealth, including legal and defensive duties (Giddens: 1998).

2. The occasional non-graduate, non-professional, or equivalent, high office holder does not disprove the tendency for relative socio-political homogeneity in political assemblies. For example, the majority of UK Members of Parliament are university graduates with only 13 per cent of Labour

representatives coming from manual labour occupations, the historical recruitment source for the Labour Party (Norton 1998: 250; Norton 2001: 346). More generally, MPs' professional background is relatively homogeneous, although more are now described as 'career politicians', their professional background, usually in communications and journalism, being aligned with political ambition. In the US, the profile of representatives is similar with 52 per cent of Congresspersons being lawyers, 49 per cent in banking or business, and 25 per cent from the education and journalism sectors (some Congresspersons list more than one profession) (*News and Observer* 1997).

3. On a few occasions, Mulgan (1994: 192) argues for Aristotle's inclusivity of women by reference to the fact that where he intends to exclude people, such as lunatics and children, he explains why. Such reasoning is not applied to women and, thus, it is concluded that women are as much part of Aristotle's ideal state in all its activities as men. However, another explanation could be that women are so invisible and/or their support role so immutable that there is no need to mention them at all. As the role of dogs and cats is not analysed in relation to the state, neither need there be discussion of women's role.

4. Plato's belief, on which his method is based, is that truth is determined through dialectic properly discharged. 'If a man can't define the form of the good and distinguish it clearly in his account from everything else, and then battle his way through all objections, determined to give them refutation based on reality and not opinion, and come through with his argument unshaken, you wouldn't say he knew what the good in itself was, or indeed any other good' (*Republic*: 346).

5. Much Greek and Greek-style tragedy is premised on the notion that women who transcend their natural place or ability will suffer horrible consequences (Euripides 1998; Racine 1986).

6. Mulgan (1994: 184) claims that Aristotle's writing was not really about politics in terms of public life at all but about humanity itself. Indeed, in *The Politics*, although the context is concerned with constitutionalism, the real subject is the virtue of the people within the state.

7. Dobbs (1996: 86) suggests that men's public duties serve to ease the plight of women by removing patriarchal men from the house.

8. The thesis that Aristotle is not writing a political treatise but one that is concerned with the holistic nature of goodness would support Dobbs's argument, in that exclusion from political office is not as significant as feminists may conclude (Mulgan 1994). However, if this is the case, there is little legitimacy for excluding women from political office, especially when, as Sabine (1951: 92) argues, the *polis* is not only about government but constitutional rule too. Thus, women's exclusion from the public is a greater injustice, always being ruled without the opportunity to rule themselves.

9. Barker (1960: 380fn) further adds that communal meals free women from the tasks associated with the supervision of cooking, so freeing them for public life.

10. Aristotle maps the process of constitutional deterioration from the best, monarchy, to the worst, tyranny, via such forms as oligarchy and democracy

(*Politics*: Book V). This is not a linear progression, not all states starting as perfect monarchies. Depending on what type of constitution is discussed, it can become either better or worse according to the factions that gain power and their motivations: specific interest will worsen a constitution; the common good will improve and strengthen it.

Chapter 6: Hobbes and Locke: Divine Right of Contract Man

Throughout the history of political thought the idea that certain people are able and functionally equipped to rule is evident. As with professions other than politics, those people with a distinct interest in, or proclivity to, particular occupations or tasks channel their efforts to achievement within these. But a fundamental difference appears to be that politicians are born, other professionals can be made. Of course, political vocation has always been susceptible to other more prosaic and materialistic objectives such as personal glory, power or remunerative reward and connections. One of the difficulties for political philosophers is to produce a basis for the balance between the 'right' people gaining rule and maintaining legitimacy based in a broad swathe of sovereignty. This is particularly difficult for liberal thinkers who acknowledge competitive individualism within states, with its potential to damage attempts at creating and maintaining socio-political unity.

By the seventeenth century the idea of an harmonious aristocracy within the overall unified state had transmuted into a European form of exclusionary politics that vested political power in the monarch whose legitimacy was derived directly from the heavens. This form of patriarchalism traces the lineage of kings to God through Adam. Basing the evidence for this in the scriptures would, one might think, have denied the possibility for any dissension. After all, who can argue with the word of God? Moreover, a hotline to God allows great scope for arbitrary powers to be utilised against friend and foe alike. The loss of liberty in civil society is complete, the ability for self-defence and preservation of individuals' rights being nullified, as only God and Its[1] earthly interpreter, subject to no checks, have the power of life and death over those they rule (Nyland 1993: 40).

By the time that philosophers such as Hobbes and Locke were writing, patriarchalists' interpretations of the scriptures were questioned as being expedient rather than supernal. As such, any opposition to the source of the king's authority had to find a basis in secularism. This did not indicate a denial of monarchy itself, the major danger of democratic forms of politics being that of civil war, or a state of nature, as conflicting political claims competed for dominance. Nor did Hobbes or Locke countermand religion. Rather, a new basis for monarchic rule was needed, preferably one that was vested in broad sovereignty to ensure a 'people's monarch' and that supported the level of liberty necessary for order to be maintained.[2] The solution for both Hobbes and Locke was found in the concept of a contract wherein every person submits equal amounts of liberty in exchange for security and the right to self-preservation. A ruler, as first among equals, preferably a monarch but with provision for an assembly if preferred, is appointed and supported with the consent of those to be ruled. What theorists such as Hobbes and Locke attempted was to eliminate the concept of natural hierarchy in society (Schochet 1975; Hampton 1986).

The predicament for women in this scenario is that, just as Aristotle noted that women can only ever belong to the part of society which is ruled, the seventeenth-century, patriarchal family in which women were permanently ruled, was effectively construed as a 'natural hierarchy' by Hobbes and Locke.[3] To be accommodated in their theories, either the family had to be granted exceptional status and remain as it was, or it had to be included in the contractual model. Both patterns have implications for the social contract: either women's sovereignty is somehow inferior to men's, rendering the legitimacy of any rulers questionable; or, as contractors, their choices are more restricted. Not only can women not compete for the right to rule but, correspondingly, they are limited to choosing male contenders for the legitimate right to rule. The historical 'maleness' of political power surely indicates a breakdown in full sovereign rights of equal individuals.

Hobbes: From Amorphous God to Embodied King

The sentiments in *Leviathan* earned Hobbes the title of 'atheist' and the ignominy of the book being burned as a 'pernicious publication' by the University of Oxford during the 1660s (Minogue 1973: iii). As Plato suggests that any myth can be incorporated into the essence of a society or state (*Republic*: 181–2) so, too, Hobbes notes that rulers develop and utilise myths of God for the purpose of maintaining political order. He argued that the type of God and religious worship common to the seventeenth century were the political inventions of the founders of commonwealths who utilised tales of God's wrath to buttress absolute rule (*Leviathan*: 59). To separate God and religion from politics, and to ensure legitimate rule without risking the dangers of dissension and a continual state of nature, Hobbes attempted to disembody God and uncover the agenda of the word of man, as opposed to the word of God. In so doing, he did not deny God or Its political role in the making of the laws of nature by which humans were to abide. Rather, he distinguished between religious-political symbolism and true faith (*Leviathan*: Ch.XLIII).

Hobbes traced the need for the creation of a God, or many Gods, from the perspective that fear of the unknown requires something, or someone, to provide a sense of security or of order, an objective of humans in the state of nature and emerging into civility. He claimed that, 'this perpetuall feare, always accompanying mankind in the ignorance of causes, as it were in the Dark, must needs have for object something' (*Leviathan*: 55). God can be utilised expediently to provide that 'object something' either by direct explanation of causes and events or by reference to Its 'mysterious ways' always having a purpose, even if humans cannot know or understand what that purpose might be. For Hobbes, concerned with elucidating unity within the state without recourse to the potentially stultifying powers presented by the divine right of kings, the way between preserving maximum liberty in civil society and strong leadership for the common good, was a form of sovereignty owned by all but pooled to determine the authority of the ruler. As such, people were free to pursue their own interests within the laws laid down by their ruler, the laws being what they have all agreed to by dint of giving their authority to the law-maker (*Leviathan*: Ch.XVIII) whereby 'every Subject is Author of every act the Soveraign [sic] doth' (*Leviathan*: 112), or where the law was silent (*Leviathan*: 115).

Herein lies a key problem in Hobbes' political theory. Apart from when political commands contravene the laws of nature (*Leviathan*: 114), there is nothing that can remove the law-maker without reimposing a state of nature, or war. The law-maker even determines his successor, either through his own blood line or by his choice should no male relatives be available (*Leviathan*: 101), to ensure continuity of civil society and the security to which individuals contracted. To close the circle fully, while the divine right of kings is rendered archaic and meaningless by Hobbes, the division between the laws of religion and the laws of nature is so thin as to be invisible. As the laws of nature are God-given, and civil law enforces the laws of nature, the law-maker is effectively maintaining God's law (*Leviathan*: 60, Ch.XXVI).[4] The fact that the law-maker does not derive his authority from God accords some modernity to the succession. However, what Hobbes fails to do is to depersonalise God and to separate It fully from the ruler. Consequently, the divine right of kings is dispelled, but the divine right of man continues.

The notion that God made man in 'His' image and gave him dominion over all else has considerable connotations for how humanity governs relations on earth. Most obviously the definition of 'man' is ambiguous: whether it refers to humans or just the part of humanity with male physiology and psychology has a profound effect on the reach of dominion. If the latter, then man *qua* man has dominion over women as well as all other living creatures. Similarly, if God has a male image then men will perceive themselves as god-like and other creatures as suitable for utilisation in man's quest for survival and development. Succour is given to such beliefs in the story of Eve's creation from Adam's rib, not only contraposing the normal pattern of earthly pro-creation witnessed in every birth since then, but rendering women a secondary creation fashioned from a spare piece of man's body (Miles 1989: 95). Contemporary feminist writers, including Armstrong (1986), Daly (1986) and Miles (1989), argue the profound effect such ideas have had throughout history on the relations between women and men, and the continuous subordination of women in all fields, including the domestic.

Why a male God should gain supremacy is not considered by Hobbes. For him, the image of God as a human is derived from lack of imagination and conceit:

but that it was the same with that of the Soule of man; and that the Soule of man, was of the same substance, with that which appeareth in a Dream, to one that sleepeth; or in a Looking-glasse, to one that is awake. (*Leviathan*: 55)

At a basic level of analysis, women have dreams and mirrors and could create God in their image too. But this is irrelevant in Hobbes' context of political gods and religions. The issue is that God should not exist as a corporeal entity (*De Cive*: 298–9). If Hobbes quibbles about the image of God being made in man's limited imagination he cannot then behold an image that is human in form. Moreover, the distinction between religion as human politics and genuinely divine politics should ensure that God does not need to be gendered or to have recognisable form. The true God 'planted Religion' giving humans the laws of nature by which all should abide including, for example, self-preservation, the first and all-encompassing law, gratitude for good done to you, and general conditions pertaining to the making and keeping of contracts that enable civil relations in society (*Leviathan*: Ch.XIV, XV; *De Cive*: Ch.II, III). As there is no differentiation between the laws of nature and civil law, there is no need for a civil ruler to invoke a larger than life man-God, the bounty of the laws being sufficient. However, Hobbes demonstrates the limits of his own imagination when describing the omnipotent entity who gave humanity the laws of nature. It may be purely convenient that God is referred to as 'he', the debate about non-gendered language probably not yet having emerged in the seventeenth century. But, of course, the sex of monarchs was not at issue, only their lineage to God.

While Hobbes' faith declared God 'king' over the earth simply by means of Its existence, his politics pronounced It 'king' over people by covenant (*Leviathan*: 60), giving individuals the power to refuse or proclaim It. Presumably, women have as much right and power to contract with God as men. As they emerge from the state of nature they can either forget about an all-embracing creator, tacitly treat with It, or overtly proclaim God as their king over people. But why would women proclaim a man-God king, with all this implied for political subjection in both the public and private spheres? Moreover, Hobbes' pro-monarchist stance required a methodology that appealed to royalist conviction but used anti-royalist persuasion (Gavre 1974: 1546–7; Hampton 1986: 25). As such, he also turned to the scriptures, based on true faith rather than political expediency, to confirm his political doctrines, thereby further excluding women from the terms of political engagement.[5] Although much of Hobbes' writing on religion is used to prove the artificiality and political origin of its interpretations, his ultimate belief in a Christian God and biblical events is still based in patriarchy. Despite being a nebulous entity, God the *father* is the originator of the laws of nature and, therefore, the definer of good with all that implies for human relations.

One conclusion to be drawn from Hobbes' exposition on religious and civil laws is that women are not contractors and therefore do not have the power of proclamation to accept God, whether It is amorphous or embodied. This proposition is fully considered below. For now, women's exclusion from the contract implies that only a male God-entity would be accepted. There would be no need for examination of the gender lines of descent as only men would be involved in the compact and its results. More fundamentally, Hobbes actually misses a step in the extraction of God and politics from his description of God and religion. If the laws of nature and therefore civil laws have come about by God's command, there is no reason for an interpreter of a specific sex to be appointed unless political difference is employed. Hobbes is quite specific in his scientific approach to causality, and his assertion that humanity is responsible for its conditions, or estate. His denunciation of 'signes' that influence beliefs, the use of 'the word of God' as presented by man to press-gang observance of civil laws and, indeed, particular messages of the gospels, are all analysed to show that they are not what they seem; people should look for real causes of events rather than rely on human interpretations. And yet his explanation of the cause of women's subjection to men is exactly the type that he would decry given any other subject. That men founded commonwealths is not given proof, and the equality of women and men in the state of nature does not render this a satisfactory excuse. Therefore, it must be conjectured that in the cause of peace or civility, by which the Sovereign symbolises unity in one body in which two sexes cannot be represented (Pateman 1991: 68), women's subjection is contrived. Thus, their exclusion from godliness and the compact that creates human leadership is itself a product of human politics.

Locke: Parental Power is not Political Power

Locke does not question the form of God although his liberalism incorporates differences of belief (*Letter Concerning Toleration*). However, his approach to refuting the divine right of kings is similar to that of Hobbes: the attempt to show the political utilisation of the scriptures to uphold illegitimate royal authority. In particular, Locke targets Filmer's *Patriarcha,* an example of the patriarchalist's religious methodology; the first book of the *Two Treatises on Government* is specifically aimed at deconstructing the arguments used to support divine right.

Patriarcha was explicit in its linkage of fatherly and royal power. Indeed, the two powers are interchangeable: children are born into subjection to their parents and this Filmer calls ' "royal authority", "fatherly authority", "right of fatherhood"' (*Two Treatises*: 6). Tracing this back to the first father, Adam, all humanity is born into subjection to this authority and its descendants, the kings, rendering the state equivalent to an extended family (Nyland 1993: 40). The power of the patriarchs, both in the family and the state, is absolute, including that of life and death over subjects, 'as kingly power is by the law of God, so it hath no inferior law to limit it' (*Two Treatises*: 7–8). A major source of support for Filmer's argument is based in a truncated form of the Fifth Commandment, honour thy father and thy mother. The truncation omits the last three words. This is a most obvious point of dissension, and Locke cites a further stream of examples from the scriptures wherein mothers and fathers are given equal grant (*Two Treatises*: 42–3). Moreover, he argues that the institution of a king by father-right either abrogates the rights of fathers by subjecting them to the supreme father, or makes all men kings in their own right, in which case the supreme king can have no higher authority than others (*Two Treatises*: 45). But this argument still ignores the subjection or equality of women, and Locke vehemently defends the rights of women to equal parental powers as a means of opposing Filmer's logic in inferring political from paternal power.

The argument over whether Adam could have been created king before any persons existed to rule over, Locke claims, could not have occurred from Adam's birth but only from Eve's. Without the means to create his posterity, Adam could not rule mankind (*Two Treatises*: 13). As both man and woman were created on the same day, after other living creatures, Locke wonders why man's dominion would extend to humans, surely it would be only over those creatures created earlier (*Two Treatises*: 19–20).[6] Indeed, by applying directly to the scriptures Locke notes that God speaks to a plurality; thus, 'God says unto Adam and Eve, have dominion' (*Two Treatises*: 21), the use of the word 'them' in the scriptures, as God bestows honour on humanity, indicating that dominion is given to humankind. Here it is possible to see that patriarchal power, not only as dominion over man but also over woman, is beginning to be dismantled. And Locke continues this theme when speaking of Adam's rule over Eve and humanity, in the context of the Fall. He does not go as far as to suggest that Eve was pushed by a male entity into sin. But he does admit Adam's part in it, concluding that 'it would be hard to imagine that God, in the same breath, should make him universal monarch over all mankind, and a day-labourer for his life' (*Two Treatises*: 32).

The inclusion of Eve in Locke's analysis is not only remarkable simply for being there, but also in its positive objective. More usually, Eve is used to elevate men's status and explain the need for control of women in perpetuity (Millett 1977: 52; de Beauvoir 1988: 111–12). However, when considered, Locke's tactic in response to Filmer is essential to the case against the patriarchalists, without implying political equality between women and men. The differentiation between paternal or patriarchal power and parental power is important. As Filmer and his ilk attempted to infer political power from that of fathers, based on highly selective reading and interpretation of the scriptures, so Locke was able to turn that argument around to show how these were being manipulated to political ends. His case relied on the inclusion of mothers to break the paternal/political interconnection and, indeed, he did grant them a level of equality in parental duty and reward. However, this lasts only as long as harmony presides. Although fathers have no power to force children not to honour their mothers (*Two Treatises*: 44), nor have they the right to take their wive's lives, when differences of opinion occur in household and family management, they will have the right of judgement 'as the abler and the stronger' (*Two Treatises*: 157). As in Plato's *The Republic,* utilising a form of female equality is, in certain circumstances, necessary to the arguments of political philosophers (Coole 1994: 191). Locke could hardly argue that paternal and political power are separate outside the family and home, but that men are really monarchs of their 'states' in microcosm. Indeed, he notes that if this was the case the Queens Elizabeth I and Mary would have been subject to their husbands' royal authority while ruling over their people, even had they married commoners (*Two Treatises*: 33). But, in his differentiation of paternal and parental power, Locke conspicuously separates the family from the political sphere: parental power rules the household while political power exists outside it. The independence of political and social relations is significant to Locke's political needs in that, if government is dissolved, society can continue without returning to the state of nature (Aaron 1955: 282; Hinton 1968: 62; Mabbott 1973: 155, 152). But in terms of the divine right of men in the political sphere, it is irrelevant that God and man are in each other's image. By breaking the lineage of kings to God, Locke argues away political patriarchalism *à la* seventeenth-century rule without disrupting patriarchy in the modern sense of male rule: only the heavenly 'blood line' is broken, as intended (Butler 1991: 88).

Problems With God's Interpreters on Earth

Neither Hobbes nor Locke denied the omnipotence of a law-giving God. Indeed, it was God who created, perhaps even personified, the laws of nature by which humanity should abide if it was to survive in some semblance of civility. Further, the fundamental message of religion and the power of faith was never in doubt for either philosopher (Dunn 1984; Tuck 1989). Only the relation of religion to politics in the form of sovereignty was put to the torch. By removing political sovereignty from God, it was placed with humanity, leaving Hobbes and Locke to justify how this would have occurred, and hence, creating a purely secular politics based on human interactions. Any ruler legitimised by the sovereign people was to guard and enforce the laws of nature, threatening their own legitimacy only if they abused this secular-sacred duty.

This is where the failure of Hobbes and Locke to demystify and degender God completely is important, especially for women. Human rulers not imbued with supernatural powers are required to interpret the laws of nature to fulfil their duties. In *Leviathan* and *Two Treatises* it is clearly spelled out that human interpretations of mystical, and factual, events are subjective and open to political manipulation. It is assumed, therefore, that the person or assembly legitimised to keep the laws of nature is beyond such political impropriety and/or that there are institutional checks and balances built into the system. What such measures cannot ensure is comprehensiveness of understanding regarding how the laws of nature, and consequent civil laws, affect different people differently. If God is personified as man, and the keeper of the laws of nature is perceived to be in Its image, then interpretations of the laws can reflect only male experience. Drawing on Jaggar's (1988) argument, the limited experience of men and male 'knowledge' binds humans to prescribed behaviours and ideas. Man's emphasis on male intellectual ability versus woman's supposed connection to the body, not only elevates mental over physical attributes but, in the analysis of the laws of nature, would favour men as the dominant actors in maintaining civil society. However, by fully disembodying God the bounds of human reason could be stretched to enable greater exposition of the laws and their relation to all humanity. As Jaggar (1988: 46) notes, it is hard to imagine that, had women played a part in developing political philosophies, the politics of egoism and almost religious faith in independence would have been central.

One must be somewhat circumspect in suggesting that, had Hobbes and Locke negated the maleness of God, women could have been rulers and that they would have interpreted the laws of nature differently. However, the potential is certainly there for such an assertion. If the nature of interpretation is based in experience, and women's and men's experience is different, leading to diverse perspectives on the laws, then under women rulers, aware of social dependencies, there is a likelihood that interdependence and co-operation, along with integration of difference within the political realm as well as in application of the laws, would be incorporated. Of course, even ignoring the man-God connection, history itself would have denied women the opportunity to rule, or stand as candidates. Dissolution of the divine right of kings would not have severed the importance of paternal blood lines that survived the transition from more feudal and aristocratic to the embryonic capitalist, liberal era of the seventeenth century. A suitable male was usually to be found to replace a dead king.[7] Furthermore, the continuation of male rule would have been assured through the lack of experience of female dominion and the consequent perception by the sovereign people of the unsuitability of female leadership. If the sovereign people perceive only males as suitable for leadership, for whatever reason, then they will be unlikely voluntarily to accept a female ruler. This brings into question the nature of sovereignty when it is vested in individuals rather than in one, all-powerful ruler.

God's Substitute – The Contract

One of the problems with political patriarchalism is that it removes any form of self-determination from humankind, rendering it passive, with no need to develop reason and, therefore, relatively static (Waldron 1994: 56). Hobbes and Locke refused this characterisation and, by locating sovereignty in each person, gave humanity the means with which to control their own destiny. The exercise of sovereignty must depend on developed, or developing, reason. If each person is their own ruler, then they must be able to demonstrate the ability to analyse their situation, to assess options and to know what course of action is required to maintain themselves (*Leviathan*: 18–20; Sabine 1951: 395; Hampshire 1956: 35, 47–8). Such an ability will, eventually, project ideas and actions into the future in the cause of self-preservation.

If this summation is transposed to the state of nature, then it is possible to see how sovereign individuals utilise their reason to survive, even to the extent of recognising the need to work co-operatively in a civil society. For example, in Hobbes' state of nature the means to end the war of all against all is to form a rule-bound society under a powerful ruler to which all sovereignty is transferred. For Locke, whose state of nature appears more friendly than Hobbes' but is, in fact, as precarious (Aaron 1955: 275–6; Mabbott 1973: 145–6), a similar view is found. That is, rational beings recognise and acknowledge that the protection of their means to self-preservation, liberty, equality and property, lies in their ability to honour the laws of nature within a civil society. This requires a body, individual or collective, to be empowered with the right to exercise rule over all others, and to which all contribute their sovereignty. In both instances, people reason from the particular to the general in their own interests.

One of the problems that Hobbes and Locke had to consider in these scenarios of mutual need for self-preservation was how to ensure that all people participated fairly. For example, in any voluntary arrangement, one person could renege on a deal made with another once their demands were met. The need to fulfil one's side of a bargain once one's needs are satisfied by the other party is less than compelling, unless it results in a threat to self-preservation. But if this is the case, then the state of nature must surely still prevail. Unless the sides of a bargain are fulfilled concurrently, there is no guarantee that the person who is to undertake their part of the bargain last will honour it. Obviously, human beings are not trustworthy and require some form of obligatory framework and enforcement to ensure compliance with agreements necessary to survival and civility. Accordingly, a compact is made amongst every person, together to install and honour a ruler to uphold the laws of nature in civil law. Where voluntary exchanges defined in contracts are necessary to maintain these laws, from localised to state level, then the power of enforcement is enshrined in the ruler. For Hobbes, in participating in such a compact, people transfer their sovereignty to the ruler, thereafter known as the Sovereign himself. The symbolism that Hobbes uses is that of all people joined as one in the sovereign (*Leviathan*: Ch.XVII).[8] Individual determination and appetites are subsumed by the sovereign who has absolute power and authority in maintaining peace in the civil society. The common good takes precedence over the private and is enforceable by any means, in effect ruling by fear (Bréhier 1966: 150; Goldsmith 1966: 73; Gavre 1974: 1553; Pateman 1989: 73). As Hobbes claims, 'Covenants, without the Sword, are but Words, and of no strength to secure a man at all' (*Leviathan*: 87).

For Locke, it appears irrational that leaving a state of nature characterised by fear, people should then contract into a submissive relationship ruled, still, by fear. He notes, 'this is to think that men are so foolish that they take care to avoid what mischiefs may be done them by polecats or foxes, but are content, nay, think it safety, to be devoured by lions' (*Two Treatises*: 163). Evident, here, is Locke's concern that Hobbes' explanation of civil society shares much with the politics of the divine right of kings.[9] Locke's contract retains individual sovereignty, for if sovereignty is renounced so is the right of liberty and self-preservation, including property rights. Thus, individuals contract with each other to create and legitimise the legislature. As in *Leviathan*, 'it is in their legislative that the members of a commonwealth are united and combined together into one coherent living body' (*Two Treatises*: 225).[10] However, unlike *Leviathan*, this legislature, although the 'supreme power' while it operates within the confines of the compact, is subject to the will of the people should it betray their trust and exceed its authority (*Two Treatises*: Ch.XIX; Dunn 1984). Therefore the relationship between sovereign individuals and the sovereign power is not that of master and servant but of equals, the legislative having some superior power only to execute exceptional duties (Aaron 1955: 271).

Locke's commonwealth is much more open than Hobbes', wherein the sovereign relies on the unwritten laws of nature to justify his actions and is effectively above the law himself (*Leviathan*: 91; *Two Treatises*: 188). For Locke, 'the ruling power ought to govern by declared and received laws' (*Two Treatises*: 187), being subject to the same laws as the rest of the people.[11] Despite the differences between the two forms of contract, both achieve a civil society in which political power, exercised by legitimate legislators, ensures the rights inherent in humanity defined by the laws of nature. Where self-preservation and security of property rely on local contract, all partners to the deal are obliged to fulfil their part under civil law. Consequently, the liberal ideal of liberty extending as far as the boundaries of others' liberty is maintained within the contract system.

It is debateable whether, for many people, political relations legitimised by contract are different from those under divine right, especially in Hobbes' model. After all, the contract defines all relations as voluntarily entered into and, therefore, consented to. But in reality, many relations are 'consented' to by custom rather than expressly. Moreover, there are some contracts, such as marriage, that are expressly entered but that arise from custom rather than from completely free choice. It is not unfeasible that people could be as unaware of their partnership in a contract relationship as they were distant from, and yet beholden to, kings under the divine right. The notion of consent assumes equal ability and equal opportunity to enter contractual exchanges. For example, legitimate government is the exchange of an amount of free and equal individuals' liberty for protection and security. But we know that some people appear to have less freedom and equality than others. For example, slaves are clearly unfree; but also the domestic position of free women is used by philosophers to place them outside the political arena and, therefore, the political contract. Under contract theory such freedom was contracted away, leading Hinton (1968: 55) to refer to Hobbes' Sovereign as a 'despot by consent', a conception also applicable to the head of household. This raises the question not only of political legitimacy granted by less than the full extent of the eligible population, but also the nature of a contract that can remove sovereignty from one partner and give it to the other. In the political theories of Hobbes and Locke, it appears that the contract is a substitute for divine right, having about as much resonance in the political relations of populations as blind faith and fear of divine retribution meted out by God's representative on earth.

Consent: On Pain of Death to Voluntary Exchange and Back Again

The fact that women are dependants in contract relationships is not necessarily an issue that sets them apart from the majority of contractors. The political contract itself places everyone in some form of dependence: the ruler for legitimacy and the people for protection and security (Chapman 1975: 81–2; Hampton 1986: 169). Indeed, any contract, and therefore contractor, is dependent on the signatories keeping to the terms of agreement. The issue is whether women, in the traditional roles described and perpetuated by mainstream political philosophers, are ever in a position to contract freely and as equal partners.

It is paradoxical that, for Hobbes and Locke, families were the first societies and were created by rational individuals in the state of nature. As Sabine (1951: 395) notes, because people in the state of nature would not have been subject to reason, it is most unlikely that marriage contracts would have been made in that state (see also Pateman 1991: 63). Certainly, the foundation for alliances based on what has come to be perceived as gender-stereotyped, heterosexual couples exchanging domestic labour for protection is implausible.[12] Moreover, the voluntarism of either sex restricting their freedom for any material or protective advantage, as Coltheart (1986: 116) suggests, is unreasonable. But Green (1995: 47) also notes that, in the state of nature, sentiment or love would not be strong enough to cement reciprocal relationships. Together, these arguments imply that the foundation of families in the state of nature must assume a form of contract. Furthermore, this constitutes an essential development towards civil society and political relations as, political philosophers argue, the family contract is the basis of the comprehensive social contract.

The problem with the contract scenario is that the development of domestic relations is not that of equals but of master and servant (Brennan and Pateman 1979: 193). The fact that, for Hobbes (*Leviathan*: 105), 'no man can obey two Masters', ensures that in any partnership of more than two people, a family for example, one person has to dominate (Green 1995: 55). Moreover, such conditions are not confined to the domestic sphere but spread to affect the relation of women to politics. When such issues are raised about the development of the contract, its origins also come under scrutiny. The fact that Hobbes' contract society is effectively subjected to the supreme Sovereign, after the freedom of the state of nature, suggests an element of coercion rather than free exchange. Indeed, when the original contract between women and men is considered, the nature of compacts built out of acquisition becomes clear. In a state of war, such as the state of nature, conquerors offer the vanquished the choice of life in servitude or death (Coole 1993: 58; Green 1995: 49). Although Hobbes asserts equality of the sexes in the state of nature, if men's greater strength, or the debilitating effects of motherhood for women, does lead to women's defeat, then the family contract is not one of voluntary exchange of equals but that of conqueror over vanquished. As such, women are subjected to men's rule. This rule necessarily extends throughout social and political relations as it would be irrational for men to give political power to their captives. The persistent nature of the contract is further explained under the acquisition theory, in that its terms extend to the offspring of women, sired by the male as superior signatory. This becomes enshrined in the civil state, where property and self-preservation are almost synonymous, and a true lineage is required for purposes of inheritance. In other words, generations in perpetuity are bound by a contract made in the state of nature between the founders of their blood line. Translated to the wider political arena, the head of the family that acquires power through conquering other families will also rule continuously through his offspring (Chapman 1975: 79).

For consent to be a real inducement in legitimating contracts and, therefore, power relations in any context, surely it must be renewed by each generation and when changes in the conditions of the contract occur. For writers like Hobbes and Locke, if this were to be realised the potential to return to the state of nature would be constant, a condition they deplore. It would enable people to try to reassert their sovereignty and become dominant partners in the contract (Hampton 1986: 170). Hobbes surmounts this crisis of legitimacy by appealing to the laws of nature and the status quo. At the family level, children are obligated to their parents, or to whomsoever brings them up, because they have not been abandoned, sold or killed (*Leviathan*: 104). In other words, they tacitly contract with their parents, owing them gratitude and loyalty in return for their lives. Of course, in the state of nature it is more probable that this contract will be with the mother, since her decision determines the survival of the child. On the other hand, if the mother chooses not to let the child survive but someone else takes care of it, then the child's obligation is to the person who saves it. However, Hobbes makes it clear that if women are in men's power, as they would presumably be after being conquered and subjected the family 'contract', so too are their children (*Leviathan*: 105, Ch.XXIX). Similarly, as the state is modelled on the family, subjects are obliged to the sovereign for his maintaining peace and security on the grounds that only in commonwealths where the people do not question or challenge the sovereign is peace sustained (*Leviathan*: 109). Without the means to challenge the sovereign effectively and peacefully, the conclusion must be made that the contract is consented to by custom, as was the divine right of kings.

Locke answers some of the challenges that Hobbes' contract theory poses by retaining individual sovereignty and rendering contracts subject to withdrawal of consent. For Locke, consent by acquisition is invalid, such natural rights as life, liberty and equality not being transferable (Hinton 1968: 64; Nyland 1993: 55; Waldron 1994: 62). Moreover, a contract could not legally bind people who had not specifically consented to it, thus eliminating the bonds of generations (*Two Treatises*: 204; Hinton 1968: 63, 65). The status of the contract is, again, evident in the family and can be inferred to apply to more general political relations. Here, women and men contract together overtly to procreate and for 'mutual support and assistance' (*Two Treatises*: 155). Within the family contract, mothers and fathers are responsible for the welfare of the children, their education and safety (*Two Treatises*: 144). Once a child achieves a level of reason it is free from its obligation to the parents and gains its liberty.[13] Similarly, for parents, once their obligation to children is over they are free to end their compact, although it is unlikely that women will want to do this, the relationship having sustained and supported them so long (*Two Treatises:* 157).[14] Apart from the man's having the final say in case of disagreement, it appears that consent is the basis for marriage contract. Another side to the family contract is, however, based on the ownership of property.

With regard to the laws of nature, and therefore civil law, property is the basis for self-preservation. Property not only describes land and its produce, material objects, but also the person (*Two Treatises*: 130). Self-ownership is integral to survival, ensuring liberty and equality. By mixing one's labour with raw materials or existing goods, ownership and use is guaranteed (*Two Treatises*: 130–1; Aaron 1955: 277; Mabbott 1967: 147). For example, cultivation places the land and its fruits under the ownership of the cultivator; or by exchanging labour for wages individuals can purchase the means of subsistence. In the state of nature, all individuals would be owners of themselves and the fruits of their labour. This is continued in civil society and the family contract, wherein women are allowed ownership and determination over their property (*Two Treatises*: 157). Consequently, women should be in a position to negotiate their contracts with men and ensure themselves a fair deal (Butler 1991: 83; Coole 1993: 65; Nyland 1993: 53). However, the status of women's property rights is muddied somewhat by Locke's assertion that ownership of property gathered within the contract accrues to husbands, effectively rendering women hired labour (Mabbott 1973: 148).

If Locke's Labour Theory of Property is taken to its logical conclusion, the fact that the domestic division of labour mixes more of the woman's labour with household property than men's would suggest that wives are more clearly entitled to ownership. But, it seems that Locke presumes that it would be the male who held ownership of the land on which the home is built and, thus, once his labour is mixed with it, ownership cannot be removed. The status of women and men in the state of nature does not nullify this assumption, for although women are equal to men, the greater punishment meted them by God for their primary part in the Fall renders them the weaker sex (*Two Treatises*: 31–2). Therefore, it is assumed that men would have been the more prolific creators of property, including shelter (Nyland 1993: 56–7), implying that families in the state of nature already subsumed women's property rights. As civil law is concerned with property rights, and is the means of continuance of rights under the laws of nature, women with very little, if any, material property will either be excluded from the rituals of consent associated with the political contract or have no interest in participation.

This explanation of women's exclusion from the political realm is dangerously close to Hobbes' contract by acquisition. There is little reason to believe that free and equal women would actively consent to the loss of their right to acquire property, or to the iniquity of mixing their labour in the domestic sphere without gaining ownership rights. Indeed, by Locke's definition, this is tantamount to 'consenting' to slavery. Furthermore, lacking material property, it would be difficult for wives to break the family contract before the children's independence, or even afterwards, if they perceived their husbands' transgressions as abnormal. The fact that the marriage contract, as Locke describes, it is enforced by law further renders women's consent questionable. That women would legitimate a sovereign ruler who upheld a contract in which they had to abdicate some, if not all, their individual sovereignty suggests that contracts cannot assume women's full consent and that their God-inflicted weakness enables the dominance of males. Locke addresses this predicament, applicable to male labourers as well as women, by announcing that, any that hath any possession or enjoyment of any part of the dominions of any government doth hereby give his *tacit consent*, and is as far forth obliged to obedience to the laws of that government, during such enjoyment, as any one under it, whether this his possession be of land to him and his heirs for ever, or a lodging only for a week. (*Two Treatises*: 177) (my emphasis)

Tacit consent provides a means of circumventing the requirement for every person to expressly and unanimously consent to, and legitimate, the sovereign ruler and effectively subsumes women's potential non-consent to a system that overtly prevents their exercising independent means to self-preservation.

Non-consent and the Rights of Man

The contract that Hobbes and Locke advocate is a tool to assist historical understanding of socio-political development (Waldron 1994: 63; Lane 1996: 52). Hobbes and Locke utilised the contract metaphor to present a viable, legitimate alternative to the non-participatory and inescapable divine right of kings. As such, the history of political development is based on an artificial construct sealed by consent, rather than a natural solution to the problems of civil society. Whether by decision of the majority or by not removing oneself from the society concerned, every-one within the broad boundaries of the state submits and consents to rule by a sovereign power. This applies equally to families, the first societies, wherein husbands and fathers claim sovereign rights.

To ensure the cohesion of the model and achieve unity within the civil state, neither Hobbes nor Locke can allow for the possibility of non-consent: they must either assume universal consent, or ignore or re-define non-consent by subsuming dissent within a contract framework (Coltheart 1986: 114, 121). However, if the notion of consent is to be fully justified, the possibility of not consenting has to be given (Pateman 1989: 72). This raises the question of when choice is actually valid. Choice must offer an alternative. It could be argued that the choice between something bad and something worse, as in accept submission under a ruler or remain in a state of nature, is no choice at all. If so, consent based on such a non-choice cannot be deemed to legitimate the relationship. In such a 'threat agreement' (Hampton 1986: 169), if circumstances were to offer the opportunity of reclaiming lost liberty and sovereignty, possibly punishing the previously benefiting signatory, then the false legitimacy of the original and subsequent 'contracts' would become obvious. It would seem then that Hobbes and Locke were reyling largely on custom in developing their contract theories, the concept of consent providing the element needed to displace the legitimacy of the divine right of kings. Had this not been so, and contract partnerships were fully equal, it can be assumed that women, and other disadvantaged people, would not have legitimised their own inequality within private and, consequently, political, relationships.

The evident inadequacies of contract theory have not prevented it from becoming an essential element of politics since the seventeenth century, although democratic ideas and practices have softened the more intractable elements of succession and qualification for rule. Moreover, economic changes in the twentieth century required the relenting of strict political gender segregation in western liberal democracies. That philosophers like Hobbes and Locke did not advocate thoroughgoing political change, requiring only that full and proper justice be incorporated into existing arrangements, would certainly have justified restrictions evident in the contract. Whether these were beneficial to political development, though, is debateable. Certainly, in the seventeenth century, the failure to tie liberty to a strict code of conduct may have introduced new and destabilising variables into the political arena. This would have been contrary to Hobbes' and Locke's objectives. However, contemporary challenges to the contract that have precipitated its extension, such as women's choices not to contract to have families, with its implications for men's rights within households, indicate the ways in which, for years, its endurance has constricted political development. Failure to adapt the contract fully to changing socio-political circumstances, a function that requires a deeper analysis of political relations than either Hobbes, Locke or any more recent political philosophers have attempted, maintains political restrictions for women in much the same way as the divine right of kings was thought to do generally in the seventeenth century.

Notes

1. My use of 'It' for God is an attempt to degender and dehumanise the concept. This is not only a personal choice stemming from my beliefs concerning the dangers of a 'human' all-powerful entity, but also a way to avoid gendering such an entity and bestowing it with political power over the gender not represented in the image. Capitalisation of the word is merely to distinguish It from the usual grammatical usage of 'it'.
2. Hobbes and Locke were writing at a time of intense political change in Britain. The earlier work, *Leviathan*, published in 1651, was developed amid the debacle between monarchists and republicans. In 1649, Charles I was beheaded in, the House of Lords prorogued and an elected Parliament established. Locke's *Two Treatises on Government* was published in 1690 (although probably written much earlier) two years after the 'Glorious Revolution' that brought William of Orange to the throne after years of

arbitrary rule by Catholic kings who relied on divine right for their legitimacy. Thus, Hobbes wrote at a time of civil war and was anxious to prevent another occurrence, whilst Locke was writing at a time of impending civil war which was prevented only by foreign intervention and the establishment of secular constitutional checks and balances in a newly protestant English polity.

3. Brennan and Pateman (1979) argue that women would have been working in the formal economy of the time, capitalism being in its early stages and cottage industries, in which women were heavily involved, being the norm. It can be assumed that Hobbes' and Locke's experience of the patriarchal family was that of a different socio-economic class, in which males were rulers, although the fact of women working does not lessen the 'prerogative' of the male head of household.

4. The necessity for a law-maker, when the laws of nature are immutable, is that social change may require addition to the civil laws. However, all new laws will be made and executed with the aim of maintaining the laws of nature.

5. There are many examples of strong women in the bible but none seems to be given due reward for her endeavours. A particular example that I have struggled with for some years is the case of Queen Esther who saved the Jews from destruction by Haman. This is still celebrated by Jews in the festival of Purim, a joyous day when school children wear fancy dress and tasty pastries are consumed. The traditional food is not concerned with Esther but is a triangular pastry modelled on the three-cornered hat of Haman, and while girls like to dress up as Esther, the boys dress as Haman rather than the male Jews who should pay homage to the queen. But then, in a religion where boys thank God every day that they were not born women, this behaviour is not remarkable.

6. In a wonderful passage, Locke dismisses Filmer's argument about Adam's dominion over all living things on earth, stating that 'methinks Sir Robert should have carried his monarchical power one step higher, and satisfied the world that princes might have eat their subjects too, since God gave as full power to Noah and his heirs to eat every living thing that moveth, as He did to Adam to have dominion over them' (*Two Treatises*: 20).

7. Hobbes does note that a king's progeny is preferable to succeed him even if this includes daughters, although younger sons would have preference over older daughters. However, the tone of his text tends to suggest that any male relative of a dying king is a better successor to the throne, and failing this any suitable man who can be nominated (*Leviathan*: 102–3).

8. The famous cover picture on *Leviathan* is of a giant person, obviously a monarch, composed of hundreds of smaller men.

9. Despite Locke's respect for Hobbes (Hinton 1968), much of the *Second Treatise* is a direct response to *Leviathan*, although neither the author nor the book is named.

10. The legislature is called together to make laws only when necessary and does not sit in permanent session, the more permanent power belonging to the executive (*Two Treatises*: 190–1).

11. Within Locke's contract, the people permit a level of prerogative to enable

the ruler to act for the public good beyond known laws, but this must be within acceptable limits and within the laws of nature (*Two Treatises*: Ch.XIV).

12. It is unlikely that 'domestic' concerns would exist in the state of nature. The image of savage men returning to a nice, clean and tidy shelter after a hard day's foraging, hunting and self-defence springs to mind, *à la* Flintstones.

13. Although a child achieves its freedom when reaching the stage of rationality, this does not completely free it from the loyalty and honour owed to its parents by their family bond (*Two Treatises*: 148).

14. It is possible for the contract to be broken before this time if the terms or 'natural right' allows it, presumably if a woman feels her liberty, equality or property have been trespassed upon (*Two Treatises*: 157).

Chapter 7: Rousseau:
Education for the Common Good

Proponents of the 'University of Life' or 'School of Hard Knocks' philosophies generally subscribe to the view that life itself is a political education. Through everyday interactions we learn appropriate behaviours, how to treat other people and maximise our self-interest and/or broad social interests, depending on our ideologies. This is certainly a familiar contemporary argument. But for traditional political philosophers, such haphazard 'education' is not enough to ensure the good society or just political institutions and relations. Within most philosophers' works, some allusion is made to ensure that citizens and other members of the state know what is expected of them in relation each other, to the sovereign and to the state. This is only to be expected as, when defining the good society, people's behaviour must conform to certain standards if the model is to hold together. It does not mean that all forms of behaviour are prescribed, but it does demand that people perform their duties in accordance with the requirements of the state.

Until the eighteenth century, Plato was probably the most prescriptive of the philosophers with regard to education for citizenship. The unity of state and citizen required that every aspect of an individual's education be ascribed a public dimension. Whatever a person's innate talent, whether for shoe-making or philosophy, education should be towards development of perfection in that field. In addition, enjoyment of, and participation in, the arts could only be such that citizenship would be enhanced. The movements of dancers and actors, and the words of poets, writers and singers were all to be directed to the promotion of the good life which, of course, was concomitant with the good state (*The Laws*: Book VII). For later philosophers, the good state and citizen provided education in themselves. As each element constituting the state, institutions and their human members, performed their duties properly, then new generations absorbed correct procedure and behaviour. For example, Chapman (1975) argues that in Hobbes' *Leviathan,* the family is where children learn duty to the sovereign and to be a good citizen. They do this by observing duties to their parents and by being good and obedient children. By consenting to their father's will, the future full citizens and lesser members of the state learn that it is to their benefit to obey a sovereign ruler: 'In Hobbes, children who are taught that fathers once had power of life or death over them are not being instructed in patriarchalism, but in sovereignty' (Chapman 1975: 90). Similarly, J. S. Mill perceives the family as 'a school of despotism' (*Subjection of Women*: 260) where power relations are upheld by force, and in which women are effectively enslaved. Thereby, children witness political relations in the home which they then apply to the wider society, believing them to be natural (*Subjection of Women*: Part I): males develop knowing their 'rights' which are enshrined in law and women accept their 'subordination'.[1] On the other hand, Mill believes that 'the family, justly constituted, would be the real school of the virtues of freedom' (*Subjection of Women*: 260). In other words, what is learnt both in the home and, by extension, in society, pervades political relations, attitudes and behaviours. Whereas writers like Hobbes and Mill look to their political models to instil proper citizen behaviour,[2] it was Rousseau who reclaimed the torch from Plato and espoused the necessary education required to create good citizens.

While Rousseau is certainly less prescriptive in his approach to education, indeed some might find him positively liberal towards his students, he actually keeps a tight rein on the content, timetable and direction that education is to take. Moreover, despite his depiction of the state of nature, in which all individuals were equal regardless of sex, his treatise on education does not even pretend to gender-neutral notions of innate ability and talent. Only men could learn to control their natures and to reason universally in order to contribute to the sovereign general will; women, due to their innate nature, could not be educated sufficiently to permit them the responsibility of citizenship, or trained to apply their skills and abilities to anything beyond their own purview. However, women are essential to the well-being of the state as carers of citizens and are capable of being educated to that task (McMillan 1982: 86). It is evident, then, that education for the common good is a two-part system: that of the citizen per se, and that for pastoral care.

Nature: A Lost Heritage

For Rousseau, the alienation of humanity from its nature was a serious obstacle to creating and maintaining the good society. In the state of nature, wherein self-sufficient individuals were motivated only by immediate need, including satisfaction of pleasure and solution of danger, there could be no concept of morality or virtue, good or bad, or obligation or duty to others (*Discourse on Inequality*: 64; Sabine 1951: 492). Being solitary individuals, having no cause to develop and use reason and having no common language, there was no impetus to 'better' themselves. Indeed, there could be no basis of comparison by which to do so. The only form of 'passion' that would resemble a comparison and lead to co-operative action would be *pitié*, whereby assistance may be given to those in physical danger or need. As such, it can be seen that people in their natural condition fully understand their needs with regard to self-preservation without recourse to external measures. This self-sufficiency, and what Rousseau calls 'self-love' or *amour de soi*, is the guarantee of complete freedom[3] and happiness.

It is with the unavoidable, but unnatural,[4] development of society that the undermining of humanity's nature occurs. The 'invention' of private property begins the corruption of *amour de soi* by introducing a measure by which people can judge themselves and others (Cranston 1995: 235). As society develops, with people living in closer proximity, the tempta-tion to compare not only levels of property and wealth but other attributes that may contribute to social standing, such as beauty, family, and material possessions, 'leads each individual to make more of himself than of any other, causes all the mutual damage men inflict one on another, and is the real source of the "sense of honour"' (*Discourse on Inequality*: 66). This *amour propre*, differing from *amour de soi* by being based on external desires and the opinion of others and in many ways based in pride (Grimsley 1973: 47), corrupts social individuals to the extent that society itself becomes a shadow of what a good community should be. Here, Rousseau's criticism of the indivi-dualistic tenet of liberalism is clear (Rapaczynksi 1987: 251). Indivi-duals are more concerned with their own interests than with those of society, and these can never be satisfied as the need to 'improve' on existing personal conditions creates a never-ending quest. Moreover, to ensure the ability of continuing accumulation and to protect possessions and status, it is preferable to have some control over other people, a condition that presupposes the underdog's striving for recompense if not vengeance. Society, therefore, destroys freedom as people are trapped in a cycle of accumulation, protection of goods and status and the need to conform to public opinion and changing fashions. This is a direct contradiction of the common idea that materialism is the route to freedom, clearly articulated in the opening sentence of *The Social Contract* (1973: 165): 'Man is born free; and everywhere he is in chains'.

Despite his gloomy prospect concerning humans in social conditions, Rousseau does not subscribe to Hobbes' idea of a war of all against all (Roche 1974: 30), retrievable only by absolute sovereignty concentrated in one man or elite assembly. Human beings are inherently good and capable of shared self-rule, although in society this is not obvious. Nor does Rousseau want to return to the state of nature, or accept that this is possible (Rapaczynski 1987: 226; Roche 1974: 42). Through social interaction and *amour propre*, humans develop capacities for reason which, used properly, can ensure that motivations to selfish ends are channelled to the common good and the reinstatement of *amour de soi* applied to a social setting. Nature itself provides a standard by which humans can think and act freely whilst creating and conforming to the common good (Sorenson 1990: 449). In a society guided by *amour de soi,* all citizens and members of the state have their role to play but remain completely free. There only remains a requirement to educate people to see this possibility and mould their thoughts and actions accordingly.

Emile and Sophy: Social Man and His Trusty Companion

The fact that people are educated within the society that, for Rousseau, was the cause of political deviance, does little to improve the political mores and behaviours of state members. Consequently, Rousseau requires that the education of the model citizen, Emile, is given away from society, not *in* nature but certainly *of* nature and directed by it.[5] Alternatively, the complementary role of Sophy, wife to Emile's citizen, is not only to free him from the mundane aspects of life so that he is able to fulfil his citizenship duties without distraction, but to maintain the social aspects of Emile's life. Sophy's education is, therefore, embedded in social etiquette and domestic obligations. Between them, Emile and Sophy provide the two halves of the personality necessary to live in society: the level-headed decision maker and the social agent. However, it cannot be claimed that Sophy's education is intended to restore her nature to that recognisable in the state of nature. Indeed, women's nature demands their unnatural restraint and confinement to strictly controlled social functions.

Education, for boys and girls, is divided into stages appropriate to their level of development. However, their distinct roles in society determine different educational content and method. Parry (1995: 103, 108) notes that the education of the citizen and the man are parallel but different. As a man, Emile has to be able to know and act on his own thoughts within his knowledge of the laws of nature and society. As a citizen, this knowledge and ability has to be used to the common good within a social and political context. Consequently, boys are encouraged to learn through satisfying their curiosity, through experience and by problem solving. Only by these means can they preserve their natural autonomy and learn the self-reliance which enables them to transcend the charade of social mores and fashionable opinion necessary to the proper use of *amour de soi* in the general will.[6] Thus, Emile is not taught to read until he is old enough to reason, relatively late in adolescence.

Memorising the words and findings of other people does not develop cognitive skills or teach one to internalise the lessons that nature presents (*Emile*: 244; de Beer 1972: 60). Rather, Emile's lessons consist of 'real' situations, usually contrived by his tutor, to be resolved. At an early stage, when Emile is completely self-absorbed and dominated by primitive *amour de soi*, he is not restrained but, for example, allowed to climb and fall out of a tree, so learning to correct mistakes and make risk calculations (*Emile*: 48–9). Later, he is encouraged to participate in, and win at, sports but in such a way that he develops not only competitiveness but also initiative, leadership and generosity, and to perceive and treat his companions as equals despite the fact that he is from a higher social class (*Emile*: 126–7). Similarly, as a young man, he is apprenticed to a furniture maker, remaining unpaid and having made, rather than bought, his own tools. Not only is his privilege never allowed to 'buy' him advantages, but throughout his education, Emile learns that his social status carries with it responsibilities to the people in the communities in which he circulates. His self-reliance and natural autonomy (Parry 1995: 104) prepares him for adulthood in which, whatever his station in life, the honourable path is to work for society and not merely self.[7]

The final element of Emile's education is to introduce him to the society of his own social class and put to use the political lessons regarding the superficiality of inequality, duty to society, and mutual independence linked to the common good. This part of his education also demands that he find a suitable mate to make bearable the life of the citizen which requires an unnatural constraint of full *amour de soi* in the fulfilment of social duty (Losco 1988: 106). As Emile learns that all things in nature are for his use, so too a partner belongs to the array of objects for his use, or to his taxonomy of utility. The choice of partner, though, is stringently shaped by his tutor's prejudices (Nichols 1985: 552):

When I supply the object of imagination, I have control over comparisons, and I am able easily to prevent illusion with regard to realities. For all that, I would not mislead a young man by describing a model of perfection which could never exist; but I would so choose the faults of his mistress that will suit him, that he will be pleased by them, and they may serve to correct his own. (*Emile*: 351)

Such grooming of both Emile and Sophy ensures that when they meet they are aware of the perfection of the match.

For Sophy, the right to education is unusual in political philosophy. Moreover, she is to be educated under the same pretext as Emile, although her education is to control her natural capacities to the common good. In other words, for women to act unselfishly is not natural. Their innate propensity is to *amour propre*, relying on the manipulation of men who are too weak to resist female charms (*Emile*: 387; Okin 1980: 145), and using men's efforts to their own advantage. Indeed, 'cunning is a natural gift of women' (*Emile*: 400) requiring their education to teach them to accept, obey and tolerate external control if they are to fulfil their role as mothers and companions to citizens. Accordingly, unlike Emile whose play is part of his education and whose development and behaviour determines the level and rate of his education, Sophy is subjected to constant interruptions in her games so that she 'should early be accustomed to restraint', and 'early learn to submit to injustice and to suffer the wrongs inflicted on her by her husband without complaint' (*Emile*: 398–9). Similarly, although, like Emile, her curiosity must be satisfied through her own efforts rather than reading from books, Sophy will not exhibit curiosity over complex ideas such as religion, girls requiring the introduction of such subjects to their education when parents or tutors deem fit (*Emile*: 407). Despite their insatiable appetite for knowledge, girls' interest is in the practical aspects of life. Their inability to make intricate connections and apply information to the broader, social good, coupled with natural curiosity, ensures that, as adults, women will need to harness the power they have over men to satisfy their *amour propre*.

Little is said in *Emile* about the life that Sophy can expect as an adult, beyond ministering to Emile's needs and bringing a moral sensibility to bear on his passionate nature. However, the details of the outcome of such a woman's education are given in *La Nouvelle Heloise* (cited in Rolland 1943). Here, the main character, Julie, is described as a mother to all members of her household, including servants and day labourers, being esteemed for her treatment of them as well as her work in the community. Like Emile, she has learnt not to abuse or flaunt her wealth and social position, taking an interest in the whole community, helping and protecting those in need as if they were part of her family. She performs her duty to her husband and household to the extent that the moral well-being of the staff is within her domain. An idyllic picture is painted of the life in the household, in which everyone joyfully and willingly performs their duties, gaining a form of kinship spirit under Julie's devoted guidance, with all this implies for mutual caring and security.

Obviously, Rousseau does not deny women's capacity to reason. The fact that he perceives education as necessary for Sophy, and that the pretext of developing girls' natural capacities to the common good is the same as that for boys, is almost without precedent in political philosophy. However, through their education, women learn to direct their reason, which is naturally appropriate to the practical tasks necessary to support men in their endeavours as individuals, fathers, husbands and citizens. Furthermore, in a society in which women's power depends on having a man to secure their needs and desires, it is essential for girls to learn,

to be pleasing in his sight, to win his respect and love, to train him in childhood, to tend him in manhood, to counsel and console, to make his life pleasant and happy, these are the duties of woman for all time, and this is what she should be taught while she is young. (*Emile*: 393)

By ensuring that 'a woman's education . . . be planned in relation to men' (*Emile*: 393), their modesty and gentleness, born from injustice, will eventually win over even the most hard-hearted husband so that he will submit to her, reasonable, demands.

Rousseau's Amour Propre: Inverted Socialisation

There is an obvious paradox in Rousseau's theory of education and the outcomes for citizens and society. In the state of nature, women and men are equal in their abilities of self-preservation, the isolated and primitive lifestyle providing the means to liberty without recourse to morality or reason. As education is meant to preserve, in fact regain, liberty, but with the social necessity for proper morals based on the ability to reason, then individuals must learn to focus on and utilise their natural abilities, to control and direct their *amour de soi* to social ends. The process for achieving this condition is clear in the education of boys: the unforced pace of education together with surreptitiously arranged incidents allow Emile, as his reason develops, to extrapolate necessary lessons and apply them to wider social and political contexts. This contrasts directly with the education of girls which is concerned with repressing their natural enthusiasm, eagerness to learn and sociability under authoritarian tutelage. As such, Sophy's reason, which Rousseau believes is arrested at adolescence (*Emile*: 206), is not stretched even to the point of fully understanding that her role is part of the common good. Her role is as it is because Rousseau says so, and because Emile needs Sophy so that he can perform his duties and be happy.

The underlying assumption made by Rousseau is that women are naturally 'bad' and men are naturally 'good'. And yet he is clear that in the state of nature there can be no concept of good or bad: this is a consequence of social development. It is women's natural tendencies, therefore, that make them subject to irretrievable *amour propre* by 'enslaving' men when they leave the state of nature and oblige men to protect them, so creating the first society (*Social Contract*: 166; Fermon 1994: 441; Green 1995: 76). It is not a purely sexual, or natural, urge in men to become 'family-orientated'. This process of society-building differs from the natural congress of men and women in the state of nature, which is governed wholly by the sexual act and admits no emotional ties. However, the sentiments that maintain a family are based on love, a concept born of society.

Of course, love for men and women is quite different, as men love selflessly whereas women cultivate that love as a means to build and maintain their status (Cranston 1995: 234). In other words, from the earliest history of society, human relations are such that women do not have to love men to accept their protection, exerting power over them to keep them captivated, while men are besotted and powerless to resist women's whims (Lange 1991: 99). If men did not love women, whether through natural sentiment or bewitchment, there would no reason to stay with them. It is as society develops, and social order and government become necessary, that women's power needs to be restrained and men allowed to perform their civic duties. Moreover, in addition to the sorry state of human relationships, the introduction of private property and inheritance further highlights women's naturally wayward tendencies so that, for men to be sure that they leave their property to their own children, women have to be constrained from casting their powers over other men and possibly introducing a cuckoo-child into the family nest (*Discourse on Political Economy*: 118; Masters 1968: 26). It is clear, then, that the characteristics Rousseau ascribes to women arise in society and not nature, almost certainly as a function of Rousseau's *amour propre*.[8] This would explain why women's education has to be prescriptive and strictly controlled, because it is meant to suppress their true nature which, logically, will be similar to, if not the same as, men's.

The General Will and Inverse Citizenship

If the line of Rousseau's imagination is projected forward, the type of society that ensues is one which is governed by the general will of socially inept, psychologically and morally weak, love-lorn men. They may well be able to consider the 'big picture', understand basic human equality and complex social issues, but whether they are able to overcome their emotional inadequacies and concentrate on these issues seems in doubt. Indeed, it appears that once men reach the age of sexual maturity they become subject to primal rutting urges at any time and are constrained only by women's level-headedness. On the other hand, in the domestic sphere sit women with the mental control and reason necessary to understand and tolerate social disadvantage for the common good, who are enthusiastic about current affairs and eager to learn about social issues, and who have the psychological dexterity to use their moral capacities to provide the life-long moral education needed by men. Indeed, throughout *Emile* the natural behaviours of the different sexes and the requisite behaviour of citizens is constantly confused. For example, during their courtship Sophy displays all the reserve, composure and self-discipline so lauded in men as prerequisites for citizenship, while Emile behaves like a deranged adolescent obsessing on his target female, behaviour that is condoned by his tutor.[9]

From Rousseau's description of the natural proclivities of the two sexes it would seem that women are actually better suited to the disciplines of citizenship and that, in the same way that men have to be trained to them, women's training away from them has to be towards an essentially unnatural condition, and their education a retardant to their intellectual development. Similarly, Nichols (1985) argues that Emile is, in fact, not a child of nature but of Rousseau, effectively making him the very reverse of his portrayal as a self-sufficient, autonomous man. This does not appear to offer a picture of freedom and happiness in society, resulting from a proper education, where everyone is accorded their natural role, albeit a role somewhat more sophisticated and psychologically developed than that in the state of nature. On the other hand, it is likely that Rousseau's concept of freedom, and therefore the basis of happiness, is specifically adapted to the requirements of the social contract and the general will.

The key to this redefinition lies in the general will which can never be wrong, even if at times individuals, as members of the sovereign, disagree with it. Consequently, a minority, or even a majority in some cases, will not be less free if they do not agree with the general will as, forming part of the sovereign body, they have still consented to the laws (*Social Contract*: 187; Roche 1974: 82; Kain 1993: 74). Therefore, if the general will ordains the role of citizen-man and domestic-woman there can be no legitimate, or even relevant, opposition to it. Anyone resisting this order is merely mistaken in their views and subject to their particular will or unreconstructed *amour propre* (*Social Contract*: 177). The logic of this system demands that anyone who does not understand the decrees of the general will, and whose will does not conform to it, is unfree and 'will be forced to be free; for this is the condition which, by giving each citizen to his country, secures him against all personal dependence' (*Social Contract*: 177). The method of ensuring freedom and happiness in the general will is that it is the will of every citizen and 'each man, in giving himself to all, gives himself to nobody' (*Social Contract*: 174). Thus, 'so long as the subjects have to submit only to conventions of this sort, they obey no one but their own will' (*Social Contract*: 188). In obeying the general will, and performing the duties relevant to one's position, individuals are only doing what they believe to be correct and proper for them. Therefore, freedom is defined as self-rule, in which one's will is in consort with all others', as opposed to its more common interpretation as absence of opposition (Cranston 1995: 237).

There are clear disparities between the general will and the definition of freedom when applied to the situation of women. Most obviously, women do not have the opportunity to obey their own will, being subject to, rather than part of, the general will. Consequently, it cannot be logically argued that women are free, or happy, by any standard that Rousseau maintains. Sophy's happiness depends on Emile, and her adherence to convention, rather than her utilisation of *amour de soi*. Her confinement and duties are continuous and onerous. As Rousseau notes, men are citizens occasionally, indicating that their social duties are intermittent, whereas women are always women with their accompanying duties (*Emile*: 388). If happiness results from performing one's duty well, then Emile is in greater need of Sophy to fill the gaps in his life when he is not participating in determining the general will than she is of him. Similarly, by this argument, Sophy, and women like her, should be the happiest of the community's members, permanently undertaking their duties to the required standards. However, as society and its incumbent political and social tasks are not themselves natural, then performing unnatural duties, especially on a continuous basis, cannot result in happiness at all, especially when these are determined by the selective 'general' will. This problem is partially solved for Emile in that his family does provide a haven for him when he is not acting as citizen (Rapaczynski 1987: 249). But if the family is a retreat for male citizens, there can be no sanctuary for Sophy. This dilemma is demonstrated amply by Julie, in *La Nouvelle Heloise,* who eventually commits suicide as her duty cannot relieve the misery resulting from its calling.

The significance of Rousseau's concept of freedom is in maintaining the status quo with regard to citizenship and society (Parry 1995: 102). Women must conserve their traditional role as mothers and wives and be, somewhat patronisingly, lauded in so doing, with their separate but equal status being emphasised, much as previous philosophers had argued. Men must continue to be political actors and be afforded the plaudits and the educational and social advantages that accompany such a distinguished role. The result of education, combined with maintenance of the general will and the common good, is that very little can change regarding political roles and relations, although Rousseau does conceive a more sympathetic attitude towards the lower classes than many previous thinkers had managed. Anyone resisting the general will is forced to comply with it, there is no scope for dissent, and political movements to challenge or fragment the general will are not acceptable (*Social Contract*: 185; Kain 1993: 72). Any non-compliance is the result of, and exacerbates, unhappiness and the thraldom of erroneous ideas. This is particularly evident in Rousseau's attack on the feminism of his time. Not only are women acting unnaturally but, because of their inherent inability to progress beyond the point where their education arrests them (based on characteristics he assigns them), they can only increase the social and political disorder that he is attempting to correct (Fermon 1994: 435). The obvious fear that women may prove themselves genuinely able citizens requires them to be put in their place and for this to be seen as part of the general will so that their challenge, on whatever grounds, is not legitimate.

It appears that freedom is concerned with maintaining what Rousseau believes is the perfect community caught in a moment of time. Such a somnambulant community, obliviously preserving what is thought to be a good community spirit, may well believe itself happy to be bound by the 'legitimate chains' (Bluhm 1984) of the general will. But without a measure of comparison, or opportunity to experiment or change, there are no objective means of understanding individuals' or society's predicament. More fundamentally, Rousseau actively retards society's progress by maintaining that half the population are unable to participate in the general will, despite their obvious qualities of self-control, putting others before themselves and moral decision-making.

J. S. Mill: A Comparative Perspective on Education for the Common Good

A comparison with Rousseau's theory of the education necessary for good citizens to be able to participate in the general will is provided in the works of J. S. Mill. Although Mill does not refer directly to Rousseau, allusions to the inadequacy of Emile's and Sophy's education are evident. Not only are the interests of those who are excluded from decision-making, such as women, potentially violated, but 'they themselves have less scope and encouragement than they might otherwise have to that exertion of their energies for the good of themselves and of the community, to which the general prosperity is always proportioned' (*Representative Government*: 248). While advocating no more than a representative government of elected elites, for Mill, participation in the political process is itself the education required for good citizenship, through informed voting, articulation of the interests to be included in political deliberation and activities such as jury service.

Like Rousseau, Mill acknowledges that the good society and its government require individuals to understand that their interests are dependent on the well-being of all. However, Mill does not accept that the common wealth can be entirely determined by an elite, whatever the breadth and method of their education. After all, Emile's experience of working as a tradesperson and witnessing the social interactions of peasants is tempered by his status, as well as his sex. As the son of a wealthy landowner, and presumably a future employer of many of the people he mixes with throughout his education, Emile cannot fully experience the lives of those he will eventually consider when making his contribution to the general will. Indeed, the method of Emile's education, and the premise of avoiding public opinion, ensure that he remains untutored in the art of listening to the concerns of others, distinguishing and prioritising demands, and making relatively inclusive policy decisions. Furthermore, Mill argues that 'tacit convention' (*On Liberty*: 39), or the dominance of orthodox opinion, stifles social and political progress (*On Liberty*: Ch.II). The limited knowledge of a restricted citizenry wastes the talents of the majority, who would bring a vitality and dynamism to decision-making, thereby replacing the more materialistic fatalism that Mill perceived in England during the nineteenth century (*Representative Government*: 241). Whereas Rousseau believes that citizens must not rely on public, or fashionable, opinion in decision-making, but must extrapolate from their broad experience and 'knowledge' rendered from an education that includes mixing across classes as well as the use of rational thought, Mill understands that the full inclusion of interests in the political process requires the participation of those who interests are being represented.

Opinion, therefore, is not the *bête noire* of good citizenship. If liberty is to be maximised, people must be given the opportunity to express their opinion and discuss issues. There is no monopoly on correct opinion held by an elite, any more than the masses may be said to succumb exclusively to personal interests with little consideration for social ends. While not all opinions may be 'correct', participation in discussion and debate can only benefit society as 'wrong opinions and practices gradually yield to fact and argument' (*On Liberty*: 25). The same argument may be used when valuing the opinions of men over those of women.[10] Indeed, it is the segregation of socio-political roles by sex that succeeds in reflecting men's opinions as larger than they are (*Subjection of Women*: 258). In other words, men are corrupted by the absence of opposition, in the home and the workplace as well as in the higher echelons of decision-making. This enables them, and others, to perceive their opinions as superior (Shanley 1991: 171). Such a self-perpetuating cycle of the reaffirmation of men's perspectives as the foundation of social and political government further damages society, as men are not forced to confront their prejudices, and women's ideas and experiences are excluded from the processes of socio-political progress.

It is clear that to implement the type of political decision-making that Mill advocates requires a change in the attitudes and perceptions which ensure that knowledge and experience is perceived in a personal, as opposed to social, context. Education should allow the free development of intellectual enquiry (Halliday 1976: 116; Williams 1976: 290).

No doubt for children of all classes and both sexes who would benefit from the education that Mill advocates, the whole of life's experience would be perceived as relevant. But Mill was writing at a time when most adults were poorly educated, if at all. For such a person, discussion and interpretation of events and interactions in a diverse range of situations, including the workplace and the home, would raise awareness of the connections between personal and social activities, so that 'he is made to feel himself one of the public, and whatever is for their benefit to be for his benefit' (*Representative Government*: 255). Moreover, as Mill's policy was also to improve adult literacy, the experiences and perspectives of others, presented in newspapers and books, would assist in informing the opinions of more, and a wider range of, citizens. The full panoply of educational methods would not only increase the interpretative skills of individuals, enabling them to see their experience in the wider socio-political context, but it would help them to understand the interrelationship of distant events and local circumstances (*Representative Government*: 328). It is evident that Mill, like Rousseau, is not primarily concerned with formal education, although he believed that everyone should have access to the basic literacy and numeracy necessary for making informed choices in the election of their representatives (*Representative Government*: 330). Rather, as Williams (1976: 290) states, Mill's emphasis was on instilling the principles of good citizenship necessary to extend the franchise and to enable better informed and responsible participation.

While Mill does not dispute the persistence of the traditional family, he is aware that the historically gendered relations in households do not stimulate interest in personal development and, therefore, in wider interests (*Subjection of Women*: 300; Shanley 1991: 172).[11] Not only are both sexes confined to their socially constructed roles, but, as kings of their own castles, the majority of men would perceive little point in wider political interests. Of course, the roles and accompanying attitudes of women and men are the result of education, such as that portrayed in *Emile*, which enforces conformity to accepted 'ideals', and are 'the result of forced repression in some directions, unnatural stimulation in others' (*Subjection of Women*: 238). Even the ideal citizen is limited in the evaluative faculties so necessary for contributing to the general will. The question remains whether Mill's pattern of education would ensure equal weight of opinion in decision-making, or merely legitimise traditional sources of power.

Certainly, Mill was anxious to avoid the perils of presenting the less well-educated classes with excessive power, this evoking 'the twofold danger, that of too low a standard of political intelligence, and that of class legislation' (*Representative Government*: 333). His objective was not to replace middle-class with working-class legislation, but to ensure

that the representatives elected to power were informed of the interests
and issues affecting the people they represented, and that 'the many
were led with their eyes open' (Ryan 1974: 143). With respect to the
issue of gender, Mill appears to argue that women should be as well
informed and able to articulate their interests as men. As an essential
part of the increasingly industrialised workforce at the time that Mill
was writing, women are incorporated into his theories. However, rem-
nants of Rousseau's disposition remain in Mill's work, evident in the
emphasis on women in the family as the source of social, and therefore
political, rectitude. That the family should be reformed to ensure its role
as the focus of socialisation of good citizens is complemented by Mill's
explanation of how educated wives and mothers influence men in
becoming better citizens. As Cameron (1980: 779–80) states, the family
is connected to representative government through educated women as
agents of socialisation. Women's equal status in the family, together
with recognition of their abilities in previously 'male' occupations,
including politics, would permit men to relinquish their monopoly of
power, which secures their interests within narrow parameters. As Mill
notes, 'neither in the affairs of families nor in those of states is power a
compensation for the loss of liberty' (*Subjection of Women*: 254). Without the need constantly to affirm and maintain power over women, men
can be liberated in order to perform their tasks better and to perceive
their status within the broad social context more clearly. Moreover,
educated women provide the competition that men require to stimulate
their intellect, female practicality 'keeping his thoughts within the limits
of real things, and the actual facts of nature' (*Subjection of Women*: 275).

It could be argued that Mill follows tradition, in that the inclusion of
women in his theory is male-orientated. As Rousseau insists that Sophy
is educated to please Emile, and in so doing indirectly benefits the
community, so nineteenth-century women are to be educated to raise
the intelligence of men and, therefore, the quality of political leadership.
The fact that women of all classes will influence men of all classes
merely increases the scope of education and influence without direct
reference to any distinct advantages for women. Moreover, as will be
discussed in the next chapter, Mill's insistence on the perpetuity of the
traditional family, with most women choosing a career maintaining the
home and family (*Subjection of Women*: 264), would probably result in
their representation in the decision-making process being made indirectly, through their husbands. Although these men will have been
educated to listen to and take seriously the interests of their wives,
women's education still does not place them at the heart of the state.
While Mill ventures much closer to full recognition of women's interests
as essential to the good society than any previous political thinker,
Mill's representative government, in which the elite is informed by the

masses, still places the majority of women outside the main activity of the state.

While criticising ideas based on nature that prevent women's parti- cipation, or even inclusion of their interests (*Subjection of Women*: 284), Mill reverts to arguments, familiar in *Emile*, about the nature of women resting in practical aspects of life. Consequently, when presented with choice of occupation, women will prefer domesticity. Indeed, the recurrent scent of fear regarding women's latent power is evident in Mill's insistence on women's domesticity despite their education and greater opportunity. The danger that Rousseau warned against in edu- cating women beyond control of their natural tendencies, recurs in the possibility that educated women in the nineteenth century would not be content with domestic responsibilities and the accompanying lack of recognition of their value. A significant decline of the domestic service industry provided by women in the home would precipitate drastic reconsideration of the central pillar of philosophers' theories, that of instilling social order into consistently androcratic polities. Whereas Rousseau could avoid such a necessity by preying on the 'natural' waywardness and need for control of women, Mill incorporated women so that, for the first time, they were perceptibly equal to men of their class. Perhaps the great advance that this represented in political theory and practice was enough, at the time, to quell concerns about the continuing imbalance of access to representation that even equality of education for females and males could not solve.

Nature versus Education and Experience

It might be conjectured that Rousseau perceived himself as a social engineer capable of correcting the injustices and corruption that had arisen from the unconstrained development of society (Bluhm 1984: 370). From an idealised notion of human nature, imbued with his own fantasies of what man is like and how woman should be, he builds an educational system suited to his ideas of how society, and therefore politics, should be. Solitary man is socialised into citizenship, with its implications for applying *amour de soi* and *pitié* into the whole of society through the general will. Women are taught that their function is to give succour and sanctuary to men, and to provide, if not to be, the moral spine on which society depends (Fermon 1994: 441).

The need for the prescriptive education of girls obviously arose from the socio-political conditions in which Rousseau wrote. The events and mores that eventually led to the French Revolution, with calls for *equalité, liberté, fraternité*, some say influenced by Rousseau's writings (Thomson 1966: 100–4; Rapaczynski 1987: 219), were in full evidence.

Within this scenario, women were also calling for equal rights, as observed most clearly by Wollstonecraft in the *Vindication of the Rights of Women* (1985). To say that Rousseau was the author of the political and educational system that enabled certain men to progress and arrested the progress of women, as well as most men, is to give him an honour not quite justified. As Wollstonecraft stated thirty years after *Emile* was published, women were not at the time given equal educational opportunities as 'the very constitution of civil governments has put almost insuperable obstacles in the way to prevent the cultivation of the female understanding' (Wollstonecraft 1985: 61). As such, it can be argued that Rousseau merely justified a system already in existence, preferring to exonerate exclusion in elite education while attempting to prove inclusiveness at other levels appropriate to status and sex.

In many ways, the implications of Mill's treatise on the education of girls echoed those of Rousseau. Despite a more liberal education in which they were introduced to a broad range of opportunities, women will still choose to place themselves in the role of carer and moral preceptor. However, it cannot be argued that Mill found solace in the status quo, and at the time when he was writing, women's assertion of the injustice of traditional ideas and practices, alongside the demands for universal suffrage, were much more conspicuous. With the conditions that Wollstonecraft had described in the eighteenth century still evident, and with the weight of tradition to consider, Mill was able to argue the repressive nature of education on the working classes in general. His inclusion of women as full members of this class, who were entitled to the requisite rights and duties, and his recognition of women's traditional duties as part of the state, represents an immense advance in political thinking, marred only by his recourse to women's tendencies to tradition. Of course, it is possible that Rousseau's and Mill's experiences were not as different as the passage of time would suggest. Both were writing in potentially pre-revolutionary circumstances – rhetoric becoming reality in Rousseau's case. Perhaps, less than one hundred years after the French Revolution, the growing unrest of the increasingly industrialised and politicised working classes in Britain required the type of educational system, and concomitant representative government model, that Mill advocated.

In contrasting Mill's work with Rousseau's, the expediency of resorting to nature is demonstrated. What Mill illustrates is that the natural characteristics of women and men to which Rousseau refers are, in fact, socialised and perpetuated through education. However, what he ultimately fails to do is to show that, given the same education as men, the majority of women would desert the relationships and functions that Rousseau ascribed to them. In other words, whatever the educational opportunities offered to women, education cannot transcend their natures. But, like Rousseau, Mill does not fully analyse the underlying inequalities between the sexes, referring only to the fact that women's nature cannot be known until freed from the agents and effects of socialisation. As such, it is their own fears and prejudices that guide these philosophers' assertions concerning women in the state. Rousseau can, therefore, justify his gendered educational treatise on the grounds that, given choice, women will not remain bound by the strictures of domestic life. Mill, too, resorts to women's nature in an understanding that access to education and opportunity might well result in the wholesale withdrawal of women from domestic servitude. Consequently, perhaps, an appeal to nature and to women's maternal instincts might prevent such a social and political catastrophe. Of course, the type of polity that Rousseau advanced certainly would have required women to be more passive, since his concept of politics was effectively non-aggressive, non-contested and passionless, perfectly befitting his ideal citizen but unsuitable for the lively and inquisitive nature of women. However, the relatively rapid and far-reaching socio-political changes occurring since the eighteenth century could not sustain such overtly limited perceptions of political inclusiveness. The necessity for the expansion of citizenship required that women, and the majority of working class men who were historically excluded from politics, be admitted. But whether the terms of entry acknowledged the philosophers' full enlightenment is still a matter of debate.

Notes

1. Whether subordination can be perceived when it is a 'natural' condition is open to question. Certainly, throughout history, some women have understood that their comparatively disadvantaged socio-political position was a political construct. When Mill was writing, the first wave of feminism was relatively strong, indicating an historical peak of understanding regarding socialisation. However, even in contemporary western societies, many people prefer to consider women as naturally equal but different rather than subordinate.
2. Mill does advocate equal education for both sexes and all socio-economic classes, but this does not include what we would now call positive enforcement to redress socio-political imbalances on a fast-track basis. Rather, with universal education, presumably not including 'women's studies' elements, everyone's political acumen would rise and full citizenship with its attendant rights and duties ensue (On Liberty: 174).
3. Rousseau's concept of 'complete freedom' will be discussed in more detail below. Certainly, in the state of nature it may be taken literally. However, for civil societies, the concept requires some limitation even while remaining, for Rousseau, 'complete'.

4. Although for philosophers such as Aristotle and Hobbes civil society was natural or evolutionary, Rousseau states that the origins of civil society occurred when 'the first man who, having enclosed a piece of ground, bethought himself of saying "This is mine", and found people simple enough to believe him'. The results of this simple act were such that it would have been better to have 'pulled up the stakes' (*Discourse on Inequality*: 76) and remained in nature.

5. The ultimate objective is to populate society with citizens thinking and behaving like Emile (Roche 1974: 51; Parry 1995: 107).

6. All citizens contribute to the general will, knowing that their will is the will of the whole, inalienable and indivisible (*Social Contract*: 182–3). Therefore, citizens, educated as Emile has been, will know that to ensure their interests is to ensure the interests of all.

7. 'All men are born poor and naked, all are liable to the sorrows of life, its disappointments, its ills, its needs, its suffering of every kind; and all are condemned at length to die. This is what it really means to be a man, this is what no mortal can escape' (*Emile*: 219).

8. Descriptions of Rousseau's life, and indeed his own *Confessions*, show that he had a particular need for women to be endowed with the characteristics he associated with them. For example, Sabine (1951: 486) notes that he was comfortable only in the company of idiots and women over whom he could shine; his patronage by powerful women obviously guides his views over 'female empires' and how women abuse their social as well as sexual powers. Rousseau had a history of exposing himself to women, and his troubled sexuality not only crossed class barriers but prevented him from fidelity to the mother of his five children.

9. Some self-restraint is instilled into Emile by sending him away from Sophy for two years to study foreign societies and governments (*Emile*: Book V). Indeed, this is an essential part of his education. Not only does Emile make a comparative study of politics to assist in his citizenship duties but, perhaps more importantly, he practises self-control under what could be deemed extreme circumstances, being wrenched from the presence of his love. Equally, a two year period of travel also ensures that Sophy is really the person he wants to spend his life with, absence either making the heart grow fonder or causing him to forget the object of a fleeting infatuation. Whatever the various outcomes of this period are, once his rationality is seen to be in ruins it is hard to perceive this young man as suitable citizen material, and certainly not as a 'natural' citizen.

10. Education for women of all classes would not necessarily fragment, but would enhance, the perspective of existing class interests, as well as presenting issues specific to women to the political agenda (*Subjection of Women*: 269).

11. Green (1994: 217) also notes that it is not possible to learn even one's own full interests, without wider experience.

Chapter 8: Mill, Marx and Engels: Equality and the Common Man

The concept of equality is integral to political philosophy. It may even be ventured that equality is an essential quest of political thinkers as, to achieve their primary objective in the ideal state, a semblance of equality must exist. Certainly liberal theorists such as Hobbes and Locke rail against the inequalities and connected injustices associated with the divine right of kings and political patriarchalism. The Greek classical philosophers attest to the equal contribution to the state from the lowliest producer of goods to the philosopher kings, or to Aristotelian political man. Wherever political philosophers, or activists, attempt to publicise and correct the injustices of the polities in which they live, they affirm the existence of injustice arising from inequality. However, most works of political philosophy do not take a broad view of equality which would lead to a comprehensive reordering of political processes and relationships. Rather, the concentration on elite politics focuses attention on a narrow band of actors, or potential actors, and interests whose liberation in political terms has little impact on the material existence of the majority of people within the state, while imposing a partisan definition of justice and its associated processes. The fact that few, if any, political philosophers come from the slave, servant or working classes, and that very few women are considered worthy of entry to the hall of philosophy fame, suggests that the conceptions of justice and equality of a certain class of men reflect their particular interests.

It is not until the nineteenth century that mainstream political thinkers begin to consider the state in other than elite terms, perceiving not only the labour but the political contributions of people from all classes as necessary to ensure justice. For the first time, it is not simply equality among equals (Koggel 1998: 43) that is important, with the upper echelons providing a form of justice for those of the lower socio-political strata. Indeed, for writers like Marx this is no form of justice at all, and for J. S. Mill, concerned with utility rather than justice per se, such inequality denies society those advantages which would accrue from the talents of those traditionally excluded from participation in the state, other than as minions. For the first time, then, it is possible that political philosophers, in their concern for inclusiveness, would incorporate women into the state or community as bona fide members. It is even credible that the inhibiting domestic-woman bond would be acknowledged and addressed as a barrier to full citizenship, which would place women fully in realm of political processes and relations.

Whatever the perception of nineteenth-century equality, it may be thought that the advance from overt discrimination evident in previous philosophers' works, would be a positive move. The problem for us lies in how far such 'new' ideas provided an adequate analysis of the different spheres which make up the state, and of the measures intended to bring about full incorporation of all activities into the political realm.

Equality and Equality of Opportunity:
A Short March to Significant Difference

Inequalities between individuals cannot be denied. Even given 'equal' circumstances, such things as taste and personal values, physical and mental abilities, and methods of achievement would ensure diversity among humans in their possessions and attainments, even assuming an unlikely form of original equality from birth (Deininger 1965: 256). However, when referring to equality, political philosophers tend to consider certain basic qualities as common to humanity. Hobbes sums this up succinctly when describing passions and their expression (*Leviathan*: Ch.VI). Between appetite and aversion, the range of emotion and physical feeling common to all people includes hunger and thirst, joy, love, pain, grief and fear, which are present to greater or lesser extent in all individuals at different times. Moreover, we all have some use of language and communication, utilise tools necessary to achieve ends and live in some sort of society (Williams 1997: 466). Without a framework in which to evaluate and compare these commonalties, they all assume equal value, serving every individual as needs demand. Such is the condition of equality in the state of nature. It is only when values cultivated in, even rudimentary, society are applied to common variables that their basis in equality comes under threat or is used to the advantage of some and the disadvantage of others. When basic need is surpassed by social want, difference itself becomes an important variable: the possession of greater oratory prowess is more highly valued in relation to the state than being a barrel-maker; characteristics associated with males have more value than those of females. Williams (1997: 466) notes that once values are placed on certain qualities or characteristics, then treatment of that quality becomes bound to a form of rationalisation that is perceived as asserting a moral principle. For example, once sex is given relevance, how women and men are treated has a moral claim. In this case the 'superior' mental and physical qualities of males determines their moral claim to political position and privilege.

In this context, equality of opportunity becomes an important concept. If the value attached to important qualities for particular jobs or roles in the state can be seen as, effectively, arbitrary, then access to the positions that require these qualities is artificially restricted, usually by those people who possess the valued attributes, thus preserving their privileges. Demands for 'equality' may mean very little in such circumstances. Placing a female home-maker in the circle of philosopher kings, or their modern equivalent, will not make her a philosopher, and certainly not a king. However, removal of the artificial barriers to greater, or different, achievement by individuals through measures such as education and training, the elimination of gendered, race or class-based language that determines the characteristics of those allowed to enter exalted circles, and other necessary support, will enable them to achieve their potential. To do this the fundamental qualities of human beings, those held in common, must be acknowledged as 'the intrinsic moral worth of each person makes equal treatment of all people foundational to equality' (Koggel 1998: 48). Without this basic criterion, equality of opportunity is only a token gesture, pursued for political purposes. It may mean that those with 'inferior' characteristics attempt to change what is fundamental and inalienable to them in order to conform to a feigned norm. For political philosophers to ignore this and to assume equality, even among equals, is to endanger political outcomes in the ideal, or good, state.

At a basic level, knowing that privilege is based on a self-perpetuating concept of in/equality places elites in a precarious position vis-à-vis the masses who are disadvantaged by the value system imposed on them. This is not only the foundation for Marxism: liberal philosophies also attempt to alleviate such a situation by trying to equalise individuals, albeit without analysing differences between them, and ignoring those who do not fit their model. Even where inequality is perceived not as unjust but as a 'natural' phenomenon, if there is no provision of opportunity for socio-economic mobility and advancement, the 'good' state is depriving itself of undiscovered talents hidden in the lower echelons. A state or community in which people are able, and encouraged, to participate as equals without recourse to traditional roles which cannot be supported by reference to nature and are, therefore, contrived, will be more morally supportable as well as better governed, so achieving the objectives of philosophers through the ages.

J. S. Mill: Liberty, Equality and Androgyny

Mill is perhaps the most unusual of mainstream political philosophers in that his ideas were positively influenced by a woman. Working with Harriet Taylor enabled him to understand that the historical and tradi-tional roles of women were not the result of nature but of custom. The presumption of men to understand the nature of women, 'which can qualify them to lay down the law to women as to what is, or is not their vocation' (*Subjection of Women*: 243) was obviously ill-founded. Only women know their nature but do not have the power or opportunity to articulate it in fora of influence (*Subjection of Women*: 240).

As with all behaviours and attitudes founded on custom, Mill noted of political and relations and institutions that 'men did not wake on a summer morning and find them sprung up . . . In every state of their existence they are made what they are by human voluntary agency' (*Representative Government*: 207). A consequence of the construction of political relations is that they are able to be refashioned and improved. As may be surmised from the scope of the potential for inclusiveness, Mill's concern was not only with the socio-political and economic damage that the exclusion of women portends, but also with the incorporation of all those interests traditionally excluded by the elitism of philosophers and statesmen. Despite the fact that in his philosophy sex was 'as entirely irrelevant to political rights, as difference in height, or in the colour of the hair' (*Representative Government*: 341), his awareness that women would not automatically be included in a generic model of liberal representative government led to the deliberate sign-posting of women's situation and their potential to participate as full citizens in all his political works, as well as his dedicated work on *The Subjection of Women* (1985).[1] As Tulloch (1989: 149) notes, even the use of the generic 'he' throughout Mill's work becomes stylistic rather than a political statement of exclusion.

For Mill, the subjection of individuals eliminated the possibility of achieving either liberal or utilitarian goals, in that this prevented them from exercising their ability to protect their interests in terms of self-preservation or attaining happiness, often not even knowing what their real interests were.[2] The dogma generated by limited contributions to politics, whether from elites or representatives of the masses, was stifling to progress (Watkins 1966: 163–4). Only by broadening the participation of educated individuals from all classes could custom be challenged and either conformed to, reformed or rejected. Diversity was not necessary for its own sake but to uncover truth, as opposed to one-sided opinion (Cowling 1963: 42; Watkins 1966: 168). A problem for Mill in advocating the level of freedom implied in his model was the tension between liberty and the security of the state and the individual. The only situation in which any intervention with an individual's conduct would be legitimate was in circumstances where the individual was in danger of harming society or other people (*On Liberty*: 83). Even to the extent of self-harm, there could be no real justification for intervention as long as no one else was affected, although, as will be argued below, there is little one can do that does not impinge on others in some way. Other than that, individual sovereignty was absolute and everyone should be at liberty to pursue their own interests which, in turn, served the interests of society. For there was no such thing as a 'good despotism' in which a ruler or assembly looked after the interests of the people. Paternalism prevented people from sustaining the consequences of their choices and actions, demanding gratitude from its beneficiaries and leaving them subject to the goodwill, or otherwise, of patrons (Williams 1976). Thus, nothing is learned, responsibility is relinquished and individuals remain uninterested in anything beyond their immediate well-being, even if this is being abused by their rulers.[3] The only people to protect the interests of individuals were the individuals themselves, and in the diversity of their contributions to the decision-making process, the all-round prosperity of society increased (*Representative Government*: 244–5).

Although interpretations of Mill's ideas on the inclusivity of political interests may assume equality, he did not actually advocate a democratic polity that would give all and sundry the right to participation, nor to office. In fact, 'right' was not a concept that Mill imposed on politics as a matter of course. The utility of actions and thoughts was more important than rights, with liberty, including suffrage, having value in the service it provided to further the good of society (Ryan 1974; Halliday 1976). Mill's model of representative democracy was designed to enable individuals who were 'qualified' to understand and articulate their interests to be heard, and to elect and legitimate those qualified for office. Unlike his predecessors, Mill's understanding of qualifications for the job of political or other decision-making was not that of inherent qualities ordained to some fortunates. While it was certain that people were not equal in their innate characteristics, he professed that most individuals would be able to achieve a basic level of literacy and numeracy to enable them to make, at least, an informed choice when voting (*Representative Government*: 330). More fundamental understanding of interests would be gained through participatory procedures. Sharing of knowledge, first-hand experience of difference and sameness, and opportunity to articulate needs and demands would become a political education in themselves. Mill states that 'political discussions fly over the heads of those who have no votes, and are not endeavouring to acquire them' (*Representative Government*: 328–9), whereas 'the person bestirring himself with hopeful prospects to improve his circumstances, is the one who feels goodwill towards others engaged in, or who have succeeded in, the same pursuit' (*Representative Government*: 250).

However, trusting to the judgement of individuals educated to a basic level was not enough to ensure that a 'tyranny of the majority'[4] did not overturn the custom of society from that established by an elite to that of the working classes, 'a class, to say no more, not the most highly cultivated' (*Representative Government*: 326). For Mill, attempting to eliminate the 'characteristic evils of class government' (*Representative Government*: 326), advocacy of plural voting would preserve 'the educated from the class legislation of the uneducated; but it must stop short of enabling them to practise class legislation on their own account' (*Representative Government*: 337). Therefore, employers, bankers, merchants, professionals and manufacturers, who had more educational and occupational qualifications, and who were able and required to consider others rather than merely subsisting, were to be entrusted with a greater contribution to the common good, in having more than one vote (*Representative Government*: 336).

Considered in a gendered framework, Mill's model of politics presents women in a contradictory situation. Whereas they may have only a basic level of formal education, there can surely be no better qualified individuals by means of 'other-regarding' acts and thoughts. And yet, here is also a clear-cut case of the potential tyranny of the majority. In *Subjection of Women*, Mill overtly refers to women's potential to retaliate against unsatisfactory conditions in the home (*Subjection of Women*: 253). If expanded to the entire population of women, this would produce a considerable strength of challenge to entrenched patriarchal custom. Presumably, Mill does not perceive women as a 'class' able to threaten prevailing custom pertaining to their subjection in the same way that the working class might. But more significantly, he assumes that given free choice, and 'if marriage were an equal contract, not implying the obligation of obedience' (*Subjection of Women*: 264) women would favour homemaking as a career. In this case, women cannot claim a greater abundance of common feeling, homemaking being a job as any other, and they are equalised with men of their class.

A further qualification pertaining to eligibility to vote, and affecting women differentially, was that electors should be tax-payers. According to Mill, this would ensure integrity in public decision-making as 'those who pay no taxes, disposing by their votes of other people's money, have every motive to be lavish, and none to economise' (*Representative Government*: 331). In other words, there is no representation without taxation. Obviously, at the time that Mill was writing, working-class women, at least, were active wage labourers. However, until the 1870 Married Women's Property Act, married women were unable to hold private property at all, any income accruing to them being controlled by their husbands and any other property reverting to men's control. Where unmarried women owned property, they were unlikely to be in a position to control it, male relatives usually having legal rights over women. Overall it would seem that, even if Mill's reforms had been in place at the time, women's participation rates in the electoral system would have been negligible.[5] Moreover, Cameron (1980) suggests that the reforms to the family and work that Mill advocated to ease the burden on working-class women who, in the nineteenth century, were carrying the double workload of home and unprotected paid employment, would perpetuate women's disadvantage. Protective legislation, shortening women's working hours and limiting their access to certain occupations, the 'family wage' for men, and the raised status of home-making would not only excuse women from the abuses of the labour market, but would depress the benefits that women could gain as taxpayers. As Pateman (1989: 216) states, the higher earnings of men can always be used to justify their greater public voice.

Equality for Women Risks Liberty of All

There is a circularity in Mill's works – no matter how much he attempts to release women from the bonds of custom, their circumstances remain relatively stable. This is probably a result of his resort to nature in the absence of empirical evidence to show that women were actually different from how they had always behaved and been perceived in society (Ring 1985; Pateman 1989: 215; Tulloch 1989: Ch.3). In spite of his honourable intentions, and the progress he made towards demonstrating the artificiality of women's subordination, Mill was still constrained by fairly conventional ideas about women and their behaviour.[6] The very least consequence of this would be that Mill's template for representative government is undermined by the inherent narrowness of the experience associated with the home (Shanley 1991: 171). More significantly, his concept of liberty which relies on 'self-regarding' behaviour, whereby complete liberty is attached to those thoughts and actions that affect the individual alone (On Liberty: passim), is imperilled by the failure to extricate women from the moral milieu of the home. As Watkins (1966: 166) notes, there are actually very few actions that can claim to be fully self-regarding, suggesting that it is only freedom of thought and liberty of conscience that affect the individual alone although Mill's insistence on freedom of publication (On Liberty: 16) further questions this claim (Carritt 1967: 137).

Considering that Mill believes women will choose to be homemakers, together with the responsibility he places on mothers to maintain the family as the source of morality and, hence, freedom (*Subjection of Women*: 260), women are so integrated into their relationships and those with society that it would be impossible for them to act in any self-regarding way. Even if they were to gain all the happiness and intellectual fulfilment they require in the home, their actions would still be other-regarding despite the 'selfish' satisfaction gained. If Mill has underestimated the extent to which women's nature has been constrained by custom and they do not, in fact, choose the career pattern he suspects, his whole concept of liberty is at risk. To maintain the family as the basis for moral interaction, either women would have to be forced to remain in the home or other measures would have to be taken. As government interference is legitimate only as a last resort, that is, if non-interventionist measures are unsuccessful, force would not necessarily be coercive, either through physical or legal measures. Women could be 'persuaded' to behave in a way that would most benefit society (Cowling 1963: 102; Ryan 1974: 144; Halliday 1976: 116). But for this to happen the people with most interest in women's domesticity, the persuaders and/or the government, must share certain values concerning women's domestic, moral and other-regarding nature. If women's nature cannot be known without giving them the opportunity to discover it by enabling choice and experimentation, then the values that place women in the home must be based on custom.

   In many ways, Mill's model required women's emancipation to have already been attained. While in his lifetime women were addressing political rallies and meetings on issues such as suffrage and the abolition of slavery, and were campaigning for workers' and trades union rights, and working-class women were staffing factories and mines, he was still unable fully to grasp the enormity of women's allotted domestic task. This, incidentally, provides a very clear example of his own stated need for proper, experienced representation. Moreover, while, as Mill predicted, women's experience fuelled their demands for representation and legal rights, instead of working towards equality within the home and workplace, men protected their interests by banning women from trades unions and demanding the status quo in gender relations. For example, the widespread use of brutality in the home was recognised by Mill as a means of men venting their frustration and asserting power in the only place, and against the only person, available to them (*Subjection of Women*: 251). This further undermines the implication of Mill's work that the elimination of gender injustice should be based not on government intervention, but on friendship (Tulloch 1989: 22; Shanley 1991: 164). His conviction that permitting women the legal right to divorce in the case of persistent domestic violence would persuade men that cruelty to their wives was not in their best interests (*Subjection of Women*: 252), especially when wives were equal partners rather than effective servants, seems somewhat naïve. As Shanley (1991: 175) states, Mill's problem is not with equality of opportunity but with his blindness to the conditions that may impair this. Equality was only ever a concern in relation to its utility (Green 1994: 270). As he was aware, the chain effect of liberty and representation was not necessarily equality or recognition and tolerance of diverse interests. Rather it was the incorporation of difference and a broadening of the scope of deliberation. The differences between classes and sexes impair good statesmanship by permitting the defence of their interests to the detriment of the whole society. Mill's solution was not to unleash the fetters on previously excluded classes, including women, in the hope that a level of equilibrium would eventually be attained, but to acclimatise them gradually to their responsibilities in the political realm; if not to govern at least to understand and know when they are being misgoverned (*Representative Government*: 342).[7]

Marx and Engels: Some Chains are Less Breakable than others

It is possible that the maintenance of the traditional state, as historically perceived by the political philosophers, places limits on their imagination. It prevents them from fully understanding the potential meaning and manifestation of human equality. Indeed, a Marxist analysis of the capitalist state might conclude that women will always be required in the home to perform essential support services vital to the public sphere, including the provision of a continuous supply of healthy and morally adept citizens, or labourers. It may be supposed, therefore, that the release of individuals from the confines of state theory would fully enable consideration of activities and relations beyond those considered 'normal' by traditional theory. Marx and Engels certainly attempted to redefine social relations through the abolition of economic dependencies, and the state that existed to maintain them. However, their radicalism, while predicting better relations between women and men, did not progress to the point where they defended bold restructuring of family relations, other than that they would be based on love rather than economic need (Elshtain 1981: 186). While women may have been perceived as equal members of communist society, they carried the additional burden of reproduction, which is not accounted for in the calculation of equal citizenship.

As Mill perceived the androgynous liberal individual, so Marx and Engels incorporated women into their ideas, by demonstrating history's legacy of forced subordination. Moreover, like Mill, women's emancipation per se was not the objective of these thinkers. Rather, their objective was freedom from all exploitative relationships. Marx perceived the relations between women and men as 'the *most natural* relation of human being to human being' ('Economico-Philosophical Manuscripts': 149)(original emphasis), indicating that the fundamental mechanisms of oppression and exploitation could be witnessed in the home. The conditions that transformed relations at that level could be translated to the wider society and, when the origin of such behaviours was understood, reference to specific sub-divisions within the major sections of society was no longer necessary. As such, where women and the family are mentioned in Marx's works, it is to illustrate the basis of inequality at its most fundamental level. Thereafter, the solutions to exploitation accommodate them as members of their economic class.

However exploitation was manifested, economic relations were always the basis. The superstructure, built to maintain a social order based on economic difference, would ensure that the oppressed regarded their condition as 'natural', or inevitable, much as custom precluded progress and the search for truth in Mill's work. For example, employment and marriage contracts gave a semblance of legal right to individuals who freely entered them (Roemer 1997: 564). However, unlike previous theorists who accepted history and its legacy, Marx and Engels produced an historical account of social development, demonstrating its maintenance by vested interests. They argued that in every epoch 'a complicated arrangement of society into various orders, a manifold gradation of social rank' ('Communist Manifesto': 204) was created in which 'the ruling ideas of each age have ever been the ideas of its ruling class' ('Communist Manifesto': 225). As such, only the ruling class will know and pursue its own interests, the rest being subject to false ideas that their interests can be realised in the system to which they are, in reality enslaved.

Under capitalism, this process is evident in the 'alienation' of the workers resulting from the division of labour, defined as 'a division of material and mental labour' ('German Ideology': 175). The new methods of production in which individuals were required to leave the home to work for wages, having only their labour to sell to the owners of the means of production, resulted in a complete loss of control, not only over their labour but, to a large extent, their lives (Avineri 1971; Jaggar 1988: 216). In addition, the requirement of the bourgeoisie to accumulate wealth in ownership reduces workers to the status of property as they become an essential part of the means of production ('Communist Manifesto': 211; Vigor 1966: 184). Herein lies the downfall of the bourgeoisie. As labourers are concentrated in places of work external to their homes, their experiences as an exploited and oppressed class of people become clear and they will be able to use their new knowledge and strength to overthrow the ruling class ('Communist Manifesto': 213–

15). The result would be a new epoch of communism. The division of labour, with its implications for individuals alone and in competition with others to accumulate more wealth or status through the labour market, is healed and an equality of interests and process can be developed: 'Only in community with others has each individual the means of cultivating his gifts in all directions; only in the community, therefore, is personal freedom possible' ('German Ideology': 193).

A prerequisite for more communal understanding is that private property be abolished. Obviously, the end of the division of labour releases individual workers from the category of property. But, more than this, the end of property ownership will release humanity from the ever-increasing desire for the accumulation of more than they can use; and which always requires the use of people as workers and consumers ('Communist Manifesto': 212). This is not to end desire, or pursuit of individual interests. Despite the common misinterpretation of Marx's and Engels' work that the communist ideal is one of uniformity rather than freedom and diversity, it is only the exploitative elements of accumulation that are deterred as 'communism deprives no man of the power to appropriate the products of society; all that it does is to deprive him of the power to subjugate the labour of others by means of such appropriation' ('Communist Manifesto': 222). However, there is one form of appropriation, the sexual division of labour, that Marx and Engels acknowledge crosses classes and epochs. Although they believe that the end of history,[8] manifested in communism, will be the end of all exploitation, including that of women, the fact that gender oppression remains constant through all forms of economic oppression tends to the view that destruction of the economic power of the bourgeoisie will not, by itself, end women's oppression.

'Til Monogamy Do Us Part

As Marx and Engels trace the history of economic relations through the stages of patriarchy, feudalism and capitalism ('Communist Manifesto': 204), or tribal, ancient communal and state ownership to private ownership ('German Ideology': 165–6), so Engels' *The Origin of the Family, Private Property and the State* (1978), a collation of the work on women and family scattered throughout his and Marx's work, traces the history of gender relations through this series of historical developments. Pre-civil societies of the savage and barbaric periods,[9] wherein communal labour and ownership prevailed, were associated with group marriages within generations rather than families. As the economy grew more sophisticated and the knowledge of animal husbandry increased, the requirement to restrict sexual relations between blood relatives to improve the human stock became imperative, resulting in an ever-decreasing circle of eligible sexual partners. However, in these periods family groups were matrilineal because, 'in all forms of family, it is uncertain who is the father of a child; but it is certain who its mother is' (*Origin*: 46).

Although the only irrefutable division of labour for Engels and Marx is that of procreation, the rest being subject to historical intervention, the savage and barbaric periods do demonstrate a quite familiar separation of female and male roles. Women controlled the method of production within the home and household goods, and men that outside the home, including obtaining food and the instruments required for this (*Origin*: 63). Although this division did not attach value status to the roles of women and men (Delmar 1976: 273; Carver 1985: 485), each having equal jurisdiction or contribution to the community, women's status in terms of clan descent, as well as their control over the distribution of good essential to subsistence, lent women a high level of respect (*Origin*: 55). Whether this translated into power, and was of the magnitude depicted in the class struggles leading to revolution, is not stated by Marx or Engels. As historical change is the result of power struggles, the implication is that men would actively struggle to overthrow such mother-right. However, it appears that if women did have power, it was benign; men's acquisitiveness, rather than subjugation, was responsible for its downfall. As such it seems that history begins with 'the world historical defeat of the female sex' (*Origin*: 65).

The major change in human relations occurred with the marginalisation of production in the home brought about by the expansion of production in the field and furnace. This not only shifted the 'power' from women to men, but added a value to production, which brought with it elements of coercion. The new sources of production in animal husbandry and agriculture created a surplus which resulted in new wealth creation but also required the use of slaves and labourers to maintain them. Thus, by the end of the barbaric period, the use of people as a means of production was already common. In addition, it somehow became necessary to pass wealth to specific children of the known owners of production and creators of wealth, the fathers. As well as the overthrow of matriliny in favour of patriliny, this required individual women to become assigned to a particular patriarchal family so that their sexuality could be controlled and the paternity of offspring guaranteed. In this description of history, then, monogamy was an obvious development of the family, and 'comes on the scene as the subjugation of the one sex by the other' (*Origin*: 75). But, as both Marx and Engels point out (*Origin*: 75–6; 'Communist Manifesto': 224), it is obvious only for women. As the only requirement of men is that of correct heredity, they are still as free as ever in history to practise, if not polygamy, extra-marital sex, adding further to women's historical social degradation as both prostitutes and wives (*Origin*: 76–7).

As much as *Origin* provides a comprehensible chronology of gender subjugation, it provides a coherent explanation only if the assumptions of patriarchy are not disturbed (Coole 1993). For example, while the placement of women in the home explains how mother-right was overthrown by men's growing economic superiority, the conditions that lead up to this situation can be explained only in terms of biological and psychological difference, so familiar throughout the history of political thought. Only the common assumption that all the responsibilities arising from childbirth are as natural as parturition could justify the division of labour Engels describes. And yet, if procreation is the only natural division of labour, with all else being economically determined, there would be no reason for women as a 'class' to be connected to home production processes at all. As Hartmann (1992a: 344) notes, the categories of social hierarchy that Marx and Engels derive from the march of history do not explain why certain types of people fill particular roles in the social order. The answer to this anomaly probably rests in the fact that Marx and Engels were not interested in the family per se, using it primarily as a means to illustrate current economic inequalities. The monogamous family was 'the cellular form of civilised society, in which the nature of the antagonisms and contradictions fully developed in that society can be already studied' (*Origin*: 75).

More specifically, the family was used to highlight the particular amoral currency of the bourgeoisie, and to demonstrate how the end of capitalism would liberate individuals from bourgeois relationships throughout society (Bowle 1963: 319). For example, Marx and Engels argued that bourgeois husbands perceived their wives much the same as they perceived proletarians; as factors of production and, therefore, available to all bourgeoisie equally ('Communist Manifesto': 224), effectively sustaining the community of wives common in the savage period of history. As the communist revolution would reorder all relations so that they would be based on reciprocity rather than economic exploitation, so the proletarian family, in the absence of private property and where wives were equal partners as wage labourers, was seen as an example of a relationship free of internal oppression; true monogamy. Such marriages based on sex-love rather than materialism were, like any post-capitalist association, supposedly reciprocal and caring. There would be no need for either partner to utilise any form of prostitution for physical or pseudo-psychological satisfaction. Marriage existed purely on the grounds that partners wanted to be together (*Origin*: 94–5). The fact that domestic violence continued in working-class families was merely the result of traditional, exploitative monogamy (Carver 1985: 486). The characteristics of these co-equal relationships were other-orientated in that the satisfaction of self depended on the satisfaction of others (Avineri 1971: 89).

The emphasis on bourgeois marriage as the epitome of human exploitation assumes that proletarian families, where true love cannot be substituted for the attractions of property ownership and hereditary needs, are the fount of all that is good in human relationships. However, Marx and Engels would not have had to search very far to see that the plight of proletarian women was not much different from that of their bourgeois counterparts. Not only did their situation as wage labourers not bring them reciprocity in the home, but male workers were actively discouraging their rights to equal pay and treatment. Instead of property proving the corrupting influence, work itself became the zealously protected focus of male power. Consequently, the conditions that Marx and Engels associated with bourgeois marriage were very much alive even in proletarian households, where women became the means by which men were able to continue working and maintain their comfort. Obviously, the utilisation of bourgeois marriage served a political objective in Marxist theory. But more than this, the failure to acknowledge the reality of proletarian women's circumstances either suggests a naïve romanticism, both with the proletariat as a class as well as the proletarian family, or portrays relationships as Marx and Engels would like them to be; similarly to Rousseau, somewhat idyllic.

Revolution and the State of Women

From the way that Marx and Engels integrated analysis of the family into their revolutionary theory, it could be assumed that the solutions to emancipation in the family, and in society at large, are synonymous and contemporaneous. However, not only is it difficult to understand the chronology of liberation from oppressive forces, but many of the variables essential to the theory do not equate in the family and the economy.

The central question here is whether women's emancipation is essential to or succeeds the revolution. Engels' statement that 'the first condition for the liberation of women is to bring the whole female sex back into public industry' (*Origin*: 86) might imply that, in so doing, not only are women freed from the bourgeois-proletarian relationship in the home (*Origin*: 85), but that in filling the workplaces, they would fuel the revolutionary potential of the proletariat. However, just as the revolution of the proletariat requires the whole class, or a substantial proportion of it, to act collectively, it must be assumed that for women as an exploited 'class' to gain their emancipation, they would also have to act collectively. Of course, Marx and Engels were not actually concerned with women in class terms, but perceived them as part of the common economic strata. The conditions of domestic labour, coupled with the additional burden of wage labour that most proletarian women were involved with, would not have created equal opportunities for women to share experiences and recognise their common oppression as women, let alone organise to revolt against it. Moreover, as Hartmann (1992a, 1992b) and de Beauvoir (1988: 147) argue, part of the bourgeoisie's method of maintaining power had been to co-opt working-class men by offering them 'control of at least some women' (Hartmann 1992a: 346).

In fighting the collaborative forces of proletariat and bourgeois men as well as the economic struggle against capitalism, women did not have the same struggle as men. On the other hand, as women were part of the labour force it may be assumed that they were already an integral part of the proletariat and ripe for revolutionary activity, providing that their historically defined domestic responsibilities allowed them the time. This leads to the conclusion that women's emancipation is appropriate to a stage after the fall of capitalism, suggesting that even a communist society could harbour exploitative gender relations.[10] After all, the monogamous family was not a product of modern capitalism, having a history stretching back to ancient Greece. Being a constant among changing socio-economic systems, there is no reason to suspect that communal ownership of most property would release women from ownership by individual men. However, without the foundations of economic elevation and inheritance that led to the development of monogamy, the reasons for women's continuing oppression would be void. It could even be assumed from this that, as the state withers away when there is no longer a use for its coercive powers, so the patriarchal family will dissolve as equal partnerships replace exploitative associations (Coole 1993: 157), thus saving women the necessity of organising a sex war. But Marx and Engels do not suggest that this will be the case, arguing that, like the bourgeoisie, women will have to be forced to be brought into, or stay in, public industry.

While the assimilation of women into public industry would be supported by the socialisation of domestic labour (*Origin*: 87), a development that is posited but not expanded by Engels, a number of anomalies exist in this solution to women's oppression. Communist modes of production end the alienation that forced wage labour induces by giving control back to individual workers and ending the competitive relations that further alienate them from other humans. As Marx notes, in the communist society where general production is regulated by social need, he will be free 'to hunt in the morning, fish in the afternoon, rear cattle in the evening, criticise after dinner, just as I have a mind' ('German Ideology': 177). In other words, freed from the specialised labour that capitalism enforces, workers reclaim control over their own productive capacities, so ending the alienation that capitalist production instils and relies on. However, Marx and Engels have stated that a natural division of labour exists between women and men, and that this results in women's association with production in the home. If this is the case, then even as history advanced and women became enslaved to husbands, despite their unwaged work and the level of 'value-added'[11] that this produced, they would have been less alienated in the home than men were in the workplace. A considerable part of this lack of alienation would be that domestic labour does not require the division between hand and brain that more specialised, industrial and agricultural labour needs (di Stefano 1991). Therefore, forcing women into public industry will create in them the same alienation that men had felt under capitalism. As such, communism cannot be perceived as women's liberator. Of course, the public industry they prefer could be domestic. It may be that women's inclinations will be to clean houses in the morning, pick up children from school and play with them in the afternoon, prepare tomorrow's meals in the evening and do the washing and ironing after dinner. But the nature of domestic labour does not allow the freedom that 'male' industry appears to, as certain domestic chores and childcare require sustained, constant and unfailing attention. Freedom based on free production in co-operation with others (Morrow 1998: 92), therefore, eludes women, as a Marxist revolution would fail to free women from the embedded assumptions of their capabilities.

The emphasis that is placed on public industry maintains the traditional inferiority of domestic labour. It is not only that privatised domestic work has no place in the collective restructuring of society but also that women's labour is eliminated from the theory of historical development. As di Stefano (1991: 153) states, the family and procreation are only the third of the premises upon which humans 'make history', after finding basic sustenance and the production of new needs ('German Ideology': 171–2). This ignores the conclusive fact that humans must be born and nurtured to reach a stage at which they are able to do anything at all. Domestic labour that does not contribute directly to capitalist markets, but provides for the welfare and the continuous supply of fit and healthy labour, is ignored in the historical account of oppression and exploitation. The absence of recognition of the contribution of women's labour to capitalism in Marx and Engels' work cannot conclude with women's liberation. It is not simply that a socialised domestic industry could not replace the work of women in the home, but the fact that intimate relationships cannot be fully equated to economic ones, which places domestic relations outside the revolutionary discourse. Of course, Marx's and Engels' concern with the alienation inherent in production processes would tend to obviate their consideration of the fact that reproduction and its associated responsibilities are the least alienated of human labour. Their inability to participate in anything other than the earliest stages, and not experiencing the full extent and repercussions of this process would perhaps not render it particularly significant in male philosophers' socio-economic consciousness. But the fact that the relations between women and men are not based on economic exploitation alone places them outside the framework of Marxist revolutionary theory. The fact is that in the absence of economic inequality, all other inequalities do not disappear.

Swings and Roundabouts

Nineteenth-century political philosophy was the first to consider the comprehensive inclusion of women, and of the many men, who had historically been deemed less rational, less concerned or less able to participate in decisions that affected the state. While Mill retained the liberal state, opening up the decision-making base to previously excluded individuals and thereby widening interest representation in government, Marx and Engels were concerned to bring freedom to all individuals by the abolition of state structures and processes that inherently exploited and oppressed some for the benefit of others. In the works of Mill, Marx and Engels the familiar strains of female irrationality, natural inferiority or weakness are not heard. Indeed, both Mill and Engels wrote specifically of the artificial use of female 'nature' in political philosophy and practice. The consequence of female, indeed any, socialisation is that it is not immutable and can be changed. For Mill, education and suffrage would incorporate women as equals, within their socio-economic class, in the decision-making process. Similarly, Marx and Engels implied that women are as able to make personal and community decisions as anyone given the opportunity. The problem with these thinkers is that, while denying claims to women's nature and correcting the perfidious dissembling of mainstream philosophers, they did not go further and reflect on the repercussions of collapsing the barriers between the public and private spheres.

For Mill, the fact that women would choose domestic labour as a career need not deprive them of a political voice, but it would not release them from dependency. Such a status itself has the potential to restrict women's equality and equality of opportunity, as the danger of losing the favour of one's patron could serve to restrict the articulation of heartfelt concerns. Moreover, the durability of the traditional family, even if based on free choice among equals, does little to challenge the customs that Mill is so keen to dispense with. Similarly, the society of Marx and Engels may dissolve the economic barriers between public and private by making all individuals socially productive, but it does not dissolve the public-private divide based on non-economic ties. That men may be unwilling to abdicate their authority in the home, despite their equal status in society, is likely to reflect the non-recognition of women's historical social production. As public industry defines the contribution of individuals to the community, so the social production that women have always undertaken, but which has not had economic value or status placed on it, will remain unrecognised. There will be no call for men to take their share of it, nor will it be acknowledged as a part of women's 'equal' status. As such, women would be unequal in the sphere of public decision-making, and much of their contribution would remain unattributed. In addition, the extra burden that this labour would entail would continue to restrict women's equality of opportunity to choose their activities. The double burden, lack of choice, and continuing gendered division of labour in the home, may well leave women dependant on husbands despite the romantic view of communist monogamy given by Engels. His own argument, stating that 'one cannot be a dependant and still an equal is very compelling' (Millett 1977: 125).

The collapsing of public and private spheres cannot entirely eliminate the essentially personal aspects of the latter. And yet it is these that are so formidable in respect to women's full equality. 'Trivial' matters, such as responsibility for making the beds, wiping the baby's nose and listening to others' problems, all impact on their bearers, often in minute ways that do not ordinarily bear consideration. Yet their consequences are substantial. Of course, there is no reason why such minutiae should fall to women. However, the fact that a value is attached to certain roles and that, following centuries of experience and philosophising, 'private' issues tend to have a female, and therefore lesser, value attached inclines to the continuing inequality of women despite formal outward appearances. For example, numerically, even if women and men participate equally in decision-making, the extra unacknowledged work that women undertake gives their contribution a lesser weight; they have to work harder for their 'equal' share. More significantly, the continuation of the private sphere as women's domain undermines the worth of women's contribution when only public activity is important in collective decision-making. Not only Mill but others since[12] who have attempted to raise the status of homemaking to that of manufacturing, commerce or trade are struggling against the embedded value that is attached to occupations that visibly produce goods and profit. While such values persist unacknowledged, 'equality' will remain sciolistic, applicable only to the common man.

Notes

1. For Mill, custom not only maintained the traditional attitudes of men towards women that prevented their progress beyond historically defined roles, but women themselves perceive their ability as insufficient for anything other than their given and accepted role (*Subjection of Women*: 222).
2. The famous utilitarian goal, or 'greatest-happiness principle', was roundly denounced by Mill as being 'too complex and indefinite an end to be sought except through the medium of various secondary ends' (*Utilitarianism*: 118).
3. Translating this to the family unit, there was also no such thing as a good household despot making decisions on behalf of a wife and family, and adult members of families were to be given the opportunity to participate in local decision-making.
4. In 1836, Mill reviewed the first volume of de Tocqueville's *Democracy in America*, in which a chapter was devoted to 'What tempers the tyranny of the majority in the United States' (de Tocqueville 1968; Gray 1998: xxiv). Mayer (1968: xviii) in his introduction to *Democracy in America* notes the strong influence that the work had on Mill.
5. The 1870 Act enabled married women under certain circumstances to hold property and control their own earnings and savings. Until the mid-nineteenth century, any property that women may have owned was automatically transferred to her husband on marriage. A further Married Women's Property Act in 1882 gave women the same rights over property as unmarried women (Millett 1977: 66; Banks 1981: 35–6; Holdsworth 1988: 12). However, as unmarried women were likely to be in the care of fathers or other male relatives, it would unlikely that many independent women of property would be eligible for involvement in affairs of the state.
6. Mill's work on women, both published, as an activist and in the House of Commons when he was MP for Westminster, is an example of living by his convictions. Moreover, he not only campaigned for and introduced a Bill to the House calling for women's suffrage, he also championed such causes as divorce whereby, for the first time, women would be able to sue for divorce and maintain control over their children and property, and had earlier been imprisoned for handing out leaflets about contraception.
7. *The Subjection of Women* was written in 1861 but not published until 1869. This was before the Married Women's Property Act of 1870, and 50 years before a woman first took her seat in the House of Commons.
8. As history had shaped the relations of individuals and effectively created humans as they are, a situation in which humans were free to find their own nature and were not subjugated by external criteria or forces, would, in effect, be free of history. 'The reality, which communism is creating, is precisely the real basis for rendering it impossible that anything should exist independently of individuals, in so far as things are only a product of the preceding intercourse of individuals themselves' ('German Ideology': 189).

In many ways, once in communism, there is no reasonable alternative, fairly much as Fukuyama (1992) notes of liberal democracy in the 1990s.

9. The savage period could be likened to the state of nature until its transformation to tool-using and rudimentary communities (*Origin*: 24–5). The barbaric period incorporated development of agriculture, animal husbandry and the mechanised production. By the end of this stage of history, large scale cultivation, use of iron tools, bellows, hand-mills and potters' wheels were common (*Origin*: 29).

10. The attitudes and behaviour of some Marxist men confirms that this is more likely the case, so giving rise to Marxist-Feminism. In fact, I have had many conversations with self-proclaimed Marxist men who, patting me on the head reassuringly, insist that women's liberation will be on the list of priorities after the fall of capitalism.

11. Surplus value is created by the extra amount of work a labourer produces which results in a profit for the employer (*Wages, Price and Profit*: 48–9; Bowle 1963: 330–1). Although women's domestic labour does not ordinarily have a monetary value, it is nevertheless completely value-added when 'several observers have declared the non-wage earning wife to be part of the standard of living of male workers' (Hartmann 1992a: 350).

12. 'Wages for housework' campaigns in the mid-twentieth century attempted to show that 'women's domestic labour does not simply represent a personal service to individual men, but is of critical importance to the capitalist economy' (Ungerson 1997: 376; Bryson 1999: 20).

Chapter 9: Rawls and Nozick: Justice and Masculinised Politics

Political philosophy has always had to contend with the fact of existing societies, and has attempted to improve on conditions and principles from a point of established relationships and procedures. For contemporary philosophers, the advances that society has made, based on previous ideas and political progression, make the task of incorporating the range of relevant interests into their formulation of the ideal state more onerous. They are faced with a polity in which the stark, political divisions between sovereign ruler, or between those deemed capable of participating in a limited democracy, and the masses have been formally eradicated, and in which the rights accruing to the political class have been extended to all individuals. Certainly in western liberal democracies, the right of self-preservation has taken on a different level of complexity from that of the seventeenth century when Hobbes could concern himself with a far more basic approach. The wider spread and greater amount of property ownership, the increased scarcity of resources requiring the extended need to work for owners of the means of production to secure even the basics of life such as food, shelter and water, compound the problems of achieving fair and proper political relations in which basic rights can be assured. In consequence, contemporary political philosophers such as Rawls and Nozick do not attempt to perceive society as a blank page from which correct political relationships and procedures can be developed. Instead, they start from existing society and impose a version of justice on the current situation. When applied to women, this approach produces notable anomalies.

In addition to generalised political progress, the situation of women has certainly changed since the early political philosophers were considering issues of the state and politics. It is evident that politics has been masculinised and maintained as a predominantly masculine activity, with the considerable assistance of political philosophy, through the ages. Despite this, and with slow progress, by the twentieth century women were evident in political assemblies, and active in non-institutional politics, in many countries, particularly those of the industrialised nations. The question of whether ideas changed to allow women into the political arena or whether women accommodated to tradition and fitted in to the existing mould is a crucial one. The fact that women's absence from politics has been justified by recourse to a variety of 'reasonable' excuses from ancient Greece to the Enlightenment and beyond effectively precludes challenge. The only response to reasonable justifications must, by definition, be unreasonable and easily disregarded. In such circumstances, women can surely only be tolerated in the political arena if they conform to accepted standards, however much this is a perversion of 'nature'. However, an effect of this would be to ignore the 'special' qualities or attributes that women bring to politics, thus perpetuating a universal philosophy that, in essence, still excludes them while tolerating their presence in practice.

It is informative that the twentieth-century political philosophers considered here, unlike previous philosophers, do not feel the need to mention the situation of women at all in their treatises.[1] This may well be due to the notion that in 'post-feminist' times opportunities for women are considered the same as those for men. Proof of this is given, for those subscribing to the idea, in the presence of women in fields of endeavour that had previously been the sole domain of men. However, the central tenet of the works of Rawls and Nozick is that justice should accrue to public holdings and positions. It is here that it is necessary not simply to deliberate on the fact that women have transcended the historical boundaries presented for entry to the public sphere. The extent and ways that this has been achieved require evaluation to determine whether women have been afforded justice.

Justice as Fairness: All Winners in the Game of Life

In 1972, Rawls reignited interest in political philosophy and debate by publishing *A Theory of Justice* in which he argued that, from what he termed 'the original position' under a 'veil of ignorance', a cross-section of a society would choose, from a list of possible alternatives, two particular principles of justice that would regulate socio-political relations in perpetuity. By these means, 'representatives' from society are placed under conditions where all specific knowledge is absent, in order to deny the intervention of particular interests in the deliberative process. For Rawls, only in this way can it be ensured that, in the real society, people are tied to a social contract based on relationships of mutuality and reciprocity. Having stated the principles of justice that the representatives would choose, Rawls goes to much trouble to illustrate why they would be chosen, elaborating and revising them slightly but significantly along the way. Over the next few years, as might be expected with the presentation of a new and extensive work in the style of good traditional political philosophy, *A Theory of Justice* attracted a great deal of attention and criticism. Accordingly, Rawls answered critics of his original thesis in a number of articles, but most significantly in a series of 'lectures' published as *Political Liberalism* in 1993.[2] In the later book, the principles of justice are again slightly but significantly revised, and the methodology of the 'original position' and 'veil of ignorance', together with the parameters of their function are placed in a specifically political, as opposed to metaphysical and hypothetical, framework.

The two principles of justice, referred to as 'justice as fairness', ensure that, firstly, every individual has equal rights to 'a fully adequate scheme of equal basic liberties which is compatible with a similar scheme of liberties for all' (*Political Liberalism*: 291). That basic liberties such as freedom of political speech and the press, freedom of assembly, and liberty of conscience, as well as 'the liberty and integrity of the person' (*Political Liberalism*: 335) are equally distributed ensures that individuals have the opportunity of pursuing what in *A Theory of Justice* is referred to as their 'rational life plan', now known as their conception of the good. That is, each person is able to maximise their interests within the constraints of others doing the same.[3] The second part of justice as fairness allows for the inevitable social and economic inequalities that arise from individuals' pursuit of different goals, utilising their unique mental and physical capacities, also ensuring that innate characteristics and/or inherited material benefits do not unduly dis/advantage anyone. In other words, there is to be equality of opportunity for public positions and offices, and inequalities are acceptable, or just, only if they are to the benefit of all, measured by 'the greatest benefit of the least advantaged members of society' (*Political Liberalism*: 291).

The inclusiveness of such a scheme of justice appears decisive, and for women, particularly advantageous. The reference to the least advantaged members of society could be interpreted as a means of redressing the injustices done to women over the centuries as a result of confining them to the private sphere, as well as injustice to certain groups of men, ethnic minorities and other clearly disadvantaged groups and individuals. However, Rawls makes it perfectly clear in *Political Liberalism* that justice as fairness is a system that applies only to 'the basic structure of society', which is 'society's main political, social, and economic institutions, and how they fit together into one unified system of social co-operation from one generation to the next' (*Political Liberalism*: 11). Apart from when involved in social interactions beyond their enclaves, non-political institutions are free to enforce their own system of rules and traditions.[4] It is difficult to see how the continuation of injustice in a non-political environment can be reconciled to justice as fairness in the political, although Jackson (1979: 731) states that intolerance and liberty can easily coexist. For example, most religions insist on the inequality of men and women and the separate spheres of activity for the two sexes, which cannot be translated to equality of liberty, opportunity and benefit for women in society (Hirshman 1994: 1865; Okin 1994). Obviously, a fundamental flaw exists in justice as fairness in that, despite women's presence in society, ascribing them with hypothetical equality of liberty and opportunity does not translate into a real condition of justice (Hirshman 1994: 1975). Rawls' assertion that, from all perspectives, justice as fairness is the best system that can be ascertained in the original position and would be accepted by people in the real world seems somewhat premature in the case of women. Moreover, as with any philosopher insisting on the reasonable basis of their argument, there is little that women can say or do that translates into reasonable political counter-argument to Rawls' justice as fairness.

The Original Position: Maintaining the Missionary Arrangement

To ensure the benchmark equality that characterises justice as fairness, Rawls invents what he now perceives as a political situation[5] in which representatives decide on the principles required to establish and maintain a well-ordered society. These representatives are 'symmetrically situated' by means of the veil of ignorance. That is, they are devoid of all specific knowledge about themselves but have an understanding of the general functions and rules of society, and they want to ensure the best position for themselves whatever their situation in the real world. Should it turn out, when they leave the comfort of the original position and the veil of ignorance, that they are at the base of the socio-economic ladder, they will have ensured that they share equal liberty to pursue their goals within the limits of their circumstances, have the opportunity to improve those circumstances by merit and will benefit from the advantages of those better off than themselves.[6] In addition to the basic liberties and opportunities necessary to achieve conceptions of the good, some 'all-purpose means' are required, for example, income and wealth and self-respect. These variables are referred to as 'primary goods'.

The conditions of the original position 'eliminate the bargaining advantages that inevitably arise within the background institutions of any society from cumulative social, historical, and natural tendencies' (*Political Liberalism*: 23), equalising any superiority of wealth and income that could influence the final decision. They also allow for individuals' rational conception of the good, or personal maximisation of primary goods, to be realised within a reasonable conception of the good encased in justice as fairness.[7] In pursuing their own interests, then, individuals will voluntarily, if not naturally, honour their sense of justice when interacting or socially co-operating with others in the knowledge that others will do the same (*Political Liberalism*: 16, passim).[8]

Rawls acknowledges that in *A Theory of Justice* the conception of justice as fairness was a means to 'generalise and carry to a higher order of abstraction the traditional doctrine of the social contract' (*Political Liberalism*: xvii). His intention was to show that justice as fairness was fundamentally superior to utilitarian doctrines in which it was acceptable for some groups or individuals, usually the better off, to sacrifice some advantages for the good of the whole (Carey 1976: 373; Ball 1993: 158). What the original theory failed to consider was that the representatives in the original position would adhere to strongly held religious, moral and philosophical beliefs, or comprehensive doctrines that include 'values and virtues within one rather precisely articulated system' (*Political Liberalism*: 13). The significance of the omission is that such comprehensive doctrines might render the choice of justice as fairness contradictory to the parties' own doctrines as well as between comprehensive doctrines outside the veil of ignorance. Beyond the original position, there must be an agreement on what justice as fairness applies to. It cannot completely override the strong convictions of individuals in society but must find some grounds on which agreement can be met with regard to fundamental issues of justice that apply to all in the political arena. Here, the concept of the 'overlapping consensus' is introduced. This identifies the relatively narrow 'shared fund of implicitly recognised basic ideas and principles' (Rawls 1991: 149) between reasonable comprehensive doctrines that can be applied to justice as fairness in the basic structure (Mandle 1999: 92). For example, it is assumed that all reasonable doctrines decry the use of slavery. Any that do not would not be deemed reasonable, if for no other reason that it denies a system of equal liberties for all. As such, Rawls believes that in a multi-cultural, multi-racial, politically heterogeneous and religiously diverse society there will be enough common ground, based on intuitive ideas embedded in democratic politics (Rawls 1991: 146), that can be applied to the basic structure and regulate social co-operation between free and equal persons.

It is perhaps Rawls' emphasis on justice as fairness and the overlapping consensus applying to political relations and institutions that creates the problems that must concern an analysis from a perspective of inequality. Overtly, the overlapping consensus is designed to take contentious issues off the agenda (Rawls 1991: 150; Exdell 1994: 459), leaving only those issues that can be agreed to be subject to justice as fairness. Consequently, if anyone wants to challenge the justice of institutional procedures they can do so only from a limited perspective agreed among the parties in the original position and may dispute justice only in the basic structure. The recourse to injustice in comprehensive doctrines is the concern only of those members or adherents to the doctrine and is not a concern of politics. For women to claim injustice in the public sphere based on their family and/or religious organisation is strictly outside the field of concern of justice as fairness. Indeed, Rawls could claim two parts to this exclusion that fully fit the parameters of his conception of justice. Firstly, it may be only women's rational, or thin, conception of good that leads to their claim of injustice. Women who feel unjustly treated in a scheme of equal liberties and opportunities may be relying on unfair comparisons in making their claims. They have their just distribution of the basic primary goods, obtained through just procedures from the original position in which they would have been represented, but have ambitions beyond their capabilities given their circumstances. As Rawls states, 'desires and wants, however intense, are not by themselves reasons in matters of constitutional essentials and basic justice' (*Political Liberalism*: 190). If women cannot adjust their 'ambitions' to a reasonable conception of the good that acknowledges their circumstances, they effectively lack a sense of justice and can be legitimately coerced to behave sociably (Jackson 1979; Alejandro 1993).

The second defence of gender difference that Rawls could claim within justice as fairness is that only *reasonable* comprehensive doctrines will be accepted in the treaty. Now this begs the question whether women wanting a better deal subscribe to a comprehensive doctrine, which could be feminism, or whether they are merely individuals demanding justice. Assuming that such women can be grouped together within the doctrine of feminism, a far-fetched idea but then Rawls often presents the reader with disputable grand assumptions, it is unlikely they will be perceived as propounding a reasonable view. Indeed, in challenging the overlapping consensus and attempting to admit justice in 'non-political' organisations to the basic structure, feminism would be dismissed as unreasonable (*Political Liberalism*: 61; Barry 1995: 898; Mulhall and Swift 1996: 232). In the event that an unreasonable doctrine is advocated, presumably insisting on its superiority and requiring the state to ensure that citizens adhere to its demands, then justice as fairness can be implemented almost as a comprehensive doctrine itself to deflect its harmful effects on social co-operation among free and equal persons (Neal 1987: 934; Alejandro 1993; Mulhall and Swift 1996: 237).

While demands for women's equal justice certainly would require a considerable change in attitude, they do not necessarily herald a fundamental alteration of belief systems. Liberalism, capitalism, Judaism and Islam would continue unabated even if women were able to achieve positions at the highest level of their organisations. However, if a reasonable conception of the good requires that women's domestic work is necessary, not only to their comprehensive doctrine but to the social co-operation of society as a whole, there appears little that women can do to argue injustice. Insistence that domestic work leads to unjust distributions of liberty, opportunity and the 'all-purpose means' can again be defended by recourse to procedural justice but, more significantly, if women's genuine equality was perceived to upset the just distribution of primary goods, perhaps limiting men's liberties and opportunities by insisting on their full participation in domestic labour, then it could in no way be perceived as reasonable. As Carey (1976: 377) notes, justice as fairness is a 'closed' system of justice that effectively prevents challenge.

Family Values and the Ambiguities of Justice as Fairness

A number of anomalies arise from Rawls' methodology and the assumptions on which he bases his certainty that, given the choice, his conception of justice as fairness would be chosen by reasonable persons. For example, commentators have argued that it is not certain that liberty would be the first priority from which it would be agreed all justice stems (Strasnick 1976: 253; Corlett 1991: 178). It is as feasible that wealth and income, the all-purpose means, would be perceived as necessary to liberty, thus placing material means prior to liberty, equality of opportunity and self-respect. While Rawls thinks it non-rational for representatives in the original position to gamble on being wealthy in the real world (*Theory of Justice*: 156, 545), the fact that they have a general knowledge of how society works may make such a gamble perfectly rational in society as it is. From the point of view of maximising one's own interests, individuals are quite often willing to take risks in the hope of greater gain. A more cautious perspective may consider that the interests, including self-respect, of the least advantaged demand a fair distribution of wealth, requiring that the liberty of some be sacrificed to benefit the well-being of others (Wright 1977).[9]

In the same way, the situation of women and the family must be known in the general knowledge about how society works. Kearns (1983: 37) notes that it is unlikely that people with similar physical attributes will not know that they have something in common even if they do not know the significance of difference in the real world. Unlike in *A Theory of Justice*, where the parties in the original position were heads of household, which would, no doubt, restrict the representation of women as individuals (Okin 1991c: 183), the representative parties depicted in *Political Liberalism* must include an equitable proportion of women. Even in the unlikely event that gendered knowledge specific to the individual can be forgotten, representatives as individuals and in common with others like them, must be aware, before they can think about their conception of the good and equality of justice, that there is a slightly greater than fifty-fifty chance of being the sex that has the burden of the mundane maintenance of society. Moreover, Hirshman (1994: 1868) suggests that general knowledge of sexual discrimination and the potential for redress evident in collective action will mean that women in the original position 'will not deconstruct into individual bargainers when asked to set the terms of politics'.

Considered from the perspective of all the primary goods, the expectation on women to perform the majority of domestic duties limits their liberty, which further restricts their equality of opportunity in the basic structure, thus giving them less ability to maximise their income and wealth. Furthermore, such relative disadvantages arising from non-public activities must have a negative affect on self-respect, which Rawls places high in the rank ordering of primary goods (*Theory of Justice*: §67; Amdur 1980: 329; Zaino 1998: 740). It must be noted that liberty and equality of opportunity in political liberalism cannot be limited to material concerns, although difficulty with extending their analysis tends to lead to such simplification (Schwarzenbach 1991: 73). These concepts are not just about being able to command equal employment opportunities and pay. Limitation of liberty and equality of opportunity to participate in political activity restricts further representation in the policy process. This negatively affects women's opportunities, not only undermining the potential for justice as fairness to be accepted outside the original position but precluding its selection at all.

A similar irregularity exists in the major part of justice as fairness which requires the most advantaged to benefit the least advantaged in society, known as the 'difference principle' (*Theory of Justice*: §13; *Political Liberalism*: 282). The least advantaged are not identified on purely economic grounds (*Theory of Justice*: 96–7; Weatherford 1991), but from a rank ordering of primary goods (*Theory of Justice*: 91). As such, for Rawls, women as a group may not be considered the least advantaged but they will be among some of the least advantaged in society. For the difference principle to operate in justice as fairness there must not only be a way of ordering liberties, opportunities and self-respect, as well as material goods, but also of measuring their relative progression as the most advantaged improve their situation. For example, perhaps the greater tax burden imposed on the well-off and their larger contribution to the funding of public services could be given as an example of benefiting the least advantaged. A healthy, educated person with access to good transport, housing and utility services is more likely to be able to grasp opportunities open to them, given their share of primary goods, and fulfil a reasonable conception of the good. However,

Zaino (1998: 739) points out that the difference principle may well restrict the least advantaged to that status interminably. Although their situation will improve marginally with the progress of the most advantaged, there is no guarantee that this will precipitate significant, or even just, social mobility predicated on increasing shares of primary goods. Again, knowing the fundamental aspects of social organisation, the representatives in the original position are hardly likely to choose a system of justice that might consign them either to permanently making greater contributions to the less well-off, or to the group that requires perpetual indulgence.

For women the operation of the difference principle is perhaps particularly significant. The presumption that the omission of the non-public extends to individuals' shares of the primary goods cannot alleviate the fact that the non-public impacts severely on women's conceptions of the good. Women's non-public responsibilities must either lessen the amount of primary goods they can justly claim or, if everyone in the public sphere has equal shares of primary goods, women's currency is less as they have less time and opportunity to utilise them. As such, it can be claimed that women are, in fact, a distinctive part of the least advantaged group if not the most disadvantaged group per se. Therefore, the public activities of men must benefit women to at least a marginal degree if the difference principle is to operate and justice as fairness prevail.

Application of the difference principle to the public sphere rules out the argument that men's better salaries pay for women's greater liberty in the form of labour-saving domestic devices, so giving women more opportunity to participate in the public sphere. However, in public, even the smallest amount of benefit that women gain from men's better market position, whether an increase in the availability of low-paid, part time jobs or a Christmas bonus, satisfies the difference principle. The problem with this is that it concentrates on material benefits alone and does not consider the primary goods that women justly hold. Certainly the provision even of the most exploitative employment may be said, by some, to increase liberty by presenting individuals with the opportunity to earn more than they would have without such work. This liberty may be expressed by the individuals concerned as a means of subsisting and/or of other more social attributes, such as interacting with other people. Whether it can be translated into equality of opportunity is open to doubt unless women are able to improve their market position relative to that of men. And yet experience shows that women have only ever been able to do this by either sacrificing some of their liberty, for example, in choosing not to have a family, or by accepting a double burden of public and non-public activities, terms of reference that do not generally apply to men in the public sphere. Furthermore, the cardinal primary good of self-respect cannot be said to improve for women as men's advantages increase. As self-respect is externally conferred by positive affirmation from others (Shue 1975: 197; Zaino 1998: 745), women are in a precarious position apropos the difference principle. Much of the work they do is not subject to external endorsement as it is non-public, and a pat on the head in lieu of equal pay for work of equal value, or for accepting the types of employment available in a marketplace segregated by sex, cannot constitute meaningful positive affirmation. Indeed, as men's advantages increase, the self-respect of women can only decrease comparatively.

The fact is that women cannot be divided into their public and non-public selves, any more than men can. However, men can easily fit into such a segregated theory, being more aligned to the public sphere, unlike women who consistently have to function in the two spheres. Consequently, women cannot be 'symmetrically situated' in the original position, and a system of justice equally applicable to all members of society will not emanate from the procedure Rawls advocates. Without a system of justice that is able to redress such a fundamental imbalance, any conclusions of the representatives in the original position must be spurious and cannot lead to a well-ordered society based on mutuality and reciprocity between free and equal persons possessing a fair distribution of primary goods. Rather than being able to forge an overlapping consensus, the best that could be hoped for in this situation would be a *modus vivendi*, or compromise, whereby any comprehensive doctrine, including feminism, would turn circumstances to its advantage over others if the opportunity arose (*Political Liberalism*: 147). Potentially, this would further entrench comprehensive doctrines as unreasonable in Rawls' definition.

Entitlements: Natural Justice and Natural Inequality

Nozick's *Anarchy, State and Utopia* can be read throughout as a response to Rawls' *A Theory of Justice*. However, Nozick not only argues that justice as fairness and the difference principle will not achieve the ends that Rawls claims for it, he propounds an alternative view of the well-ordered society that maintains the individual as the sole object of justice. This admits no claims on individuals by others as 'individuals have rights, and there are things no person or group may do to them (without violating their rights)' (*Anarchy, State and Utopia*: ix).

Nozick's theory is fundamentally that of the free market. It ignores the possibility of shared values and objectives as well as any unifying community (Fowler 1980: 558).[10] In many ways, it propounds an unmitigated version of Locke's *Second Treatise*. Bringing the Labour

Theory of Property into the twentieth century, wherein it is less viable for individuals to mix their labour with raw resources to claim them as their own, Nozick presents a proviso that holdings are just if they are acquired fairly and if no one is worse off than they would have been had the property not been owned by others (*Anarchy, State and Utopia*: 178). This theory does not permit contingencies such as natural endowment and accidents or privileges of birth to impose on debates about justice. People are entitled to the holdings that they own through just original acquisition or transfer.[11] As in the state of nature, all individuals are equally free to pursue their interests subject to their abilities. Naturally, this negates the potential for coercive utilisation of others' skills and abilities as 'there is no justified sacrifice of some of us for others' (*Anarchy, State and Utopia*: 33). No more can a person command that someone accepts their assistance, possibly even charging for it, than can anyone demand action to be taken by other people for their own, even basic welfare, purposes. This certainly solves the problem that could occur in Rawls' system of justice as fairness which could permit 'free-riders' to benefit from the productivity of other people (Davis 1991) through the difference principle. Moreover, there is no question of individuals or representatives meeting together in a state of un-knowing, or nescience, to agree a system of justice applied to political institutions and relations that will nullify the detrimental effects of inequality. Rather, Nozick refers to the practical aspects of civil life where self-interested people will not forfeit, or risk forfeiture of, rewards that they are entitled to in the hope of a better civil order. Civil order is best protected by the maximisation of liberty for individuals to acquire holdings, being restricted only if actions violate the rights of others, by minimal rules and regulations that are agreed by citizens in relation to rights protection.

Deduction from the premises that no person has a claim on any others, despite inherent inequalities and the material and social differentials that accrue from them, leads to the conclusion that the state can have little function without violating the rights of individuals. Indeed, this is the crux of Nozick's thesis. Liberal theories err when they allow the state to perform more than 'the narrow functions of protection against force, theft, fraud, enforcement of contracts and so on' (*Anarchy, State and Utopia*: ix). Nozick's narration of the development of the dominant protective agency, later identified as the minimal state, perceives all institutional relationships as voluntary, based only on the protection of property.[12] Given that a demand by anyone for more than their entitlements requires a transfer of holdings to them that is tantamount to a violation of rights, and that no person would risk having their rights violated by someone else's demands on them, no member would have agreed to the protective agency doing any more than what is necessary to preserve their rights. This will include the restriction of actions by other people that might violate their rights and restitution for violations that occur, as well as an insurance policy to cover claims against them for alleged violations. No provision of welfare would be included, this effectively comprising a transfer of holdings to those unable to provide for themselves.[13] For Nozick, the framework provided through the limited jurisdiction of the state enhances individual freedom, giving people the liberty to distribute or preserve their talents and assets as they wish, as well as permitting freedom of association, choice of lifestyle and the full rewards of choices made.

The attempt to revert almost to a contemporary state of nature, defined in terms of freedom, could invoke some optimism among feminists. Justice based on entitlement may not equalise holdings between women and men, but it would render women able to utilise their inherent talents and any inherited holdings to pursue their interests. In such circumstances universal sex inequalities could be surmounted, leaving only the more indiscriminate, but just, differentials of the free market.[14] Again, however, this raises the familiar problem of just outcomes of equal treatment in the absence of basic socio-political equality, so evident in the twentieth century as political relationships have expanded and become more publicised. It is not simply that casting women loose in a free market fails to address the disadvantages that their non-market responsibilities and relationships pose in competitive situations. In addition, Nozick effectively recreates the argument, familiar from Plato to Rousseau, that women's natural rights are less than men's. Emphasis on entitlement can only interpret the universality of women's lesser holdings as integral to their being.

The No-Contract Society: Sleight of Mind

Nozick parts company with Locke's theory most obviously in that the liberal state requires compliance with a social contract to which existing citizens were not party. As the liberal state has developed, it has taken on more than the justifiable role of the minimal state, further diminishing its legitimacy in terms of agreement between citizens and the state. Consequently, in liberal states all citizens are forced to act in ways that they might not choose to do, so restricting their liberty. It may be ascertained, then, that any universal contracts are unjust. Indeed, within the minimal state, as in any free market, only direct agreements, or contracts, between involved parties are just. Nozick's hypothetical example of the extrication from the 'obligation' to devote a day to operating a public address system that requires a donation of one day's work from each member of a community explains how, under the framework theory, people are relieved from the burdens that society places on them in the form of tacit contracts and obligations (*Anarchy, State and Utopia*: 93–4). Individuals need act only if the benefits of an action outweigh the costs to them (Bell 1978: 66).

When such arguments are applied to parenthood,[15] the assumptions accruing to motherhood, especially, require revision. The role of mother is relevant not only to family but to society; in particular, the benefits accruing from the aspects of motherhood that relate to housekeeping extend to individual men, not only as husbands but as economic actors, as well as to the economy and social order. Moreover, the moral imperatives of motherhood regarding childrearing have inestimable social ramifications. In other words, motherhood in many ways implies a social contract. While this may be unavoidable, it is unjust for the minimal state to act in such a way that makes it more viable for women to take on the major burden of domestic and parental responsibilities. In relation to the family unit, the framework can only be said to operate justly by recourse to nature, and women's overbearing desire to limit their own freedom in pursuit of the higher happiness achieved by subjecting themselves to the dependence required if they are to care for children at all. However, Nozick, like Rawls, attempts to circumvent situations of contemporary society that contradict his theory. As Rawls can always respond to fundamental inequalities that prevent full and fair participation in the public sphere as just from a situation of procedural justice, so too Nozick resorts to the concept of compensation for acts that individuals are prohibited from undertaking if the dominant protective agency perceives them as endangering, or potentially endangering, its members (*Anarchy, State and Utopia*: 78–9). Applied to women, the costs to society of asserting their rights to maximum freedom in relation to their abilities could quite legitimately allow the minimal state to restrict their actions as long as they were sufficiently compensated. What would constitute sufficient compensation for limitations to a single act is difficult to ascertain in any circumstances (*Anarchy, State and Utopia*: 63–5), but when the restrictions have implications over a lifetime, the task becomes much more difficult.

Nozick identifies two types of compensation, full and market. Full compensation may be defined as nominal in that it is sufficient to acknowledge that there has been a restriction on liberty without replacing the loss by other means. Alternatively, market compensation is negotiated between parties providing a more direct link between the loss and the restitution (*Anarchy, State and Utopia*: 68; Nock 1992: 686–7). Of course, if harmful acts are to be prevented from occurring, the negotiation has to be prior to the event. Nozick acknowledges that this is unlikely to achieve a proper level of compensation as the full costs or effects of prohibition cannot be completely anticipated (*Anarchy, State and Utopia*: 68). For women, who effectively alter their entire way of life to meet the requirements placed on them by the demands of motherhood and its social obligations, calculating an accurate level of compensation would prove exceptionally difficult.

It could be argued that prohibiting women's actions that could harm others through, for example, neglect, is adequately compensated, certainly over the period of restriction by the provision of shelter, food and the comforts of family life, having been negotiated as an agreement not to pursue self-interests but to rear children. On the other hand, the pressure on women to conform to traditional roles once children are produced suggests that the agreement is prior even to their existence and is, thus, assumed. And yet, it has already been established by Nozick that obligations cannot be enforced to which individuals have not agreed directly. As Nock (1992: 687) notes, in situations such as this, where choice is unavailable, a violation of rights occurs. The solution is given by removing the option of compensating acts, the fear of which cannot be placated, and making them 'prohibited and punishable' (*Anarchy, State and Utopia*: 66). Therefore, it becomes unnecessary even to compensate women for the violation of their rights imposed by the need for caring and domestic services and their related social consequences.

While compensation is a means to redress violations of rights, or infringements on individuals' borders, it is actually unlikely that it need even be considered for women who consistently have fewer entitlements, and whose actions are circumscribed by their social responsibilities. For example, reference to natural endowments, including women's smaller physiques and 'different psychology', might still be used to account for the historical form of family relationships and sociopolitical repercussions. If this is so, the distribution of male owners and senior employees, together with their higher earnings, would entitle them to holdings accumulated as a consequence. Women are equally entitled to the holdings that they acquire fairly even if these are usually less than those of men. The reproductive endowments of women cannot be used to ascertain women's unjust inequality, even in terms of remuneration for work. If they choose to utilise this natural capacity they must accept that it will limit their liberty and entitlements. Furthermore, if women choose to enter an association with men in families, their lesser holdings may well restrict their entitlements within the household. This cannot necessarily be translated as men's entitlement to a family, but it certainly justifies the dominance of men in a household and beyond. In the framework of the dominant protective agency, then, women choose the 'community' of wives and mothers, their entitlements protected by the agency but having no recourse to the agency to redress differential holdings and the privileges these accrue.

Another way of considering the predicament of women within the entitlement theory is that women are actually born with fewer rights attached to them. This certainly aligns with the lesser entitlements that women universally experience. As Nozick invokes the state of nature as his starting point for considering the acceptable level of state intervention (*Anarchy, State and Utopia*: 11; Biesenthal 1978: 161; Kavka 1991: 300), an assumption must be made that, as with the seventeenth century liberal philosophers, despite inherent and accumulated differences in physical and mental capacities, all individuals are equally able to pursue their interests. The logical conclusion to be drawn from the fact that women consistently have fewer holdings than men, therefore, is that their natural assets actually entitle them to less and that the rights of women, attached to the person, are fewer than those of men. Indeed, when reliance is made on natural rights theory, as in *Anarchy, State and Utopia*, the most logical conclusion concerning inequality, especially on a mass scale such as class or sex, is that rights distributions are naturally unequal between groups as well as individuals. As a result, there is no action that can be taken to benefit less advantaged individuals and groups without violating the natural rights of others, and neither men nor the state can be held responsible for the result of sexual inequalities (Biesenthal 1978: 157). Indeed, Nozick maintains that it is only envy that motivates demands for redistribution as 'people generally judge themselves by how they fall along the most important dimensions in which they *differ* from others' (*Anarchy, State and Utopia*: 243)(original emphasis).[16] Logically then, feminism is an ideology of jealousy, and women claiming equal rights make unjust demands on fellow citizens to redistribute what is rightfully theirs by entitlement.

In ironing out the anomalies of liberal theory, and maintaining the libertarianism of the state of nature within civil society, Nozick has managed to create a system that should permit maximisation of self-interest within a framework that protects rights. As with liberalism, it is able to claim equality in terms of entitlements to liberty and holdings while remaining steadfast in the view that distribution of goods cannot be uniform. Therefore, any action to equalise distribution, even by common consent, cannot be described as just. The omission of specific reference to women from *Anarchy, State and Utopia* must be accepted as a statement of the equality of women within the framework. After all, in the state of nature women were able to maintain themselves and compete with men for resources as equals. So too, without the overt declaration of exclusion, in the minimal state they should be able to uphold, or return to, this tradition. For Nozick, the fact that women have fewer holdings can be translated only as their lesser entitlements resulting from fewer rights. However, Davis (1991) argues that Nozick's theory can be interpreted as leading to a form of welfare through its universal provision of protection and by maintaining the infrastructure of the framework through economies of scale unavailable with private provision. Therefore, far from being left to manage within the framework and sustaining lesser holdings through just entitlements, it could be reasoned, especially as the minimal state imposes conditions on women, that their disadvantages should be expressly considered within Nozickean theory. Without so doing, the claims to justice cannot be legitimately postulated.

Post-feminism: The Philosophers' Stone

Despite their very clear differences, Rawls' and Nozick's theories of justice show remarkable similarities. Both admit that inequality of holdings is just, provided certain conditions apply to them, and both understand that the focus of justice is the individual with rights that cannot be violated (MacIntyre 1992). For both philosophers, holdings and rights are the legitimate subject of just procedure. For Rawls, rights are conceived in the original position and applied to the basic structure of society, including political and economic institutions. Nozick perceives holdings as contingent on rights attached to the person and, therefore, incapable of being legitimately subjected to consideration of, or by, anyone else except in instances of alleged or potential violation. Moreover, unlike their predecessors, both must be assumed to incorporate women fully into their theories. The reasons for this assumption are that neither overtly excludes women, and the society about which they are theorising demonstrates a greater level of female participation than previous philosophers would have experienced. The imperative to argue the equality of fundamental concepts did not require provisos in the twentieth century as it did in the seventeenth.

Women hold a peculiar status in contemporary political philosophy. While implicitly they are not omitted, the failure to analyse the effect of their historical exclusion and pre-ordained responsibilities on theory, and therefore, anticipated practice, means that implicitly they cannot be fully included either. This curious suspension between being addressed as legitimate citizens and women's more usual invisibility cannot be sufficiently exonerated by reference to their status in society. The fact that more women in twentieth-century, western liberal democracies have a public profile, attain high positions in public service as well as private business, and are employed in greater numbers, does not necessarily equate with their achieving equality in justice. Certainly by the procedural standards of justice as fairness, the continuing gender imbalance in public office, pay differentials and restricted opportunities, means that justice cannot genuinely be claimed for women. This is not a reference to inequality amongst individuals, who may well be as free as anyone to pursue their interests within their distribution of primary goods, but between the gendered halves of the population which persistently experience an unequal distribution of primary goods. Moreover, the assumption that competitive markets are open to all, with freedom of choice regarding lifestyles and associations within a neutral framework enforcing contracts, does not address fundamental factors that prevent the market operating fairly for all. Contemporary philosophers should be obliged to consider the differential impact that their ideas might have on women. Even the nineteenth-century philosophers specifically addressed the issue of women's potentially equal status, arguing that their historical exclusion was politically motivated as opposed to natural. If political philosophers like Nozick and Rawls wish to propound equality in basic variables relevant to humanity, they must be able to demonstrate its feasibility in all pertinent permutations. This cannot be done by separating off and ignoring the relevance of the private, non-public sphere from activities and relationships in the public, political world.

Of course, it might be argued that, considering the advances made by women, it is acceptable to concentrate universal theories of justice on the public sphere. However, recourse to 'post-feminism' was not a possibility for Nozick. When he wrote *Anarchy, State and Utopia* feminism was enjoying possibly its most auspicious period. Women were clearly articulating how inequalities were manifested and socially perpetuated. As such, Nozick should have clarified the relevance of his theory to women at the time. On the other hand, it could be proposed that the social movements concerned with race and sex equality may have provided a motivation for a theory of natural endowments and politico-economic justice. Rather than explicitly stating the case for women's full equality, justification of inequality and the illegitimacy of claims for indemnity would be in order. While Rawls' first major opus comes from the same era as *Anarchy, State and Utopia*, and attracted feminist criticism, his later work implies a post-feminist standpoint merely by enveloping gender equality, along with race equality, within the theory (*Political Liberalism*: xxxi). The problem here is that, without having addressed the issues that feminism was raising at the time when Rawls must have been formulating his theory, the leap to post-feminism is somewhat precocious, and dubious. More likely, both Rawls and Nozick preferred not to consider the relation of women to their theories, and their liberal premises disguise the potential for continuation of the customary exclusion of women. If they had so considered women, the intricacies of the private sphere would have further complicated the already complex ideas they wanted to propound. Moreover, any attempt to apply their theories to the situation of historically excluded groups would have demonstrated the androcratic nature of their ideas.

While the nineteenth-century philosophers appeared to advance political thought in their inclusion of women, Rawls and Nozick effectively symbolise a return to the past. The liberalism they advocate is, in many ways, a more consummate form than that of the seventeenth and eighteenth centuries, socio-political development indicating the deficiencies of, for example, Locke's and Rousseau's theories. However, like the earlier liberal thinkers, contemporary philosophers find it difficult to render liberalism fully inclusive. Much as earlier theorists found it impossible to deliver comprehensive theories because the socio-economic situation of the masses made the concept of equality, and therefore full participation, impracticable, so do contemporary philosophers appear to find the concept of women and equality. Moreover, as, historically, political theory has been used to maintain a certain level of elite politics under the guise of universal sovereignty, so the 'post-feminist' umbrella, under which women are implicitly incorporated as equally sovereign individuals, maintains androcracy. The absence of analysis of the different relations of women to the public sphere disavows claims to universality and accommodation of diversity. If equality in justice is to be argued, and the precepts of liberalism properly instilled, then injustice, in all its guises, must be fully considered, despite the tide of history and custom rendering certain forms of injustice 'normal'.

Notes

1. Where women or gender are referred to in *Political Liberalism* (p. xxxi) it is to claim that revisions of Rawls' theory accommodate sex and race differences. In *Anarchy, State and Utopia* (p. 273) Nozick mentions women only to illustrate an example of legitimate choice and the inappropriateness of external intervention.
2. Throughout *Political Liberalism*, Rawls acknowledges many 'mainstream' critics and responds to them directly. However, despite obvious responses to feminist criticism, the honour of direct confirmation of its contribution to his theory's revision is never made (Frazer and Lacey 1995: 234fn).
3. Maximisation of interests implies the dominance of wants and desires regardless of the circumstances from which these are derived. However, the conception of the good tempers such unbridled interests by noting that they can be realised only with reference to the share of primary goods an individual holds. As such, a rational plan is to maximise the share of primary goods that an individual holds. This requires adaption and change of individuals' conception of the good according to the circumstances, in which they find themselves (*Theory of Justice*: §63; *Political Liberalism*:

82–3). As circumstances change, so do individuals' share of primary goods.

4. Rawls specifically uses the term 'non-political' to distinguish it from 'private'. Included in the non-political sphere would be such public things as religious organisations, businesses and 'leisure' clubs. This distinction neatly excludes the private organisation of the family. However, possibly as an ill-thought-out response to feminist criticism about the anomaly of unjust families and their relation to the public sphere, Rawls confuses the issue by stating that the family is part of the basic structure of society (*Political Liberalism*: 258; Frazer and Lacey 1995: 241). As such, it is argued that if intervention in non-public organisations is permissible to teach constitutional and civil liberties in order to maintain the basic structure, then justice as fairness must be allowed some impact on the family (Okin 1994; Frazer and Lacey 1995: 242–3).

5. For reasons concerned with the unviability and remoteness of the original position, it has been criticised as being hypothetical and non-historical (Neal 1987: 403; Ball 1993; 165). Rawls counters this in *Political Liberalism* (p. 24), by noting that the significance of the original position is its representative function.

6. This is likened to cutting a cake so that the last person to take a slice, the cutter, is ensured of the same size slice as all other consumers (*Theory of Justice*: 85; Marty 1981).

7. Individuals' rational life plans are sometimes referred to by Rawls as the 'thin' conception of the good (*Theory of Justice*: §60). People who manage to adhere only to this stage are not necessarily unjust or otherwise socially deficient, they are seen as rationally autonomous. However, fully autonomous individuals (*Political Liberalism*: 77) observe a 'thick' conception of the good in which their rational plans are integrated into the full social system of justice as fairness.

8. A sense of justice is not absorbed merely by being in a just society, although the just and well-ordered society is necessary for its development. Rather, individuals learn a sense of justice through the moral authority of the family. This then operates in social and associational relationships, leading to an understanding that reciprocated, just relations are deserving of perpetuation (*Theory of Justice*: 462–79). 'Being governed by these principles means that we want to live with others on terms that everyone would recognise as fair from a perspective that all would accept as reasonable' (*Theory of Justice*: 478).

9. Marty (1981) gives an example of two men on a desert island, one industrious and the other not. Under justice as fairness, the man who cultivates land and produces food is required not only to give half of his existing produce to the non-worker, but has to increase the amount of his contribution as his productivity rises. The question is posed whether the worker would find the distribution just when out of the veil of ignorance.

10. '[But] there is no *social entity* with a good that undergoes some sacrifice for its own good. There are only individual people, different individual people, with their own individual lives' (*Anarchy, State and Utopia*: 32–3)(original emphasis).

11. In many cases it is not possible to ascertain the conditions of original acquisition. Moreover, history informs us that many transfers of property, whether originally acquired fairly or not, certainly do not meet the criteria of the principle of justice in transfer (O'Neill 1976: 473). For such cases, Nozick briefly acknowledges a retributive principle without presenting details of its operation or outcome. Lund (1996: 121) suggests that retribution, or restitution, implies the imposition of inheritance taxes, thus intimating a more than minimal, redistributive role for the state.

12. The development of the state from a state of nature is described more fully in Chapter 2.

13. One of the criteria for the dominant protective agency having the status of minimal state is that it provides its services for all people within its territory. As such it would provide cover for independent individuals unable to afford its services in the case of a claim by one of its members. Nozick acknowledges that this could be perceived as a form of redistribution, members' 'subscriptions', or taxes, providing for *pro bono* cases. However, 'such provision need not be redistributive since it can be justified on other than redistributive grounds, namely, those provided in the principle of compensation' (*Anarchy, State and Utopia*: 114).

14. Criticism of women's relation to the free market is given in Chapter 2. This analysis deals only with the more general aspects of justice in Nozick's framework theory.

15. Marriage may still be perceived as a contract made between two parties, compared to parenthood which has implications affecting more remote social actors.

16. The concern with envy replies to Rawls' assertion that procedural justice maximises individuals' self-esteem. It is only in comparison with others regarding specific criteria that it is possible to measure self-worth, or value. 'The most promising ways for a society to avoid widespread differences in self-esteem would be to have no common weighting of dimensions; instead it would have a diversity of different lists of dimensions and of weightings' (*Anarchy, State and Utopia*: 245).

Chapter 10: Never Decreasing Circles: The Legacy of Political Philosophy

Whether to transform or to restore political order, the task that political philosophers undertake is to find solutions to the problems besetting, or threatening, the states in which they live. Inevitably, immediate concerns concentrate the mind on conspicuous issues and events leading to distinct, and in many ways obvious, solutions, for example, instituting a verifiable source of legitimacy to counter threats to the state and civil order posed by the divine right of kings. Direct solutions to evident political problems may furnish political stability. According to Fukuyama's thesis (1992), the success of established western liberal democracies is witness to this. However, in their hypothetical forms, as propounded by the philosophers, they explicitly exclude many members of the state. Some effort may be given to justifying such exclusion on the grounds that certain types or groups of people do not meet the criteria designated for full citizenship, the prerequisite for legitimate problem-solving at state level. For the philosophers, of course, this does not inhibit the fulfilment of their ideals, nor does it constitute an explicit form of injustice within their otherwise potentially just models. But, for those people less convinced of the astuteness of decision-makers in incorporating 'pertinent' needs, and also for those who perceive a clear pattern in the type of person and the qualities selected for inclusion in the legitimising as well as the governing echelon, questions are raised concerning the justice of selection and, ultimately, the comprehensiveness and authentic application of the theories.

What philosophers fail to demonstrate in assuming the limited parameters and relationships of citizenship, is that the people who meet the criteria for belonging to the citizenry, with all this implies for the legitimacy of rulers and their decisions, actually act in the interests of the common wealth; that their interests and those of 'the state' are congruous. Without challenge, who is to argue that the interests of the propertied, male, head of household are the most appropriate, just and equitable? Similarly, there is no attempt by philosophers to consider the effects of a more inclusive full citizenship. Certainly, at a pragmatic level, political philosophers are arguing that too little citizenship causes or permits arbitrary rule and endangers the state; whereas too much would probably have the same effect as a multitude of ill-informed and vested interests vie for supremacy. What is argued for is enough citizenship to bestow legitimacy on rulers to enable the perception of just rule. Little credence is given, by most of the philosophers, to the idea that the interests of husbands and wives might be consonant, or that women's presence in the citizenry would not sabotage the tenets of the moral, unified, democratic *polis*, or the liberal state, or weaken the revolutionary spirit. More baneful is the neglect of reflection on the possibility that women might, indeed, have different interests to contribute to, rather than oppose, the affairs of the common wealth, or that they might claim a different perspective on the interests of property, household and the state that would add to the quality and legitimacy of citizens' decisions.

It is folly not to reflect on issues of exclusion and its effects on the comprehensiveness of relations between the state and citizens in contemporary western societies where more women, including mothers, are choosing not to marry or to marry later in life, where women have jobs and careers, own property and run businesses, and are endowed with formal legal rights, including the right to vote and to stand for political office. Following an era in which the legitimacy gap between rulers and ruled has had to be addressed, as the working classes no longer accepted the integrity and universal cognition of a limited citizenry, and when it would be insupportable for rich countries not to provide welfare or accessible services for those in need, women have been included in a new political *rapprochement*. 'Feminist' or 'women's' interests, such as women's health issues, childcare, positive action and affirmative discrimination in the workplace and political processes, have been included on political agendas. However, the expedient politics of observable inclusion does not admit the genuine justice of acknowledging women as equal citizens in their own right. Firstly, the fact that interests are identified with the prefix 'women's' or 'feminist' suggests that they are not perceived as integral to the common wealth, and that women's rights are residual and subject to repeal if necessary.[1] Moreover, women's relationship to the state is more usually considered with respect to their public activities, interest and legislation on 'women's issues' in the private sphere being woefully tardy, incomplete and weak. Despite the politic concession that women's domestic activities are essential to the state, even as women routinely manage both domestic and public activities, they are still perceived as belonging outside the political domain.

Notwithstanding the achievements of women, especially in the twentieth century and alongside extensive political change, the agenda set by political philosophers, from Plato to Nozick, prevails, at the expense of fundamental inclusiveness and the potential for real scrutiny of the notion of comprehensive citizenship and state. The contiguous and relatively homogeneous nature of political philosophy has resulted in standards that must be adhered to in the practice of politics. Failure to do so represents the threat that philosophers through the ages have fought to defend against: disharmony, disorder, insecurity and instability. For women to be permitted to join the citizenry, they have had to prove that they can fit the model of citizen that has been presented historically; that which is based on the economically active, rational, and so-called value-free male (Narayan 1997: 48; Baker 1999: 4). Thus, pragmatic politics satisfies the substance of creating 'enough citizenship' without considering, or disturbing, the main tenets of its underpinning philosophies. Women can be included as citizens without endangering the legitimacy of androcratic rule by introducing too many new interests at a level that cannot be accommodated.

Women Citizens and the State: A Precarious Relationship

The division of the public, political arena from the private, domestic sphere that essentially defines relationships in the state has never been strictly adhered to by political philosophers, despite advocacy of such a separation. Emphasis on the home as the breeding ground for good citizens, and for hard-working and law-abiding members of the state, confers the status 'political' on that arena. However, the fact that men are usually given jurisdiction over the household, even Locke giving men the final say on issues of dispute in the home, precludes women from political designation. Dependence on women to maintain the good state is not translated into their citizenship; they are expected to labour for the good of the state without a say in its affairs.

A possible conclusion to be drawn from analysis of the state as androcratic and, consequently, androcentric, is that the state per se is bad for women and that, whatever its constitution, they would be better without it. A response to this might be that women have never actually been a legitimate part of the state, in which case we have no way of knowing that a properly constituted and inclusive state would be disadvantageous. Indeed, although Rousseau, Hobbes and Locke refer to families as the first societies existing within the state of nature, Rousseau even intimating that women's cunning lured men into this unnatural association, the evidence could suggest that women have, in fact, always existed in a form of state of nature. The way that philosophers construct the state, in which women are precluded from property ownership, forfeits their need for protection by the state. As the state developed to regulate relations and behaviour between freely maximising, property-owning individuals, then women have no need for, or place in, the state. Moreover, if the state provides a legal framework to regulate property exchanges, then, as unpropertied and non-public actors, relationships with which women are involved in society remain unprotected by the law. Their struggle for survival, while no longer resembling the purely animal instinct of dodging the odd interloper and foraging for food, requires cleaving to rules, determined by others, to maintain their and their offspring's security. Avoiding the territoriality and terrorism of self-seeking, atomistic individuals ensuring their own survival is replaced by performing tasks well enough to avoid the wrath of the men in their household and the territorial behaviours of those beyond. A 'loose' woman, or a poor housekeeper, can be disengaged from the household and left to manage alone.

In the twenty-first century such scenarios may appear somewhat Dickensian. However, the feminisation of poverty and the vagaries of legal and welfare systems that still assume women are cared for by men who earn a family wage (Lewis and Åström 1997; Lister 1997), together with relatively closed political institutions and processes, leave many women in a recognisable and unenviable situation of fending for themselves and their dependants as best they can, while the state provides only a basic minimum as required by the 'ethics' of contemporary politics. As Schochet (1975: 25) notes, the state of nature was not perceived as ubiquitous; it existed somewhere, but not universally, at all times (*Leviathan*: 65; *Two Treatises*: 124). Consequently, the concept of women existing in a form of state of nature within contemporary states is not infeasible.

An alternative interpretation of the development of the state is that, as the philosophers argue, women are separate but equal members, having their own contributions to make in assuring security and stability. However, in many situations in contemporary societies, women are certainly not 'separate' in that they are public actors; and they are not equal, having also to endure the traditional expectations that philosophers and politicians traditionally place on them in maintaining the good and secure state. Obviously, this is reflected in public sphere relations where, whatever their occupation, rank and performance, women are routinely disadvantaged by their circumstances and the reputation that accompanies their gendered status. Moreover, public policy reinforces the primary parenting role of women, and their unequal status as citizens, by provision of support services for working mothers, not usually for fathers (Baker 1999: 11). Similarly, parental leave for caring for sick children is primarily targeted at working women, paternity leave being considered rather 'odd' by employers, with male economic advantages making it less attractive than historical care patterns (Lister 1997: 181).

An explanation for the continuing recourse to the separate but equal argument for disparity between the sexes is that, almost a century after being permitted citizenship status, for women this is still only a 'formal' rather than authentic, public arrangement. In other words, women may be citizens but they are not sovereign individuals with the liberty, self-possession and veneration that is implied in philosophers' expositions of the concept. This contention is supported by the demands of women for genuine equal rights in the context of, for example, differential treatment before the law (Walklate 1995; Edwards 1996; Kelly 1999),[2] the continued demands for equal pay for work of equal value,[3] the right to recruitment and promotion on the same criteria as men without implicit reference to their sex, and the right to participate in political institutions and processes without the stigma of being an electoral or political liability.[4] The spirit of the age might require toleration of women in traditionally male preserves, so contributing to an observable concession to women's right to equal status. However, it does not demand acceptance of such. Indeed, the repeal of measures to achieve equal opportunities for women in Britain during the 1980s and 1990s[5] (Sperling 1998: 479; Baker 1999: 13), the reaction to girl's and women's higher educational,[6] and sometimes occupational, achievements, and the blaming of women for social breakdown (Etzioni 1993), all point to the 'fact' that if only women accepted their traditional place in the state, the regretful politics of rising expectations, with its associated break-down of civil order, manifested in, for example, youth and adult crime, illegal drug usage and promiscuity, would have been avoided.

The State: Can't Live With It – Can't Live Without It

Despite their precarious relationship to the state, women, like other members of the state, need a framework for regulating socio-political and economic relations and providing whatever psychological benefits, in terms of a sense of belonging and security, membership brings. The problem lies in identifying the aspects of state-citizen relationships that require incorporation, where the integration of public and private activities occurs, and establishing acceptable levels of legitimate state intervention where necessary, to ensure that women's contribution to the structure and development of the framework is consolidated. In other words, the public-private divide must not only be realigned, or abolished, to provide women with the security and protection of the state, but also supplanted in a way which places women's sovereignty on the same level as other citizens. Whether this is coterminous with 'the personal is political' has been keenly debated by feminists (Elshtain 1991; Okin 1991b; Dietz 1998). So has the concept of the state protecting women, when it has clearly not only neglected this responsibility, but does not genuinely acknowledge such an obligation (Presley and Kinsky 1991; Mies 1998: 26; Pateman 1988).

It could be argued that, as political philosophers have constructed the division between the public and private, and politicians exploited it to their advantage, it can be dismantled. Of course, it would require time before new ways of thinking about the state as an integrated entity became fully accepted, and the assignation of 'soft' and 'hard' politics to so-called gendered interests ceased. However, this should not deter action if the common wealth is to benefit. Reaching the position in which women's citizenship is fully integrated would be more trouble-some, requiring men to relinquish their dominance in positions of power. To ensure the full conflation of public and private spheres that would herald comprehensive citizenship, women have to be at the heart of the structures and processes that influence socio-political develop-ments and progress. The problem with such a form of discontinuance of the public-private divide, if it were at all possible, would be that, although it was only an invention of men, it is clearly not without significance. It has effectively defined a gendered normality within states and socio-political relationships that has been ingrained in most female and male psyches as well as in political institutions and pro-cesses. Any group that is 'other', whether by definition of their gender, sexuality, race, class, physicality or skin colour, is only too aware that when demanding their rights as citizens, they are contesting social and political 'norms'. The pervasiveness of the public-private divide makes it exceedingly difficult to conceive a means to achieve its abolition, or the elimination of its discriminatory consequences, even if the ends can be more readily hypothesised.

Unlike androcratic political philosophies that are able to build a description of the state based on male experience, feminist thinkers and politicians do not have the convenience of alluding to a genuinely gender-balanced state of nature and simply starting again. The oppor-tunity of avoiding or contesting the development of illogical arguments that create and justify women's exclusion from citizenship, and the implication that this has for contemporary politics, does not present itself. Furthermore, the ubiquitous nature of the public-private division practically ensures that attempting to ignore or evade it will change little in terms of women's overall relation to the state. For example, creating non-authoritarian substitutes for government services, such as self-help clinics and childcare centres run by and for women (Presley and Kinsky 1991), replicates the gendered separation of private and public that is familiar through political philosophy. In the absence of state provision, women have always had to support each other independently. For example, mothers in paid employment have historically been forced to manage childcare through 'informal' means, such as reliance on older children, grandmothers, neighbours and private employment of child-minders; care for the sick and elderly has been women's responsibility; control of reproductive technologies and abortion resided in medicine women or back-street sympathisers/profiteers; and even responsibility for recording women's history has traditionally been women's, through storytelling rather than books. Indeed, the absence of services for women has precipitated demands that the state should provide them, and that women should be able to participate in the decision-making processes that decide the substance of state provision and, therefore, levels of acceptable intervention.

Separatist services run in parallel to state provision are more likely to enable androcratic politics and politicians to persist without challenge, rather than providing a solution to the exclusive androcentricity, and concomitant injustices, of the state. Women, as workers, taxpayers, moral guardians and providers of sustenance and care for the popula-tion, must surely be entitled to the services required to enable them to perform all the tasks demanded of them if only in a pragmatic sense, without recourse to philosophical argument. Moreover, rejection of political institutions and structures does not entirely disengage women from them. As Watson (1990: 5) states, women's groups and service providers are often dependent on the state for funding as well as for their authority. This is not to denigrate or dismiss attempts to provide alternatives to state provision for women who want to utilise them. If they raise awareness of deficiencies in state policy, and if they empower women to perceive themselves and demand their rights as sovereign citizens, then they are part of the solution to the gendered legitimacy gap. However, while not advocating purely liberal feminist solutions to the discrimination intrinsic to the public-private divide, the prevailing structures and processes that must be influenced are built on an admixture of liberal and democratic ideas, and it is to these that the objectives of inclusiveness, by whatever method and underlying phi-losophy they are informed, must be directed.

The elimination or evasion of the public-private divide is not feasible, nor a required option, for many feminists. For example, Elshtain (1991: 63), argues that the closure of public and private would leave nowhere, and no activities, safe from possible intervention by the state. The danger of women being subject to androcentric policies and practices would continue but, whereas the absence of law or policy in certain intimate areas of the domestic sphere may be said to provide some security for women, this would no longer be the case. In addition, it can be argued that the removal of the public-private division would not necessarily guarantee the acceptance of women as political contributors in their own right. The alignment of traditional public issues with 'hard' politics accorded great significance, versus the 'soft' private politics of domestic and domestic-related interests, would not evaporate with socio-political amalgamation. For political thinkers like Elshtain and Gilligan, who advocate a social feminist philosophy (see Baumeister 2000: 54), women's identity is ingrained in the status and duties, indeed the accomplishments, they historically exercise, as well as in the undeniable natural biological functions that distinguish female and male. Accordingly, social feminists argue that these should be acknowledged and incorporated into the political agenda. Instead of abolishing the public-private divide, the narrow parameters of the state should be broadened to incorporate the social, as opposed to the private, aspects of the state. In this way, whatever issues are perceived as indisputably private and which, subsequently, should not be subject to intervention by the state, remain so. However, wherever interests and concerns traditionally perceived as the realm of private individuals are acknowledged as relevant to the state, they can be incorporated in public sphere deliberation and activity. By these means, the common wealth will be better served, as the social interests of women and men traditionally claimed as separate from the state exert their humanising effects on the public sphere (Elshtain 1991). In contrast to Locke who, while unable to distinguish between parental and paternal power, could not sanction either as relevant to politics, social feminism brings parental thinking, indeed maternal thinking, firmly into the public realm.

In advocating a socio-political/private divide, social, or maternal, feminist theory addresses many aspects of the situation of women in contemporary western societies. That working mothers should be able to influence public policy and 'humanise' the public sphere, and that non-employed women should influence the political agenda as they interact with the public sphere, is indisputable. What the theory fails to argue is the propriety of political ideas that place primacy for domestic concerns with women and, ultimately, arrest their full citizenship and equal sovereignty. The identification of interests as 'social' rather than 'political' does not challenge the gendered status quo that determines 'hard' and 'soft' politics or public and private, and the politicisation of the social remains unconsidered (Dietz 1998: 58). Indeed, this theory does not situate the social and the political equally: the status of social interests within the political realm cannot be guaranteed while a private sphere to which they can be pushed, indeed rightfully belong, exists. As Okin (1991b: 77) notes, the use of distinct spheres entrenches the attitudes towards the actors in each, reinforcing the gendered division of society and politics. Moreover, the division protects certain undesirable aspects of private relationships from political and public scrutiny, as the continuing incidence of domestic violence and abuse testifies. In other words, relabelling concepts and shifting the boundaries between the public and private may widen the interests that constitute 'politics', but they do not equalise the importance of newly admitted issues. Nor do they present previously excluded groups with the ability or opportunity to challenge traditional concepts of politics.

Perhaps instead of ignoring or moving the public-private divide, it would be possible to 'work through' and overcome its discriminatory effects. As Baker (1999: 23) argues, the public-private distinction is an essential element of the dialogue that women and men, rulers and ruled, have to engage with if gender equality is to be achieved and the philosophies consummated. Unfortunately, the depth and breadth of androcracy means that women do not often have the luxury of making representations to decision-makers and administrators who understand them. At best, women and their demands or needs can be assimilated into and by traditional fora; they can only be added-in to existing templates, effectively requiring them to mould their needs to suit available existing, or obvious, solutions. Therefore, as Phillips (1998) argues, the politics of ideas must be combined with the politics of presence: women must be present in democratic institutions to articulate and implement the objectives of women, and men, in wider fora. To ensure that politics incorporates new demands from a different experience and history requires people throughout the system to introduce structures and processes which take account of their language and experience.

In many respects, this has begun to happen. Whereas political philosophers have excluded women from the three basic echelons of the state, government, administration and common membership,[7] decision-makers in liberal democracies are recognising that they can no longer exclude women. As women have been officially admitted to public office, including state officialdom, more of them have reached decision-making and administrative positions, thus providing some opportunity for institutional support for change, whether this is initiated at institutional and/or grassroots level. More women, as individuals and 'serialities' (Young 1997a), are making evident their dissatisfaction with their traditional, historically and universally endorsed, roles. For example, they are not marrying and producing children, or are doing so later in life; maintaining careers when in life partnerships; and rejecting heterosexuality and male definitions of femininity. Other women are now in place to interpret this in policy deliberation. Thus, research in Australia demonstrates the effectiveness of so-called 'femocracy', in which women civil servants act to channel grassroots activism into gender-sensitive policy implementation (Watson 1990; Pringle and Watson 1992). Similarly, women's policy networks in the European Union, including women in national and transnational networks, have succeeded in influencing policy and implementation agendas (Hoskyns 1994; Sperling and Bretherton 1996). Indeed, the work of such networks, and the realisation that there is much more to achieve, has culminated in the European Union's strategy of 'mainstreaming', in which gender is intended to be integrated into all policy initiatives by means of gender-auditing (Beveridge, Nott and Stephen: undated).[8]

Of course, the normality of androcracy continues to pose a problem with solutions such as mainstreaming and gender-auditing to philosophers' eradication of women as citizens. Continuous and historical appeal to nature renders equality unnatural and dangerous. Consequently, it is the mandate of decision-makers to ensure that only those people who are fit and able to maintain existing order are given the opportunity to participate fully in determining the affairs of the state. This was evident in the early twentieth century when the first female MPs in the UK were replacing their husbands who had either died, been elevated to the House of Lords or, in one case, banned from standing for Parliament for fraudulent practices (Vallance 1979: 25–6). More commonly, women have to be eminently qualified to suit job descriptions, as well as looking, dressing and behaving suitably for public office. Hence the situation where, as the old saying goes, women have to work twice as hard, and be perceived as being twice as good, as men to enter the echelons formerly preserved exclusively for male occupants.[9] However, the definition of 'suitable' may not be women's, tending towards a stereotyped, androgynous fashion.[10] Whatever the criteria for entry to, and promotion within, public office, and the public sphere more generally, male gatekeepers are in a position to determine access. This somewhat limits women's potential for entering the higher levels of public service in sufficient numbers, and with sufficient motivation or opportunity for promoting change. Moreover, working with, and through, the public-private divide still does not assure women's presence and endowment as citizens in their own right. The problem with concepts such as mainstreaming is that, while purporting to include women, they can still be premised on the fundamental tenets of androcracy. For example, policy-auditing by means of applying gender impact assessments to all public policy will reveal gaps in provision that need addressing to allow working women the ability to participate in the public sphere, especially if their skills are required in the workforce. What decision-makers may not want, or be able, to confront are the fundamental requirements necessary to ensure that women, and women's needs as they apply to the whole state, are integrated into the public sphere as fully equal in status, rather than merely assisting them with their 'additional' domestic responsibilities.

The paradox facing women has been bequeathed to them by philosophers and politicians. Rejection of the state perpetuates the status quo in terms of androcracy and female exclusion, and attempts to attain equality of opportunity by shifting, or working through, the public-private divide leaves gender inequality relatively unimpaired as women are assimilated by, or assimilate, the traditional values of state and citizenship. And yet it has become untenable for liberal democracies to appear as exclusive as their liberal and democratic antecedents. Thus, women have had to be admitted to previously male occupations and offices. As the opportunity for rebuilding the state and citizenship from a position of ungendered equality is not feasible, especially as the values and qualities of androcracy are so entrenched in female and male socio-political psyches, women have had to use their recent admission to the existing structures and processes of the state in their attempts to make political philosophies and practices more inclusive: in other words, to make the philosophers and politicians live up to their own ideals. Accordingly, political philosophy, and practice, is challenged by feminist academics, journalists and philosophers, as well as by women politicians, administrators and activists, whether as organised groups or as individuals challenging accepted norms of behaviour and thought.

In trying to ensure that political philosophy realises its full potential by addressing whole commonwealths, as opposed to selected parts within them, women are utilising the inconsistencies in the arguments that have historically excluded them. Of course, this is not always a conscious political objective. In maximising their self-interest by rejecting subservience, some women may be asserting their liberal rights without perceiving this as part of a collective act of claiming citizenship rights for women. Indeed, for many women, as well as men, citizenship rights are perceived as enshrined only in the right to vote, to have access to the law and to certain welfare provisions. In other words, democratic rights are explicit, leaving liberal rights relatively abstruse. However, if liberalism is concerned with individual liberty, then individualistic acts by women are also part of claiming the potential inclusivity of the philosophy and its demands for justice within the state.

Women's traditional domestic role has remained relatively unchallenged until the twentieth century. The alienation of sovereignty from women that has resulted from this is possibly of even greater significance than the lack of such challenge itself. Of course it cannot be argued that women remain excluded from citizenship. Even reference to their 'second-class' citizenship can be challenged as their legal status is enshrined in constitutions or precedents, despite the lack of implementation. However, women have been allowed a place in the public sphere and its benefits not as a right, but conditional upon managing the private sphere. The status of women as citizens, beyond universal suffrage and formal legal rights, depends on their meeting criteria determined by the political philosophers and incorporated into politics: indeed, they are judged as citizens on their ability to meet the criteria appropriate to public sphere activity (Narayan 1997). Moreover, if order within the state is endangered, women are expected to resume their rightful place in the private sphere, and policy or administrative initiatives designed to assist women's progress are rationalised and reversed (Etzioni 1993).[11] In a way then, women are citizens of convenience. Their citizenship is expendable in crises; it is residual and can be rescinded in service to the state, and it is, therefore, defined in a different way from men's citizenship, which takes precedence. Consequently, it can be argued that despite advances in women's status in contemporary polities, the political philosophies which inform politics are still relatively unadulterated, remaining partial and exclusive. What women may have been granted is formal citizenship: what is still missing is their sovereignty.

Citizenship and Sovereignty: You Can't Have One Without the Other

Traditional political philosophy endows individuals with sovereignty in order to legitimate political rule. Political philosophers' emphasis on the role of sovereign citizens in creating and maintaining the good state requires that those people eligible to participate in decision-making, as rulers and/or legitimators, know and understand how interests relate to, and affect, the common wealth. Ancient Greek philosophy integrates personal and state interests, requiring citizens to give the state primary consideration in their deliberations, so ensuring that their interests are protected. Members of the state who are not part of the deliberative citizenry have their interests protected within the order and security maintained by citizens' deliberations. On the other hand, liberal thinkers' principal emphasis on the protection of property requires only a legal and political framework to allow all individuals to pursue their interests without hindrance by others doing the same. When sovereign citizenship implies the politics of a relatively small number of people applying their fairly homogeneous interests to the rest of the state, it is an effortless concept. It becomes much more complex when it is endowed in all members of the state, who are equally concerned to further their own interests, which may have previously been considered irrelevant or marginal to the state.

The quality that is intrinsic to sovereignty in all political philosophies, whether it is applied to a limited citizenry or more extensively throughout the state, is that it is inalienable. For Hobbes, sovereignty is partially surrendered to a ruler who is commissioned to keep the state secure. Less authoritarian liberal philosophers do not permit the capitulation of any amount of individuals' sovereignty, rulers always remaining subject to the will of the people. The absence of women's sovereignty with respect to legitimating rulers is evident in the works of all the mainstream philosophers until J. S. Mill, who granted women equal opportunity based on merit. Prior to the nineteenth century and the beginnings of liberal democracy, women were not perceived as capable of using sovereignty rationally in relation to maintaining the security and stability of the state. However, it must be argued that sovereignty is not only the power to grant, or cancel, the legitimacy of rulers. Sovereignty is necessary to liberty. Even in Hobbes' state, sovereign individuals would have been free to maximise their interests within the constraints of laws made by legitimate rulers. Moreover, where no law existed, they were free to pursue their interests unhindered. Indeed, it would be incongruous if sovereignty were to be utilised only in legitimating rulers, resting on a shelf for the majority of citizens' lives and being aired only for elections or referenda, after which a return to subjection would be required. As an inalienable essence of individuals' citizenship, sovereignty is utilised to alert free people to the actions of others, including rulers, that may infringe rights and, therefore, liberty. Women, disqualified by philosophers from defining their own interests and pursuing individual interests within the state, are clearly not bestowed with sovereign status.

Again, the formal legal, political and social rights and freedoms of contemporary women appear to render the issue of sovereignty antiquated and irrelevant. However, as argued above, these rights and liberties are residual and subject to different stipulations from those of men. Similarly, they are not complete. The right to work as long as childcare is organised, the right to control reproduction unless you are a single woman or a lesbian or have some other disqualification,[12] the right to own property despite not having equal pay, distinguishes women from men who are not subject to the same caveats on their sovereign rights. Of course, there is a contradiction in arguing that women, despite their formal status as citizens, do not have full sovereignty. In exercising their political rights, women do, in fact, legitimate androcratic states and rulers. In other words, it can be argued that women are complicit in maintaining their unequal status. This reflects the perplexing question of why women, emerging from a condition of equality in the state of nature, would agree to subservience in the state.

If it is accepted that women's universal role as predominantly private sphere workers came about through conquest rather than by contract, then as formal citizenship is bestowed on them, the option to participate in a less androcratic and androcentric state is, naturally, unavailable. As the state and politics progressed, and claims to a broader justice and political integrity required women's recognition as citizens, then it is not surprising that they should be granted citizenship rights on the grounds that they conform to existing structures and processes. Women could not be allowed to assume individual sovereignty if the underlying status quo were to continue, or unless fundamental challenge to androcratic rules, regulations and practices were to be accepted. Of course, it can be argued that males of different classes are also faced with a legitimacy gap, since a ruling elite is unable to incorporate working class needs fully into state policy. However, one method used by political philosophers to overcome such potential crises of male legitimacy has been to bring class issues together to stand against the gender issue. Male members of the state share a common space in the public sphere, whether as full citizens or as labouring members of the state. Moreover, customarily, their public duties require the support of non-public female workers. In other words, the values and interests of androcracy are shared among men, across classes: as breadwinners they do not have to defend women's equal pay, treatment or opportunities in the labour force; as protectors of families there is no need for them to sanction equality before the law for women; and as the only sanctioned defenders of the state they deserve the full benefits of citizenship more than women.[13] However, in the relatively short period of time that women in the west have been granted formal rights as citizens, they have demonstrated the illegitimacy of androcentric rule by demanding genuine equality and repudiating the traditional parameters and restrictions on their liberty in both the public and private spheres. Women are, in fact reclaiming their sovereignty despite the androcentricity of the state.

The issue here is not to determine how women become fully sovereign citizens, but to consider the problem of unequal sovereignty within political philosophy and, therefore, politics. In contemporary liberal democracies, where formal citizenship is universal and all citizens have the right to participate in decision-making, as voters, activists, letter-writers and abstainers,[14] then inequality of sovereignty, especially as it applies to women who want to resist or reject androcratic rule, negates the objectives of both liberalism and democracy. Women do not have the level of liberty implied by sovereign individuals and citizens, and their democratic choices are limited to those of androcratic philosophies and policies. The opportunity to participate as sovereign citizens who are able to recognise and realise their interests, as opposed to androcracy's interests, and whose interests are as integral to the state as male citizens' have been for centuries, will remain inaccessible. Obviously, this is a policy and a philosophical issue: policy must acknowledge and address the problem of women's unequal sovereignty as well as recognising their formal citizenship. It will certainly be necessary for women and the supporters of political justice throughout the political, administrative and social echelons of the state to maintain a vigilant advocacy of women's claim to full sovereignty. This must include denial of the legitimacy of tokenistic ideas and policies which purport to be working for such sovereignty. At the same time, however, this is an issue for the philosophies that underlie and inform politics. As full sovereignty is the key to fulfilment of good states, whatever the philosophical and political objectives and means, understanding of its purposes and its distribution is vital to meet the requirements that ensure states are good for all members.

By extending full sovereignty to women and applying rights comprehensively, the problems encountered in diversity are potentially eliminated. Sovereign citizenship would acknowledge people and interests in their own right, rather than the formal equality of citizenship that requires uniformity, and results in women being treated the same as, rather than equally with, men (Goodin 1976, 108; Koggel 1998: 168).[15] This would free women from the bounds of essentialism, which contends that all women can be identified as an oppressed collective and as non-citizens, or that they should all understand what is necessary to assert their freedom. It also alleviates the perils of post-modernism and post-feminism that leave individual women stranded in a sea of androcracy without the possibility of collective support and action if, and as, they perceive its necessity. As the political philosophers argue, sovereign citizenship enables citizens as individuals and as collectives to pursue their interests, which inevitably rely on the security and stability of the state. Plaintive cries that women's different interests would disrupt the state, should they be granted full sovereign status, are, therefore, bogus. Women, too, need security and stability to assure their interests. Indeed, the only uniformity in traditional sovereign citizenship, as espoused by political philosophers, is that they are male and interested in preserving the good state, usually for their own advantage. Therefore, it can be argued, not only would women's full sovereignty complete the philosophers' ideals, but it would enhance them as the interests of all those people essential to the state, in all their roles and diversity, are incorporated and the 'good' state becomes good for all.

Political Philosophy, Politics and Women

From Plato to the New Right, political philosophers have expounded their ideas of the good state, usually in response to acute, long-term or imminent political crisis. Solutions suggested to circumvent such crises tend to focus on improving, or even instituting, the legitimacy of rulers, so eliminating the legitimacy gap. Methods of ensuring the legitimacy of rulers, ranging from election or lot (Plato, Aristotle, Mill and Rousseau), to tacit consent (Hobbes and Locke), rely on the superior intellect and rational ability to perceive the common good, of a small number of qualified citizens. Such qualification appears to rest in the ownership and control of property, or wealth-creating potential. Possessors of such credentials will also qualify to be educated so that they can understand the relationship of their privileges to the security and stability of the good state. Indeed, in all political philosophies, the interests of property and wealth-holders appear to coincide with those of the state. Even in the *polis*, where citizenship was restricted by birthright, wealthy or propertied foreigners could be granted limited rights of citizens (*The Laws*: 193–4). Only in philosophies advocating minimal (Nozick) or no-state (Marx) solutions to political crises is it suggested that legitimacy does not imply transfer of rights to qualified others.[16] The relationship of property to the state rests in states' development: as individuals gather and accumulate what they need to survive, including shelter, provisions and other assets, structures and processes are required to secure these against other individuals who are also preoccupied with self-preservation.

The conjunction of citizenship and property overtly places the majority of people living and working in the state outside an exclusive domain. This is justified by political philosophers who maintained that only the propertied classes have the leisure, as well as the qualifications, to participate in reasoned and informed deliberation, both as electors and as legislators. That this may, indeed, maintain rule by vested interests, even if these differ from the interests of absolute monarchs or tyrants, appears to go unnoticed. However, if the interests of all members of the state are defined in security and stability, allowing them to pursue their work and leisure activities free from fear of incursions by other individuals or the state, and without incurring the responsibilities pertaining to full citizenship, then this arrangement may be considered satisfactory. It may be a small price to pay to allow a relatively closed group of property-owning citizens to safeguard their interests if, in so doing, they procure and maintain peace and civil order. The problem lies with those people who remain unfree in pursuing their work and leisure activities, who are not secure even within a stable state, and who suffer constant violations, by other individuals and by the state, of any rights they may be permitted. This is more problematic when such a situation does not refer to slaves or minorities but to women, who constitute more than half of the population of most states.

Without clear and full justification, philosophers not only exclude women from property ownership and the potential for such, but from the freedom to pursue their own preservation and interests. This is made easy for them by the biological fact that women conceive, gestate and give birth to children. It does not stretch the imagination to situate women's role in the home, so defending the case that their primary responsibility is that of childcare and, by inference, household management. More perniciously, even if incognisantly, male philosophers are unlikely to advocate ideal polities that depose men from seats of power. Thus, philosophers justify the gendered status quo either by reference to women's unsuitability to engage with affairs of the state due to physical and psychological inferiority (Aristotle, Hobbes, Locke), or to the need for their moral superiority in maintaining the moral veracity of male citizens (Rousseau). However, as well as refusing women's access to legitimation processes, philosophers claim men's right to ultimate power in the domestic sphere. Experience demonstrates that men use this power not only in political decision-making as it affects the household, but also to control women's actions, sometimes by violent means. Political philosophers' legacy to women is that the security of the state and civil order is maintained at their expense.

Does this mean that political philosophers are wrong, and that their works are meaningless to a truly just and good state? The argument has not been to discredit any of the basic philosophies, even if it has been fun to illustrate some of the absurdities promulgated by certain philosophers. The intention has been to demonstrate how the anomalous and illogical arguments pertaining especially to the exclusion of women serve to frustrate the full realisation of philosophers' ideals. Where women have not been mentioned by philosophers, or their inclusion as equals with men is assumed, an attempt has been made to show how the historical exclusion of women thwarts claims to equality and legitimacy. Considered another way, and based on the assertion that contemporary politics is informed by the panoply of political philosophy, it is argued here that politics is based on misleading, incomplete and exclusive ideas.

Until women, and other previously excluded groups, are fully accepted as sovereign citizens, any political solutions to exclusion and crises of legitimacy can be only partial, if not tokenistic. While it might be conceded that philosophers prior to the mid-nineteenth century could not have conceived of women as citizens, let alone statespersons in political institutions, in the twenty-first century this is no longer the case. The only possible reason for women being obstructed in exercising their sovereign rights is the maintenance of androcratic power. It can be argued that women as citizens, property owners, public sphere actors, statespersons, and private sphere workers by choice, demonstrate their sovereignty routinely. But, if this were the case, demands for equal rights would no longer be necessary. The objectives of philosophers, and therefore states, in which civil order rests on the equal right of citizens or members of the state to pursue interests freely, would not be characterised by multifarious manifestations of, and complaints about, inequality. Equality policies bestowed within androcracies signify not the sovereignty, but attempts at the pacification, of women. Thus, while western liberal democracies can boast the stability and internal security that philosophers of all persuasions coveted, without full and comprehensive inclusiveness, manifested in formal citizenship plus full sovereignty, the project remains incomplete.

Notes

1. Although Afghanistan is not an example of liberal democracy, the revoking of access for women to health care, education, legal and other public services in that country is an, albeit extreme, example of the residual nature of women's rights. In liberal democracies, appeal to women's sense of right is more likely to be used to undermine their 'rights'. For example, as economic markets require, women can either be used as cheap, 'flexible' and generally unprotected labour, or, as in the case of the aftermath of the two world wars, they can be expected to forego occupational progress when it impedes the rights of men to employment and a family wage. Concomitantly, 'rights' to childcare are adaptable and can be expanded, restricted or withdrawn, so rendering women's economic 'rights' a moveable feast (Carter 1988: 12–13; Pettman 1996; Dale 1997).
2. The most obvious anomaly, apart from the negligence of the law in matters of domestic violence, is the severe sentences given to women who kill abusive partners compared with the leniency of judges when faced with men who murder 'nagging' wives (Walklate 1995; Edwards 1996). However, apart from other judicial injustices, women's lower pay further reduces access to the protection of the law.
3. A United Nations (2000: 93) survey on the progress of women in the global economy indicates that women's pay remains less than men's in all states, including those of western Europe and developed countries.
4. Women have been eligible to stand for election, and otherwise participate in institutional politics, since the early part of the twentieth century in most liberal democratic states. However, almost a century later, women's representation in elected assemblies in western liberal democracies ranges from 6.3 per cent in Greece to 42.7 per cent in Sweden, and 30 per cent in the European Parliament. Excluding Scandinavian states, the average rate of representation is 18.6 per cent (European Commission 1999; UN 2000: 77).
5. Local authorities' women's equal opportunities units were closed or amalgamated with generic equal opportunities units, and the Labour Party's initiative to increase the number of women MPs at and after the 1997 general election by instituting all-woman shortlists was successfully challenged in tribunal (McDougall 1998: 161–2; Bryson 1999: 121). This hearing did not comprise a comprehensive legal requirement to abolish the initiative, and could possibly have been successfully appealed, especially under the terms of the Amsterdam Treaty which includes provision for positive action in member states of the European Union. However, it was not continued.
6. Since 1996 in the UK, girls have consistently outperformed boys in public examinations, overcoming the inbuilt male advantages of educational processes (Thompson 1983; EOC 1994, 1998; Spender 1989). Despite many

decades of women's knowledge about, and attempts to remedy, girls' disadvantage, once boys were perceived to be disadvantaged considerable public concern was demonstrated. Initiatives such as reviewing the content of school literature texts to portray positive images of men were instituted to improve boys' educational experiences and attainments.

7. Even as ordinary members of the state, women's contribution is marginalised, if not ignored, as in the contemporary philosophy of Nozick and the early work of Rawls. It is recorded only to justify exclusion from the suggested new orders that such philosophers prescribe.

8. Mainstreaming is also essential to the European Union as it expands to incorporate countries from the former Eastern bloc. In such countries, transition from command to market economies has had a detrimental effect on the status of women as men's employment rights are prioritised over women's (UN 1995: 13; Sperling 2000). This emphases the need for the European Union to require such states to indicate their commitment to gender equality as part of the accession criteria (Bretherton, forthcoming).

9. Perhaps unkindly, but in many cases appropriately, the saying is continued with the notion that this is not too hard to achieve!

10. The striking similarity of the 101 women Labour MPs elected to the House of Commons in the UK in 1997 was their besuited dress sense, unobtrusive make-up and tidy coiffure (McDougall 1998). More significantly, women have to adapt to parliamentary procedures which, in Britain, have not only been likened to the schoolroom and a Gentleman's Club, but which were instituted to enable men to meet their professional commitments before having to attend the House for the day's political business (Vallance 1979; McDougall 1998; Bryson 1999).

11. This contrasts with external dangers to the state in which both women and men are required to contribute their time and labour in defence efforts, as service personnel, medical staff, agriculture and manufacturing industries. However, as the experience at the end of the last world war shows, women are still expected to return to traditional duties once the men return and require employment.

12. While contraception may be available, indeed encouraged, for such people, access to reproductive technologies such as in vitro fertilisation is more strictly controlled (Rowland 1992; Lovenduski and Randall 1993: 254; Bryson 1999: 154).

13. Defence of the state should not be defined only in relation to armed engagement. Women have historically been integral to the defence of the state in times of conflict on the home front as well as in munitions and agricultural work. However, in terms of participation in actual conflict and defence of the state, women have historically been involved in front-line activity as fighters and 'auxiliaries', and can often also be involuntarily involved as civilian casualties, victims of war crimes and other effects of war (Miles 1989; Pettman 1996).

14. As electoral turnouts diminish, it is assumed that voter apathy is rampant. An alternative interpretation could be that non-voting, as in non-decision-making (Bachrach and Baratz 1970), is a politically motivated (in)action.

15. Equal treatment defined as identical treatment does not necessarily result in

equality. If differences remain untreated, they perpetuate inequalities defined in androcracy. As Koggel (1998: 43) argues, a condition of equality may be achieved only after a period in which inequalities are treated unequally.

16. What is not considered in such philosophies is that purely administrative functions of co-ordination of markets and economic exchange, and of labour to maintain communist societies, have a political function. Wherever authority for any level of decision-making is delegated to others, the legitimacy of decision-makers and their judgements is at risk.

Bibliography

Aaron, R. I. (1955), *John Locke* (2nd Edn), Oxford: Oxford University Press.

Ackerman, B. A. (1980), *Social Justice and the Liberal State*, New Haven: Yale University Press.

Alejandro, R. (1993), 'Rawls's Communitarianism', *Canadian Journal of Philosophy*, Vol. 23 (1), pp. 75–100.

Allen, J. (1990), 'Does Feminism Need a Theory of "The State"?', in S. Watson (ed.), *Playing the State: Australian Feminist Interventions*, London: Verso.

Amdur, R. (1980), 'Rawls and his Radical Critics: The Problem of Equality', *Dissent*, Vol. 27 (3), pp. 323–34.

Archer, R. L. (1928), *Rousseau on Education*, London: Edward Arnold.

Aristotle [c.335–323 BC](1962), *The Politics*, Trans. T. A. Sinclair, London: Penguin Books.

Aristotle [undated](1976), *Ethics*, Trans. J. A. K. Thomson, London: Penguin Books.

Armstrong, K. (1986), *The Gospel According to Woman: Christianity's Creation of the Sex War in the West*, London: Pan Books.

Avineri, S. (1971), *The Social and Political Thought of Karl Marx*, Cambridge: Cambridge University Press.

Bacchi, C. (1991), 'Pregnancy, the Law and the Meaning of Equality', in E. Meehan and S. Sevenhuijsen (eds), *Equality, Politics and Gender*, London: Sage.

Bacchi, C. (1999), *Women, Policy and Politics: the Construction of Policy Problems*, London: Sage.

Bachrach, P. and Baratz, M. S. (1970), *Power and Poverty: Theory and Practice*, Oxford: Oxford University Press.

Baker, S. (1999), 'Risking Difference: Reconceptualising the Boundaries Between the Public and Private Spheres', in S. Baker and A. van Doorne-Huiskes (eds), *Women and Public Policy: The Shifting Boundaries Between the Public and Private Spheres*, Aldershot: Ashgate Press.

Baker, S. and van Doorne-Huiskes, A. (eds) (1999), *Women and Public Policy: The Shifting Boundaries Between the Public and Private Spheres*, Aldershot: Ashgate Press.

Ball, S. W. (1993), 'Maximin Justice, Sacrifice, and the Reciprocity Argument: A Pragmatic Reassessment of the Rawls/Nozick Debate', *Utilitas*, Vol. 5 (2), pp. 157–84.

Banks, O. (1981), *Faces of Feminism: A Study of Feminism as a Social Movement*, Oxford: Basil Blackwell.

Barker, E. (1946), *The Politics of Aristotle*, Oxford: Oxford University Press.

Barker, E. (1960), *Greek Political Theory: Plato and his Predecessors* (5th Edn), London: Methuen.

Barrett, M. [1980](1992), 'Women's Oppression Today: Problems in Marxist Feminist Analysis', in M. Humm (ed.), *Feminisms: A Reader*, London: Harvester-Wheatsheaf.

Barry, B. (1995), 'John Rawls and the Search for Stability', *Ethics* Vol. 105 (4), pp. 874–915.

Barry, N. (1981), *An Introduction to Modern Political Theory*, Hants: Macmillan.

Baumeister, A. (2000), 'The New Feminism', in N. O'Sullivan (ed.), *Political Theory in Transition*, London: Routledge.

Behn, A. [1688](1992), *Oroonoko, The Rover and Other Works*, J. Todd (ed.), London: Penguin Books.

Bell, N. K. (1978), 'Nozick and the Principle of Fairness', *Social Theory and Practice*, Vol. 5 (1), pp. 65–73.

Beveridge, F., Nott, S. and Stephen, K. (undated), *Predicting the Impact of Policy: Gender-Auditing as a Means of Assessing the Probable Impact of Policy Initiatives on Women. Country Report: United Kingdom*. University of Liverpool: Feminist Legal Research Unit.

Biesenthal, L. (1978), 'Natural Rights and Natural Assets', *Philosophy of the Social Sciences*, Vol. 8 (2), pp. 153–71.

Bluestone, N. H. (1988), 'Why Women Cannot Rule: Sexism in Plato Scholarship', *Philosophy of the Social Sciences*, Vol. 18 (1), pp. 41–60.

Bluhm, W. T. (1984), 'Freedom in the Social Contract: Rousseau's "Legitimate Chains"', *Polity*, Vol. 16 (3), pp. 359–83.

Boucher, D. and Kelly, P. (eds) (1994), *The Social Contract from Hobbes to Rawls*, London: Routledge.

Bowle, J. (1961), *Western Political Thought: From the Origins to Rousseau*, London: Methuen.

Bowle, J. (1963), *Politics and Opinion in the Nineteenth Century: An Historical Introduction*, London: Jonathan Cape.

Boynton, G. R. and Kim, C. L. (1991), 'Legislative Representation as Parallel-Processing and Problem-Solving', *Journal of Theoretical Studies*, Vol. 3 (4), pp. 437–61.

Bréhier, E. (1966), *The History of Philosophy: The Seventeenth Century*, Trans. W. Baskin, Chicago: University of Chicago Press.

Brennan, T. and Pateman, C. (1979), 'Mere Auxiliaries to the Commonwealth: Women and the Origins of Liberalism', *Political Studies*, Vol. 27 (June), pp. 183–200.

Bretherton, C. (forthcoming), 'Gender Mainstreaming and EU Enlargement: Swimming Against the Tide', *Journal of European Public Policy*.

Bryson, V. (1999), *Feminist Debates: Issues of Theory and Political Practice*, Hants: Macmillan.

Butler, M. A. (1991), 'Early Liberal Roots of Feminism: John Locke and the Attack on Patriarchy', in M. L. Shanley and C. Pateman (eds), *Feminist Interpretations and Political Theory*, Oxford: Polity Press.

Cabinet Office (1995), *Public Bodies, 1994*, London: HMSO.

Cameron, B. (1980), 'Mill's Treatment of Women, Workers and Private Property', *Canadian Journal of Political Science*, Vol. XIII (4), pp. 775–83.

Carey, G. W. (1976), 'The Just and Good State: Rawls and Nozick Read Anew', *Modern Age*, Vol. 20 (4), pp. 371–82.

Carnoy, M. (1969), *The State and Political Theory*, USA: Princeton University Press.

Carritt, E. F. (1967), 'Liberty and Equality', in A. Quinton (ed.), *Political Philosophy*, Oxford: Oxford University Press.

Carter, A. (1988), *The Politics of Women's Rights*, London: Longman.

Carver, T. (1985), 'Engels' Feminism', *History of Political Thought*, Vol. 6 (3), pp. 479–89.

Chapman, R. A. (1975), '*Leviathan* Writ Small: Thomas Hobbes on the Family', *American Political Science Review*, Vol. 69 (1), pp. 76–90.

Charvet, J. (1995), 'Rousseau, the Problem of Sovereignty and the Limits of Political Obligation', in R. Wokler (ed.), *Rousseau and Liberty*, Manchester: Manchester University Press.

Coltheart, L. (1986), 'Desire, Consent and Liberal Theory', in C. Pateman and E. Gross (eds), *Feminist Challenges: Social and Political Theory*, London: Allen and Unwin.

Coole, D. (1993), *Women in Political Theory: From Ancient Misogyny to Contemporary Feminism* (2ⁿᵈ Edn), London: Harvester-Wheatsheaf.

Coole, D. (1994), 'Women, Gender and Contract: Feminist Interpretations', in D. Boucher and P. Kelly (eds), *The Social Contract: From Hobbes to Rawls*, London: Routledge.

Corlett, J. A. (ed.) (1991), *Equality and Liberty: Analysing Rawls and Nozick*, Hants: Macmillan.

Corlett, J. A. (1991), 'Does Ambiguity Lurk Behind the Veil of Ignorance in Rawls' Original Position', in J. A. Corlett (ed.), *Equality and Liberty: Analysing Rawls and Nozick*, Hants: Macmillan.

Cowling, M. (1963), *Mill and Liberalism*, Cambridge: Cambridge University Press.

Cranston, M. (1966), 'John Locke and Government by Consent', in D. Thomson (ed.), *Political Ideas*, London: C. A. Watts.

Cranston, M. (1995), 'Rousseau's Theory of Liberty', in R. Wokler (ed.), *Rousseau and Liberty*, Manchester: Manchester University Press.

Crick, B. (1964), *In Defence of Politics*, London: Penguin Books.

Crick, B. (1987), *Socialism*, Milton Keynes: Open University Press.

Crocker, L. (1977), 'Equality, Solidarity and Rawls' Maximin', *Philosophy and Public Affairs*, Vol. 6 (3), pp. 262–6.

Crombie, I. M. (1964), *Plato: The Midwife's Apprentice*, London: Routledge and Kegan Paul.

Dahl, R. A. (1997), 'Procedural Democracy', in R. E. Goodin and P. Pettit (eds), *Contemporary Political Philosophy: An Anthology*, Oxford: Blackwell.

Dale, A. [1990–1](1997), 'Women in the Labour Market: Policy and Perspective', in C. Ungerson and M. Kember (eds), *Women and Social Policy: A Reader* (2ⁿᵈ Edn), London: Macmillan.

Daly, M. (1986), *Beyond God the Father: Towards a Philosophy of Women's Liberation*, London: The Women's Press.

Daly, M. (1978), *Gyn/Ecology: The Metaethics of Radical Feminism*, London: The Women's Press.

David, M. (1986), 'Moral and Maternal: The Family in the Right', in R. Levitas (ed.), *The Ideology of the New Right*, Oxford: Polity Press.

Davies, C. (1999), 'The Masculinity of Organisational Life', in S. Baker and A. van Doorne-Huiskes (eds), *Women in Public Policy: The Shifting Boundaries Between the Public and Private Spheres*, Aldershot: Ashgate Press.

Davis, M. (1991), 'Nozick's Argument for the Legitimacy of the Welfare State', in J. A. Corlett (ed.), *Equality and Liberty: Analysing Rawls and Nozick*, Hants: Macmillan.

de Beauvoir, S. [1949](1988), *The Second Sex*, Trans. H. M. Parshley, London: Picador.

de Beer, G. (1972), *Jean-Jacques Rousseau and His World*, London: Thames and Hudson.

Deininger, W. T. (1965), *Problems in Social and Political Thought: A Philosophical Introduction*, New York: Macmillan.

Delmar, R. (1976), 'Looking Again at Engels's "Origins of the Family, Private Property and the State"', in A. Oakley and J. Mitchell (eds), *The Rights and Wrongs of Women*, London: Penguin Books.

de Tocqueville, A. [1835](1968), *Democracy in America*, Trans. G. Lawrence, London: Fontana.

Dietz, M. G. [1985](1998), 'Citizenship with a Feminist Face: the Problem with Maternal Thinking', in J. B. Landes (ed.), *Feminism, the Public and the Private*, Oxford: Oxford University Press.

di Stefano, C. (1991), 'Masculine Marx', in M. L. Shanley and C. Pateman (eds), *Feminist Interpretations and Political Theory*, Oxford: Polity Press.

Dobbs, D. (1996), 'Family Matters: Aristotle's Appreciation of Women and the Plural Structure of Society', *American Political Science Review*, Vol. 90 (1), pp. 74–89.

Dunn, J. (1984), *Locke*, Oxford: Oxford University Press.

Dunn, J. (1991), 'Political Obligation', in D. Held (ed.), *Political Theory Today*, Oxford: Polity Press.

Edwards, S. M. (1996), *Sex and Gender in the Legal Process*, London: Blackstone Press.

Eisenstein, Z. R. (1995), 'The Sexual Politics of the New Right: Understanding the "Crisis of Liberalism" for the 1980s', in N. Tuana and R. Tong (eds), *Feminism and Philosophy: Essential Readings in Theory, Reinterpretation and Application*, Boulder, CO: Westview Press.

Elshtain, J. B. (1981), *Public Man, Private Woman: Women in Social and Political Thought*, Oxford: Martin Robertson.

Elshtain, J. B. [1982](1991), 'Antigone's Daughters', in W. McElroy (ed.), *Freedom, Feminism and the State* (2nd Edn), New York, NY: The Independent Institute.

Elshtain, J. B. (1998), 'Women and War: Ten Years On', *Review of International Studies*, Vol. 24, pp. 447–60.

Engels, F. [1884](1978), *The Origin of the Family, Private Property and the State*, Peking: Foreign Languages Press.

EOC (1994), *Some Facts about Women*, Manchester: Equal Opportunities Commission.

EOC (1998), *Women and Men of Britain*, Manchester: Equal Opportunities Commission.

Etzioni, A. (1993), *The Spirit of Community: The Reinvention of American Society*, New York, NY: Simon and Schuster.

Euripides [c.431–410 BC](1998), *Medea, The Phoenician Women, Bacchae*, London: Methuen.

European Commission (1999), *Women of Europe Newsletter*, No. 87, July/August.

Exdell, J. (1994), 'Feminism, Fundamentalism and Liberal Legitimacy', *Canadian Journal of Philosophy*, Vol. 24 (3), pp. 441–64.

Fawcett Society (2000), *Fawcett Society Annual Report 1999–2000*, London: Fawcett Society.

Fermon, N. (1994), 'Domesticating Women, Civilising Men: Rousseau's Political Program', *The Sociological Quarterly*, Vol. 35 (3), pp. 431–42.

Field, G. C. (1969), *The Philosophy of Plato* (2nd Edn), Oxford: Oxford University Press.

Firestone, S. (1979), *The Dialectic of Sex*, London: The Women's Press.

Flanders, M. L. (1994), *Breakthrough: The Career Woman's Guide to Shattering the Glass Ceiling*, London: Paul Chapman.

Fowler, M. (1980), 'Stability and Utopia: A Critique of Nozick's Framework Argument', *Ethics*, Vol. 90 (4), pp. 550–63.

Frazer, E. and Lacey, N. (1993), *The Politics of Community: A Feminist Critique of the Liberal-Communitarian Debate*, Hemel Hempstead: Harvester-Wheatsheaf.

Frazer, E. and Lacey, N. (1995), 'Politics and the Public in Rawls' Political Liberalism', *Political Studies*, Vol. 43 (2), pp. 233–47.

French, M. (1992), *The War Against Women*, London: Hamish Hamilton.

Fukuyama, F. (1992), *The End of History and the Last Man*, London: Penguin Books.

Gauthier, D. P. (1969), *The Logic of Leviathan: The Moral and Political Theory of Thomas Hobbes*, Oxford: Clarendon Press.

Gavre, M. (1974), 'Hobbes and His Audience: The Dynamics of Theorising', *American Political Science Review*, Vol. 68 (4), pp. 1542–56.

Giddens, A. (1998), *The Third Way: The Renewal of Social Democracy*, Oxford: Polity Press.

Goldmann, L. (1968), *The Philosophy of the Enlightenment: The Christian Burgers and the Enlightenment'*, Trans. H. Maas, London: Routledge and Kegan Paul.

Goldsmith, M. M. (1966), *Hobbes's Science and Politics*, New York, NY: Columbia University Press.

Goodin, R. E. (1976), *The Politics of Rational Man*, London: John Wiley and Sons.

Goodin, R. E. and Pettit, P. (1997), *Contemporary Political Philosophy: An Anthology*, Oxford: Blackwell.

Gorr, M. (1991), 'Rawls on Natural Inequality', in J. A. Corlett (ed.), *Equality and Liberty: Analysing Rawls and Nozick*, Hants: Macmillan.

Gourevitch, V. (1998), 'Recent Works on Rousseau: Review Essay', *Political Theory*, Vol. 26 (4), pp. 536–56.

Gray, J. (1998), *John Stuart Mill on Liberty and Other Essays*, Oxford: Oxford University Press.

Green, K. (1995), *The Woman of Reason: Feminism, Humanism and Political Thought*, Oxford: Polity Press.

Green, M. (1994), 'Conflicting Principles or Competing Counterparts? J. S. Mill on Political Economy and the Equality of Women', *Utilitas*, Vol. 6 (2), pp. 268–85.

Greer, G. (2000), *The Whole Woman*, London: Anchor.

Grimke, S. [1837](1991), 'Legal Disabilities of Women', in W. McElroy (ed.), *Freedom, Feminism and the State*, (2nd Edn), New York, NY: The Independent Institute.

Grimsley, R. (1973), *The Philosophy of Rousseau*, Oxford: Oxford University Press.

Halle, L. J. (1972), *The Ideological Imagination: Ideological Conflict in Our Time and its Roots in Hobbes, Rousseau and Marx*, London: Chatto and Windus.

Halliday, R. J. (1976), *John Stuart Mill*, London: George Allen and Unwin.

Hampsher-Monk, I. (1992), *A History of Modern Political Thought: Major Political Thinkers from Hobbes to Marx*, Oxford: Blackwell.

Hampshire, S. (1956), *The Age of Reason: The Seventeenth Century Philosophers*, New York, NY: Mentor Books.

Hampton, J. (1986), *Hobbes and the Social Contract Tradition*, Cambridge: Cambridge University Press.

Harman, H. (1993), *The Century Gap*, London: Vermillion.

Hartmann, H. [1979](1992a), 'The Unhappy Marriage of Marxism and Feminism: Towards a More Progressive Union', in J. A. Kourany, J. P. Sterba and R. Tong (eds), *Feminist Philosophies*, New Jersey: Prentice-Hall.

Hartmann, H. [1976](1992b), 'Capitalism, Patriarchy and Job Segregation by Sex', in M. Humm (ed.), *Feminisms: A Reader*, Hemel Hempstead: Harvester-Wheatsheaf.

Haworth, A. (1994), *Anti-Libertarianism: Markets, Philosophy and Myth*, London: Routledge.

Hay, C. (1996), *Re-stating Social and Political Change*, Buckingham: Open University Press.

Hayek, F. A. [1944](1976), *The Road to Serfdom*, London: Routledge and Kegan Paul.

Hayek, F. A. [1960](1999), *The Constitution of Liberty*, London: Routledge.

Held, D. (1989), *Political Theory and the Modern State: Essays on State, Power and Democracy*, Oxford: Polity Press.

Hinton, R. W. K. (1968), 'Husbands, Fathers and Conquerors', *Political Studies*, Vol. XVI (1), pp. 55–67.

Hirshman, L. R. (1994), 'Is the Original Position Inherently Male-Superior?', *Columbia Law Review*, Vol. 94 (6), pp. 1860–81.

Hobbes, T. [1651](1973), *Leviathan*, London: J. M. Dent and Sons.

Hobbes, T. [1651](1991), *Man and Citizen*, Indianapolis, IN: Hackett.

Holdsworth, A. (1988), *Out of the Doll's House: the Story of Women in the Twentieth Century*, London: BBC Books.

Horowitz, A. (1986), 'Will, Community and Alienation: Rousseau's Social Contract', *Canadian Journal of Political and Social Theory*, Vol. X (3), pp. 63–82.

Hoskyns, C. (1994), 'Gender Issues in International Relations: the Case of the European Community', *Review of International Studies*, Vol. 20 pp. 225–39.

Ivison, D. (1997), 'The Secret History of Public Reason: Hobbes to Rawls', *History of Political Thought*, Vol. XVIII (1), pp. 125–47.

Jackson, M. W. (1979), 'The Least Advantaged Class in Rawls's Theory', *Canadian Journal of Political Science*, Vol. 12 (4), pp. 727–46.

Jaggar, A. M. (1988), *Feminist Politics and Human Nature*, New Jersey: Rowman and Littlefield.

Jennings, J. (1994), 'Rousseau, Social Contract and the Modern Leviathan', in D. Boucher and P. Kelly (eds), *The Social Contract from Hobbes to Rawls*, London: Routledge.

Kain, P. J. (1993), *Marx and Modern Political Theory: From Hobbes to Contemporary Feminism*, New Jersey: Rowman and Littlefield.

Kamenka, E. (ed.)(1983), *The Portable Karl Marx*, London: Penguin Books.

Kavka, G. (1991), 'An Internal Critique of Nozick's Entitlement Theory', in J. A. Corlett (ed.), *Equality and Liberty: Analysing Rawls and Nozick*, Hants: Macmillan.

Kearns, D. (1983), 'A Theory of Justice and Love; Rawls on the Family', *Politics*, Vol. 19 (2), pp. 36–42.

Kelly, L. (1999), 'Violence Against Women: a Policy of Neglect or a Neglect of Policy?', in S. Walby (ed.), *New Agendas for Women*, Hants: Macmillan.

Koggel, C. M. (1998), *Perspectives on Equality: Constructing a Relational Theory*, Lanham: Rowman and Littlefield.

Kymlicka, W. (1990), *Contemporary Political Philosophy: An Introduction*, Oxford: Clarendon Press.

Lane, J. E. (1996), *Constitutions and Political Theory*, Manchester: Manchester University Press.

Lange, L. (1991), 'Rousseau and Modern Feminism', in M. L. Shanley and C. Pateman (eds), *Feminist Interpretations and Political Theory*, Oxford: Polity Press.

Laski, H. J. (1917), *Studies in the Problem of Sovereignty*, Oxford: Oxford University Press.

Laski, H. J. (1920), *Political Thought in England: Locke to Bentham*, Oxford: Oxford University Press.

Laslett, P. and Runciman, W. G. (eds) (1969), *Philosophy, Politics and Society* (2nd Series), Oxford: Basil Blackwell.

Lee, D. (1977), *Plato: Timaeus and Critias*, London: Penguin Books.

Levy, H. L. (1990), 'Does Aristotle Exclude Women from Politics?', *Review of Politics*, Vol. 52 (3), pp. 397–416.

Lewis, J. and Åström, G. (1997), 'Equality, Difference and State Welfare: Labour Market and Family Policies in Sweden', in C. Ungerson and M. Kember (eds), *Women and Social Policy: A Reader* (2nd Edn), London: Macmillan.

Lister, R. (1997), *Citizenship: Feminist Perspectives*, Hants: Macmillan.

Locke, J. [1690](1924), *Two Treatises of Government*, London: J. M. Dent and Sons.

Locke, J. [1689](1983), *A Letter Concerning Toleration*, Indianapolis, IN: Hackett.

Losco, J. (1988), 'Rousseau on the Political Role of the Family', *History of Political Thought*, Vol. IX (1), pp. 91–110.

Lovenduski, J. (1986), *Women and European Politics: Contemporary Feminism and Public Policy*, Brighton: Wheatsheaf Books.

Lovenduski, J. and Randall, V. (1993), *Contemporary Feminist Politics: Women and Power in Britain*, Oxford: Oxford University Press.

Lukes, S. (1974), *Power: A Radial View*, Hants: Macmillan.

Lund, B. (1996), 'Robert Nozick and the Politics of Social Welfare', *Political Studies*, Vol. 44 (1), pp. 115–22.

Mabbott, J. D. (1967), *The State and the Citizen* (2nd Edn), London: Hutchinson.

Mabbott, J. D. (1973), *John Locke*, London: Macmillan.

MacIntyre, A. (1992), 'Justice as a Virtue: Changing Conceptions', in S. Avineri and A. de-Shalit (eds), *Communitarianism and Individualism*, Oxford: Oxford University Press.

MacKenzie, W. J. M. (1975), *Power, Violence and Decision*, London: Penguin Books.

MacKie, J. L. (1976), *Problems from Locke*, Oxford: Clarendon Press.

Mahowald, M. B. (ed.) (1994), *Philosophy of Woman: An Anthology of Classic to Current Concepts* (3rd Edn), Indianapolis, IN: Hackett.

Mandle, J. (1999), 'The Reasonable in Justice as Fairness', *Canadian Journal of Philosophy*, Vol. 29 (1), pp. 75–108.

Marshall, T. H. (1950), *Citizenship and Social Class and Other Essays*, Cambridge: Cambridge University Press.

Marty, W. R. (1981), 'Rawls and the Harried Mother', *Interpretation*, Vol. 9 (2–3), pp. 385–96.

Marx, K. [1844](1983), 'From Economico-Philosophical Manuscripts of 1844', in E. Kamenka (ed.), *The Portable Karl Marx*, London: Penguin Books.

Marx, K. [1845–6](1983), 'The German Ideology, Volume 1', in E. Kamenka (ed.), *The Portable Karl Marx*, London: Penguin Books.

Marx, K. [1848](1983), 'The Communist Manifesto', in E. Kamenka (ed.), *The Portable Karl Marx*, London: Penguin Books.

Marx, K. [c.1871](1983), 'Critique of the Gotha Programme', in E. Kamenka (ed.), *The Portable Karl Marx*, London: Penguin Books.

Marx, K. [1898](1975), *Wages, Price and Profit*, Peking: Foreign Languages Press.

Masters, R. D. (1968), *The Political Philosophy of Rousseau*, New Jersey: Princeton University Press.

Mayer, J. P. (1968), Introduction to *Democracy in America*, Trans. G. Lawrence, London: Fontana.

McDougall, L. (1998), *Westminster Women*, London: Vintage.

McElroy, W. (ed.) (1991), *Freedom, Feminism and the State*, New York, NY: The Independent Institute.

McLean, I. (1991), 'Forms of Representation and Systems of Voting', in D. Held (ed.), *Political Theory Today*, Oxford: Polity Press.

McMillan, C. (1982), *Women, Reason and Nature*, Oxford: Basil Blackwell.

Mendus, S. (1994), 'John Stuart Mill and Harriet Taylor on Women and Marriage', *Utilitas*, Vol. 6 (2), pp. 287–99.

Mies, M. (1998), *Patriarchy and Accumulation on a World Scale: Women in the International Division of Labour* (2nd Edn), London: Zed Books.

Miles, R. (1989), *The Women's History of the World*, London: Paladin.

Mill, J. S. [1863](1962), *Utilitarianism*, London: Fontana.

Mill, J. S. [1869](1985), 'The Subjection of Women', in M. Wollstonecraft, *A Vindication of the Rights of Women* and J. S. Mill, *The Subjection of Women*, London: J. M. Dent.

Mill, J. S. [1858](1998), 'On Liberty', in J. S. Mill, *Utilitarianism, On Liberty, Considerations on Representative Government*, London: J. M. Dent.

Mill, J. S. [1861](1998), 'On Representative Government', in J. S. Mill *Utilitarianism, On Liberty, Considerations on Representative Government*, London: J. M. Dent.

Millett, K. (1977), *Sexual Politics*, London: Virago.

Minogue, K. (1963), *The Liberal Mind*, London: Methuen.

Minogue, K. R. (1966), 'Thomas Hobbes and the Philosophy of Absolutism', in D. Thomson (ed.), *Political Ideas*, London: C. A. Watts.

Minogue, K. R. (1973), *Introduction to Leviathan*, London: J. M. Dent.

Morrow, J. (1998), *History of Political Thought: A Thematic Introduction*, Hants: Macmillan.

Mulgan, R. (1994), 'Aristotle and the Political Role of Women', *History of Political Thought*, Vol. XV (2), pp. 179–202.

Mulhall, S. and Swift, A. (1996), *Liberals and Communitarians* (2nd Edn), Oxford: Blackwell.

Myers, J. L. (1968), *The Political Ideas of the Greeks*, New York, NY: Greenwood Press.

Narayan, U. (1997), 'Towards a Feminist Vision of Citizenship: Rethinking the Implications of Dignity, Political Participation, and Nationality', in C. Ungerson and M. Kember (eds), *Women and Social Policy: A Reader* (2nd Edn), London: Macmillan.

Nash, K. (1998), 'Beyond Liberalism? Feminist Theories of Democracy', in V. Randall and G. Waylen (eds), *Gender, Politics and the State*, London: Routledge.

Neal, P. (1987), 'In the Shadow of the General Will: Rawls, Kant and Rousseau on the Problem of Political Right', *Review of Politics*, Vol. 49 (3), pp. 389–409.

News and Observer (1997), *The Demographics of the 105th Congress*, http://www.newsobserver.com/newsroom/nao/top/010897/congress/demographic.html

Nichols, M. P. (1985), 'Rousseau's Novel Education in the *Emile*', *Political Theory*, Vol. 13 (4), pp. 535–58.

Nock, C. J. (1992), 'Equal Freedom and Unequal Property: A Critique of Nozick's Libertarian Case', *Canadian Journal of Political Science*, Vol. XXV (4), pp. 677–95.

Norton, P. (1998), 'The House of Commons', in Jones, B., Gray, A., Kavanagh, D., Moran, M., Norton, P. and Seldon, A. *Politics UK* (3rd Edn), London: Prentice-Hall.

Norton, P. (2001), 'The House of Commons', in Jones, B., Gray, A., Kavanagh, D., Moran, M., Norton, P. and Seldon, A. *Politics UK* (4th Edn), London: Prentice-Hall.

Nozick, R. (1974), *Anarchy, State and Utopia*, Oxford: Basil Blackwell.

Nyland, C. (1993), 'John Locke and the Social Position of Women', *History of Political Economy*, Vol. 25 (1), pp. 39–63.

Oakeshott, M. (1975), *Hobbes on Civil Association*, Oxford: Basil Blackwell.

Okin, S. M. (1980), *Women in Western Political Thought*, London: Virago.

Okin, S. M. (1991a), 'Philosopher Queens and Private Wives: Plato on Women and the Family', in M. L. Shanley and C. Pateman (eds), *Feminist Interpretations and Political Theory*, Oxford: Polity Press.

Okin, S. M. (1991b), 'Gender, the Public and the Private', in D. Held (ed.), *Political Theory Today*, Oxford: Polity Press.

Okin, S. M. (1991c), 'John Rawls: Justice as Fairness For Whom?', in M. L. Shanley and C. Pateman (eds), *Feminist Interpretations and Political Theory*, Oxford: Polity Press.

Okin, S. M. (1994), 'Political Liberalism, Justice and Gender', *Ethics*, Vol. 105 (1), pp. 23–43.

O'Neill, O. (1976), 'Nozick's Entitlements', *Inquiry*, Vol. 19 (4), pp. 468–81.

Padia, C. (1994), 'Plato, Aristotle, Rousseau and Hegel on Women: A Critique', *Indian Journal of Political Science*, Vol. 55 (19), pp. 27–36.

Parker, B. and Fagenson, E. A. (1994), 'An Introductory Overview of Women in Corporate Management', in M. J. Davidson and R. J. Burke (eds), *Women in Management: Current Research Issues*, London: Paul Chapman.

Parry, G. (1995), 'Thinking One's Own Thoughts: Autonomy and the Citizen', in R. Wokler (ed.), *Rousseau and Liberty*, Manchester: Manchester University Press.

Partridge, P. H. (1971), *Consent and Consensus*, London: Pall Mall Press.

Pateman, C. (1988), *The Sexual Contract*, Oxford: Polity Press.

Pateman, C. (1989), *The Disorder of Women*, Oxford: Polity Press.

Pateman, C. (1991), '"God Hath Ordained to Man a Helper": Hobbes, Patriarchy and Conjugal Right', in M. L. Shanley and C. Pateman (eds), *Feminist Interpretations and Political Theory*, Oxford: Polity Press.

Pateman, C. (1994), '"Does Sex Matter to Democracy?" – A Comment', in M. Githen, P. Norris and J. Lovenduski (eds), *Different Roles, Different Voices: Women and Politics in the United States and Europe*, New York, NY: Harper Collins.

Peele, G. (1995), *Governing the UK* (3rd Edn), Oxford: Blackwell.

Pettman, J. J. (1996), *Worlding Women: A Feminist International Politics*, London: Routledge.

Phillips, A. (1991), *Engendering Democracy*, Oxford: Polity Press.

Phillips, A. (1993), *Democracy and Difference*, Oxford: Polity Press.

Phillips, A. (1995), *The Politics of Presence*, Oxford: Clarendon Press.

Phillips, A. (1998), 'Dealing with Difference: A Politics of Ideas or a Politics of

Presence?', in J. B. Landes (ed.), *Feminism: The Public and the Private*, Oxford: Oxford University Press.

Phillips, A. (1999), *Which Equalities Matter?*, Oxford: Polity Press.

Pierson, A. (1996), *The Modern State*, London: Routledge.

Pietarinen, J. (1990), 'Early Liberalism and Women's Liberty', in UK Monographs, *Women's Rights and the Rights of Man*, Aberdeen: Aberdeen University Press.

Plato [c.399 BC](1993), *Phaedo*, Trans. D. Gallop, Oxford: Oxford University Press.

Plato [c.348 BC](1971), *Timaeus and, Critias*, Trans. D. Lee, London: Penguin Books.

Plato [c.347 BC](1970), *The Laws*, Trans. T. J. Saunders, London: Penguin Books.

Plato [c.375 BC](1974), *The Republic*, Trans. D. Lee (2nd Edn), London: Penguin Books.

Presley, S. and Kinsky, L. (1991), 'Government is Women's Enemy', in W. McElroy (ed.), *Freedom, Feminism and the State* (2nd Edn), New York, NY: The Independent Institute.

Pringle, R. and Watson, S. (1992), 'Women's Interests and the Post-Structural State', in M. Barrett and A. Phillips (eds), *Destabilising Theory: Contemporary Feminist Debates*, Oxford: Polity Press.

Racine, J. [1677](1986), *Phaedre*, New York, NY: Harcourt Brace.

Randall, V. (1987), *Women and Politics: An International Perspective* (2nd Edn), Hants: Macmillan.

Randall, V. (1998), 'Women Engage the State', in Randall, V. and Waylen, G. (eds), *Gender, Politics and the State*, London: Routledge.

Randall, V. and Waylen, G. (eds) (1998), *Gender, Politics and the State*, London: Routledge.

Rapaczynski, A. (1987), *Nature and Politics: Liberalism in the Philosophies of Hobbes, Locke, and Rousseau*, Ithaca, NY: Cornell University Press.

Raphael, D. D. (1976), *Problems of Political Philosophy* (Revised Edn), London: Macmillan.

Rawls, J. (1972), *A Theory of Justice*, Oxford: Oxford University Press.

Rawls, J. (1991), 'Justice as Fairness: Political not Metaphysical', in J. A. Corlett (ed.), *Equality and Liberty: Analysing Rawls and Nozick*, Hants: Macmillan.

Rawls, J. (1996), *Political Liberalism*, New York, NY: Columbia University Press.

Ring, J. (1985), 'Mill's *The Subjection of Women*: The Methodological Limits of Liberal Feminism', *Review of Politics*, Vol. 47 (1), pp. 27–44.

Roche, K. F. (1974), *Rousseau: Stoic and Romantic*, London: Methuen.

Roche, M. (1992), *Rethinking Citizenship: Welfare, Ideology and Change in Modern Society*, Oxford: Polity Press.

Roemer, J. E. (1997), 'Exploitation, Alternatives and Socialism', in R. Goodin and P. Pettit (eds), *Contemporary Political Philosophy*, Oxford: Blackwell.

Rolland, R. (1943), *The Living Thoughts of Rousseau* (2nd Edn), London: Cassell and Co.

Rousseau, J. J. [c.1778](1954), *The Confessions*, Trans. J. M. Cohen, London: Penguin Books.

Rousseau, J. J. [1750–62](1973), *The Social Contract and Discourses*, Trans. G. D. H. Cole, London: Dent.

Rousseau, J. J. [1762](1993), *Emile*, Trans. B. Foxley, London: J. M. Dent.

Rowland, R. (1992), *Living Laboratories: Women and Reproductive Technology*, London: Cedar.

Ryan, A. (1974), *J. S. Mill*, London: Routledge and Kegan Paul.

Sabine, G. H. (1951), *A History of Political Theory* (3rd Edn), London: George G. Harrap and Co.

Saxonhouse, A. (1986), 'From Tragedy to Hierarchy and Back Again: Women in Greek Political Thought', *American Political Science Review*, Vol. 80 (2), pp. 403–18.

Saxonhouse, A. (1991), 'Aristotle: Defective Males, Hierarchy and the Limits of Politics', in M. L. Shanley and C. Pateman (eds), *Feminist Interpretations and Political Theory*, Oxford: Polity Press.

Schochet, G. J. (1975), *Patriarchalism in Political Thought: The Authoritarian Family and Political Speculation and Attitudes Especially in Seventeenth Century England*, Oxford: Basil Blackwell.

Schwarzenbach, S. (1991), 'Rawls and Ownership: The Forgotten Category of Reproductive Labour', in J. A. Corlett (ed.), *Equality and Liberty: Analysing Rawls and Nozick*, Hants: Macmillan.

Self, P. (1993), *Government by the Market? The Politics of Public Choice*, Hants: Macmillan.

Shanley, M. L. (1991), 'Marital Slavery and Friendship: John Stuart Mill's *The Subjection of Women*', in M. L. Shanley and C. Pateman (eds), *Feminist Interpretations and Political Theory*, Oxford: Polity Press.

Shanley, M. L. and Pateman, C. (eds) (1991), *Feminist Interpretations and Political Theory*, Oxford: Polity Press.

Shaw, George Bernard (1944), *Everybody's Political What's What?* London: Constable and Co.

Shue, H. (1975), 'Liberty and Self-Respect', *Ethics*, Vol. 85 (3), pp. 195–203.

Siltanen, J. and Stanworth, M. (eds) (1984), *Women and the Public Sphere: A Critique of Sociology and Politics*, London: Hutchinson.

Sjöö, M. and Mor, B. (1987), *The Great Cosmic Mother: Rediscovering the Religion of the Earth*, New York, NY: Harper Collins.

Skinner, Q. (1997), 'The State', in R. E. Goodin and P. Pettit (eds), *Contemporary Political Philosophy: An Anthology*, Oxford: Blackwell.

Sorenson, L. R. (1990), 'Rousseau's Liberalism', *History of Political Thought*, Vol. XI (3), pp. 443–66.

Spender, D. (1982), *Women of Ideas and What Men Have Done to Them*, London: Pandora.

Spender, D. (1985), *Man Made Language*, London: Routledge and Kegan Paul.

Spender, D. (1989), *Invisible Women: The Schooling Scandal*, London: The Women's Press.

Sperling, L. (1997), 'Quangos: Political Representation and Women Consumers of Public Services', *Policy and Politics*, Vol. 25 (2), pp. 119–28.

Sperling, L. (1998), 'Public Services, Quangos and Women: A Concern for Local Government', *Public Administration*, Vol. 76 (3), pp. 471–87.

Sperling, L. (2000), 'Women and Work: The Age of Post-Feminism', in L. Sperling and M. Owen (eds), *Women and Work: The Age of Post-Feminism?* Aldershot: Ashgate Press.

Sperling, L. and Bretherton, C. (1996), 'Women's Policy Networks and the European Union', *Women's Studies International Forum*, Vol. 19 (3), pp. 303–14.

Spooner, L. [1882](1991), 'A Right to Make Laws?', in W. McElroy (ed.), *Freedom, Feminism and the State* (2nd Edn), New York, NY: The Independent Institute.

Squires, J. (1999), 'Rethinking the Boundaries of Political Representation', in S. Walby (ed.), *New Agendas for Women*, London: Macmillan.

Squires, J. (2000), *Gender in Political Theory*, Oxford: Polity Press.
Stacey, M. and Price, M. (1981), *Women, Power and Politics*, London: Tavistock.
Steans, J. (1998), *Gender in International Relations: An Introduction*, Oxford: Polity Press.
Stivers, C. (1999), 'Reframing the "Public" in Public Administration', in S. Baker and A. van Doorne-Huiskes (eds), *Women and Public Policy: The Shifting Boundaries Between the Public and Private Spheres*, Aldershot: Ashgate Press.
Strasnick, S. (1976), 'The Problem of Social Choice: Arrow to Rawls', *Philosophy of Public Affairs*, Vol. 5 (3), pp. 241–73.
Strathern, P. (1996), *Locke in 90 Minutes*, London: Constable.
Thomas, C. G. (1981), 'The Greek Polis', in R. Griffeth and C. G. Thomas (eds), *The City State in Five Cultures*, Oxford: ABC-Clio.
Thompson, J. L. (1983), *Learning Liberation: Women's Response to Men's Education*, London: Croom Helm.
Thomson, D. (1966), 'Rousseau and the General Will', in D. Thomson (ed.), *Political Ideas*, London: C. A. Watts.
Thomson, D. (ed.) (1966), *Political Ideas*, London: C. A. Watts.
Tolleson-Rinehart, S. (1992), *Gender Consciousness and Politics*, New York, NY: Routledge.
Tuck, R. (1989), *Hobbes*, Oxford: Oxford University Press.
Tulloch, G. (1989), *Mill and Sexual Equality*, Hemel Hempstead: Harvester-Wheatsheaf.
Ungerson, C. (1997), 'Payment for Caring – Mapping a Territory', in C. Ungerson and M. Kember (eds), *Women and Social Policy: A Reader* (2nd Edn), London: Macmillan.
Ungerson, C. and Kember, M. (eds)(1997), *Women and Social Policy: A Reader* (2nd Edn), London: Macmillan.
UN (1991), *The World's Women 1970–1990: Trends and Statistics*, New York, NY: United Nations.
UN (1995), *Women in a Changing Global Economy: 1994 World Survey on the Role of Women in Development*, New York, NY: United Nations.
UN (1996) *The Beijing Declaration and The Platform for Action*, Fourth World Conference on Women, Beijing, China, 4–15 September 1995.
UN (2000), *Progress of the World's Women 2000: UNIFEM Biennial Report*, http://www.unifem.undp.org/progressww/2000
Vallance, E. (1979), *Women in the House: A Study of Women Members of Parliament*, London: Athlone Press.
Vigor, P. H. (1966), 'Marx and Modern Capitalism', in D. Thomson (ed.), *Political Ideas*, London: C. A. Watts.
Vincent, A. (1987), *Theories of the State*, Oxford: Basil Blackwell.
Vincent, A. (ed.) (1997), *Political Theory: Tradition and Diversity*, Cambridge: Cambridge University Press.
Vogel, U. (1995), 'But in a Republic, Men are Needed: Guarding the Boundaries of Liberty', in R. Wokler (ed.), *Rousseau and Liberty*, Manchester: Manchester University Press.
Walby, S. (ed.) (1999), *New Agendas for Women*, London: Macmillan.
Waldron, J. (1994), 'John Locke: Social Contract versus Political Anthropology', in D. Boucher and P. Kelly (eds), *The Social Contract from Hobbes to Rawls*, London: Routledge.
Walklate, S. (1995), *Gender and Crime: An Introduction*, London: Prentice-Hall.
Walsh, C. (1962), *From Utopia to Nightmare*, Westport, CT: Greenwood Press.

Watkins, J. W. N. (1966), 'John Stuart Mill and the Liberty of the Individual', in D. Thomson (ed.), *Political Ideas*, London: C. A. Watts.

Watson, S. (1990), 'The State of Play: An Introduction', in S. Watson (ed.), *Playing the State: Australian Feminist Interventions*, London: Verso.

Waylen, G. (1998), 'Gender, Feminism and the State: An Overview', in V. Randall and G. Waylen (eds), *Gender, Politics and the State*, London: Routledge.

Weale, A. (2000), 'Conversations and Democracy', *C. S. D. Bulletin*, Vol. 7 (2), pp. 1–2.

Weatherford, R. C. (1991), 'Discussions Defining the Least Advantaged', in J. A. Corlett (ed.), *Equality and Liberty: Analysing Rawls and Nozick*, Hants: Macmillan.

Williams, B. (1997), 'The Idea of Equality', in R. E. Goodin and P. Pettit (eds), *Contemporary Political Philosophy: An Anthology*, Oxford: Blackwell.

Williams, G. L. (ed.) (1976), *John Stuart Mill on Politics and Society*, Brighton: The Harvester Press.

Wingrove, E. (1995), 'Sexual Performance as Political Performance in the *Lettre à M. D'Alembert sur les Spectacles*', *Political Theory*, Vol. 23 (4), pp. 585–616.

Wokler, R. (ed.) (1995), *Rousseau and Liberty*, Manchester: Manchester University Press.

Wolff, J. (1991), *Robert Nozick: Property, Justice and the Minimal State*, Oxford: Polity Press.

Wolff, J. (1996), *An Introduction to Political Philosophy*, Oxford: Oxford University Press.

Wollheim, R. (1969), 'A Paradox in the Theory of Democracy', in P. Laslett and W. G. Runciman (eds), *Philosophy, Politics and Society* (2nd Series), Oxford: Basil Blackwell.

Wolin, S. (1960), *Politics and Vision: Continuity and Innovation in Western Political Thought*, Boston, MA: Little, Brown and Co.

Wollstonecraft, M. [1792](1985), *A Vindication of the Rights of Woman*, London: Dent.

Wright, R. G. (1977), 'The High Cost of Rawls' Inegalitarianism', *Western Political Quarterly*, Vol. 30 (1), pp. 73–9.

Wright, T. (1994), *Citizens and Subjects: An Essay on British Politics*, London: Routledge.

Young, F. C. (1991), 'Nozick and the Individualist Anarchist', in J. A. Corlett (ed.), *Equality and Liberty: Analysing Rawls and Nozick*, Hants: Macmillan.

Young, I. M. (1997a), 'Gender as Seriality: Thinking about Women as a Social Collective', in I. M. Young, *Intersecting Voices: Dilemmas of Gender, Political Philosophy and Policy*, Chichester: Princeton University Press.

Young, I. M. (1997b), 'Asymmetrical Reciprocity: On Moral Respect, Wonder and Enlarged Thought', in I. M. Young, *Intersecting Voices: Dilemmas of Gender, Political Philosophy and Policy*, Chichester: Princeton University Press.

Yuval-Davis, N. (1999), 'The "Multi-Layered Citizen": Citizenship in the Age of Glocalisation', *International Feminist Journal of Politics*, Vol. 1 (1), pp. 119–36.

Zaino, J. S. (1998), 'Self-Respect and Rawlsian Justice', *The Journal of Politics*, Vol. 60 (3), pp. 737–53.

Index

Related Reading from Edinburgh University Press

Sexual Politics
An Introduction

Richard Dunphy
Senior Lecturer in Politics at the University of Dundee

September 2000   248pp   Pb   0 7486 1247 5   £15.95

An exciting new textbook introduction to contemporary sexual politics.

This book offers an exploration of the theoretical approaches to the study of gender and sexuality, and a critical appraisal of contemporary debates within and between some of the main sexual politics movements. The arguments are illustrated with case studies that demonstrate the ways in which gender and sexuality have affected the political and public policy agendas in the UK in recent decades.

The book is unique in drawing upon three research areas: feminist theory, lesbian and gay studies, and critical studies of masculinity. Queer theory and post-feminism are critiqued and the author argues that the battle for sexual diversity must encompass the fight against male domination and gender inequalities.

Sexual Politics: An Introduction will be an ideal text for students of politics, sociology, gender studies and cultural studies, and anyone with an interest in gender and sexuality.

- Unique - combines work on sexual politics from feminist studies, lesbian and gay studies, and men's studies
- Accessible - illustrates theoretical approaches with up-to-date case studies
- Contemporary - covers up-to-date debates within feminism, post-feminism and queer theory
- Shows connections between gender politics and the politics of sexuality

Order from
Marston Book Services, PO Box 269, Abingdon, Oxon OX14 4YN
Tel 01235 465500 • Fax 01235 465555
Email: direct.order@marston.co.uk

Visit our website www.eup.ed.ac.uk
All details correct at time of printing but subject to change without notice